Politics and Policy in China's Social Assistance Reform

Edinburgh East Asian Studies Series
Series Editors: Natascha Gentz, Urs Matthias Zachmann and David Der-Wei Wang

Covering language, literature, history and society, this series of academic monographs and reference volumes brings together scholars of East Asia to address crucial topics in East Asian Studies. The series embraces a broad scope of approaches and welcomes volumes that address topics such as regional patterns of cooperation and social, political, cultural implications of interregional collaborations, as well as volumes on individual regional themes across the spectrum of East Asian Studies. With its critical analysis of central issues in East Asia, and its remit of contributing to a wider understanding of East Asian countries' international impact, the series will be crucial to understand the shifting patterns in this region within an increasingly globalised world.

Series Editors

Professor Natascha Gentz is Chair of Chinese Studies, Director of the Confucius Institute for Scotland and Dean International (China) at the University of Edinburgh.

Professor Urs Matthias Zachmann is Professor of History and Culture of Modern Japan at the Institute of East Asian Studies, Freie Universität Berlin.

Professor David Der-Wei Wang is the Edward C. Henderson Professor of Chinese Literature at the Fairbank Center for Chinese Studies at Harvard University.

Editorial Board

Professor Marion Eggert, Bochum University
Professor Joshua A. Fogel, York University, Toronto
Professor Andrew Gordon, Harvard University
Professor Rikki Kersten, Murdoch University
Dr Seung-Young Kim, University of Sheffield
Dr Hui Wang, Tsinghua University, Beijing

Titles available in the series:

Asia after Versailles: Asian Perspectives on the Paris Peace Conference and the Interwar Order 1919–1933
Urs Matthias Zachmann (Editor)

On the Margins of Modernism: Xu Xu, Wumingshi and Popular Chinese Literature in the 1940s
Christopher Rosenmeier

Politics and Policy in China's Social Assistance Reform: Providing for the Poor?
Daniel R. Hammond

www.edinburghuniversitypress.com/series/eeas

Politics and Policy in China's Social Assistance Reform

Providing for the Poor?

Daniel R. Hammond

EDINBURGH
University Press

For Peter and Martin, you are missed.

Edinburgh University Press is one of the leading university presses in the UK. We publish academic books and journals in our selected subject areas across the humanities and social sciences, combining cutting-edge scholarship with high editorial and production values to produce academic works of lasting importance. For more information visit our website: edinburghuniversitypress.com

Edinburgh University Press Ltd
The Tun – Holyrood Road
12(2f) Jackson's Entry
Edinburgh EH8 8PJ

First published in hardback by Edinburgh University Press 2019

Typeset in 10/12 Ehrhardt by
Servis Filmsetting Ltd, Stockport, Cheshire

A CIP record for this book is available from the British Library

ISBN 978 1 4744 2011 2 (hardback)
ISBN 978 1 4744 7466 5 (paperback)
ISBN 978 1 4744 2012 9 (webready PDF)
ISBN 978 1 4744 2013 6 (epub)

Contents

Acknowledgements   vii
Note on Chinese and Translations   ix
Glossary of Terms and Abbreviations   x

Introduction   1
    Introduction   1
    Previous Studies of the MLG   3
    Explaining Policy in China   8
    Theoretical Approach of the Book   12
    A Note on Methods   17
    Structure of the Book   18

1 *Historical Background to* Dibao *and the Question of Poverty in*
   China   21
    Introduction   21
    Social Assistance before 1992   22
    A History of *Dibao*   26
    Nature of Poverty in Reform Era China   40

2 *Urban* Dibao: *Emergence and Transition to National Policy,*
   1992–1999   46
    Introduction   46
    Emergence and Spread of the MLG   47
    National Implementation of the MLG: 1997–1999 59
    Conclusion   65

3 *Urban* Dibao: *The Resolution of Unwanted and Unintended*
   Outcomes, 1999–2003   67
    Introduction   67
    Unintended and Unwanted Outcomes   68
    Interventions   73
    The Ministry of Civil Affairs during Zhu's Intervention
      and after   82
    Conclusion   87

4   *Rural* Dibao*: The Countryside and Fragmentation*   89
    Introduction   89
    The Timeline, Design and Function of Rural *Dibao*   90
    Successes and Challenges of Rural *Dibao*   93
    How Fragmentation Facilitated and Challenges Rural *Dibao*   98
    Conclusion   104

5   *Institutionalisation? Achieving Policy in a Fragmented State*   106
    Introduction   106
    The Importance of Institutionalisation   107
    Dibao's Lack of Institutionalisation   109
    A Consequence of Fragmentation?   121
    Can Institutionalisation Resolve Fragmentation?   123
    Should Institutionalisation Resolve Fragmentation?   125
    Could China Learn from Other Countries?   126
    Conclusion   129

    Conclusion   132
    Introduction   132
    Goals of the Study   132
    Main Findings   134
    Contribution to China Studies   137
    Contribution beyond China Studies   139
    Reflection and Future Research   140

    Appendix: Interview List   143
    Bibliography   144
    Index   166

Acknowledgements

There are many people who have contributed to this book getting written. I am sure, in the process of thanking people, there will be some who I forget and for that I ask their forgiveness. As a supervisor and mentor who has worked with me since I was a postgraduate student I would like to thank Jane Duckett. Other members of staff who supported me during my time at Glasgow include Barry O'Toole, Cian O'Driscoll, Alasdair Young, Chris Thornton and Tom Lundberg. Heather Zhang and Myrto Tsakatika not only gave my PhD thesis a thorough examination but have also helped me develop as a scholar and researcher in the years since. Colleagues in the PhD process who provided invaluable support and friendship (and continue to do so) include Sam Robertshaw, James Bilsland, Scott Brown, Donghyun Kim, Tom Johnson, Poppy Winanti, Wang Guohui, Aofei Lu, Valentina Feklyunina, Chris Lamont, Wang Hua and Ariel Ko.

While conducting research in China I have been fortunate to work with and get to know several scholars, without them I wouldn't have been able to complete this work, and for that I thank Guan Xinping, Yang Tuan and Tang Jun. I would like to extend special thanks to Wang Fei, Wang Jing and Chen Xi for their support and friendship.

My research has been funded over the years by the Universities China Committee in London, the University of Glasgow and the University of Edinburgh. Without the funds to travel and stay in China I would not have been able to complete the research that formed the basis of this book.

In the time since I completed my PhD I have benefited from working at the University of Edinburgh where I am surrounded by colleagues in Asian Studies who have all helped me to complete this book. Thank you to Julian Ward, Joachim Gentz, Natascha Gentz, Christopher Rosenmeier, Mark McLeister and Huang Xuelei for providing a genuinely pleasant place in which to work. I would like to thank Chris Perkins in particular for his friendship and for making sure I got this book written.

I have also been fortunate enough to benefit from the advice and guidance of a number of China scholars who, in their own ways, have had a profound impact on how I view my research and work. In particular, I would like to thank Dorothy Solinger and Tim Wright.

Edinburgh University Press and the four reviewers whose suggestions have been worked into the text all have my thanks for their patience and hard work.

I have been lucky in that I have a family which has supported me throughout my time as a student and an early career researcher. For their love and support I would like to thank my parents Judith and Phil, my brother and sister Matthew and Sarah, my grandparents Doreen, Hilda, Ron and Peter, and uncles Steve, David and Martin. For making sure I get out of the house, get a walk and clear my head, thank you to Junior, Lily and Ludo.

Finally, I have been blessed to spend the last nine years of my life with Senia Febrica. Thank you.

Note on Chinese and Translations

Throughout this study pinyin has been used for the romanisation of Chinese terms, unless a quote used an alternative method in which case the original is maintained.

All translations are by the author unless otherwise stated.

The former Minister for Civil Affairs Doje Cering is an ethnic Tibetan and his name can be represented as either Doje Cering or Duoji Cairang following the *hanzi* used to represent his name. Throughout the text the pinyin is used.

Glossary of Terms and Abbreviations

CCP Chinese Communist Party
Fenlei baozhang cuoshi (Classification guarantee measures)
Hukou (Household registration)
Lianghui (The Two Meetings, shorthand for the Chinese People's Political Consultative Congress and National People's Congress)
FA fragmented authoritarianism (model)
MCA Ministry of Civil Affairs
MLG Minimum Livelihood Guarantee (*dibao, zuidi shenghuo baozhang*)
MoF Ministry of Finance
MoHRSS Ministry of Human Resources and Social Security (replaced the Ministry of Labour and Social Security in 2008)
MoLSS Ministry of Labour and Social Security (replaced the Ministry of Labour in 1998)
NPC National People's Congress
PE policy entrepreneur
PRC People's Republic of China, China
Sannong (Three problems of the countryside)
Sanwu (Three No's, or Three Withouts)
SOE state-owned enterprise
Wubao (Five Guarantees)
Xiagang zhigong (Laid-off worker)
XGBLG *Xiagang* basic livelihood guarantee
Xin pinkun (New poverty)
YBJB *Yingbao jinbao* (Ought to protect, fully protect)
YBWB *Yingbao weibao* (Ought to protect, not protecting)
ZGMZ *Zhongguo Minzheng* magazine (*China Civil Affairs*, a monthly magazine on Civil Affairs matters)
Zhongguo Shehui Bao (*China Society News* newspaper, a triweekly publication on Civil Affairs matters)

Introduction

Introduction

The People's Republic of China's (China or PRC hereafter) transformation since 1978 has been dramatic and far reaching. The headline grabbing growth achieved under the leadership of the Chinese Communist Party (CCP) has transformed people's lives, but it has not been without consequence. The introduction of market principles has seen the re-emergence of poverty as a policy problem in urban and rural areas. The size of China means that the scale of the challenge presented by poverty was and continues to be enormous. While the reforms have lifted hundreds of millions of Chinese out of poverty there are tens of millions who have been left behind (ADB 2004; Gustafsson and Zhong 2000; Hussain 2003; Khan and Riskin 2001, 2005; Tang 2003). One response to the issue has been the introduction of new policies to expand the scope and provision of social assistance for those most in need. The Minimum Livelihood Guarantee (MLG or *dibao* hereafter) system emerged during the 1990s initially providing a means tested benefit to urban residents who applied for assistance. First appearing in Shanghai in 1993, the MLG was a radical departure from traditional urban social assistance and went on to spread to a small number of cities before being officially marked for national implementation in 1997. Since 1997 the MLG has undergone significant expansion in the number of people receiving the benefit as well as large increases in scope and expenditure, and, in 2007, a rural MLG system was implemented nationally. It is a means tested, locally-administered and -financed policy which provides a household with a top-up to their income providing a minimum income guarantee. The MLG was originally designed to provide the absolute minimum that a household might require to survive and as such should not necessarily be thought of as a poverty alleviation measure. Rather the MLG was a continuation of traditional Chinese social assistance which provided those most in need with the means to survive and served the state's political aims of governing a stable society.

The MLG is important for two reasons. First, it is a radical departure in the mechanics of social assistance provision in China. The preceding policy of the Three No's (*sanwu*) in urban areas and the Five Guarantees (*wubao*) in rural areas provided assistance to the poor as long as the person in question fell into one of three categories: those with no income, no ability to work, and no carer or guardian. These measures were a final safety net for those in China who were not eligible for social welfare and social insurance provided by state-owned enterprises (SOEs) or government run organisations and who had no family to fall back on. The MLG being means tested rather than category based implies a significant change in the Chinese approach to social assistance provision. Poverty was recognised by the state as existing outside of a small number of categories and the traditional association of social assistance and welfare with labour ability has been broken. There were urban and rural residents capable of working and their household may have had an income, but these households were impoverished. The means tested element of the MLG is also a departure in terms of the way in which the state conceives and administers social policy. Instead of determining need according to inflexible unchanging criteria, the MLG is in theory flexible and capable of adapting to the changing economic and social circumstances of individual residents, cities or even provinces.

Second, the MLG is significant because of the numbers involved. The MLG is a massive programme in its scope and reach. At the end of 2015 urban MLG payments covered 17.08 million people in 9.6 million households. The total spent on the urban MLG was RMB 65.2 billion with a household receiving an average of 303 RMB per month. The rural MLG at the end of 2015 reached 49.03 million people in 28.43 million households. The total spent was RMB 87.73 billion with a recipient receiving an average of 144 RMB (MCA 2016). Based on population figures for 2014 the percentage of those receiving the MLG was 5.18 per cent in the overall population, 2.51 per cent in urban areas and 8.42 per cent in rural areas (NBS 2016; World Bank 2017).

The current research and discussion of the MLG system is evolving. On the one hand the programme's origins, implementation and development is often described briefly and typically defaults to the economic determinist approach that has been typical of studies of social policy in China since reforms began. However, even the year national implementation of the urban programme occurred varies depending on which piece of research is being read. On the other hand, the literature frequently suggests that the programme is falling short in achieving particular policy objectives because it is seen to fail as a poverty alleviation measure. But if we do not fully understand where a policy came from and what it is for how can we really, effectively and constructively criticise it? These two themes in the literature on *dibao* are interrelated and serve to establish a muddled view of what the programme is for and how it might be adjusted or adapted in the future. What is the story of *dibao's* development and how might we explain it? What explains the criticism in academia, the derision that *dibao* receives by some of the public, and the feeling among some recipients that they do not receive enough help? What explains the seeming incoherence in what *dibao* is viewed as being for? It is these questions which this book will address, arguing that what *dibao* is for and how this came about is a consequence of the fragmented authoritarianism of the PRC. In order to address problems in the future, the politics and policy making behind *dibao* needs to be understood.

Previous studies of the MLG

The MLG has attracted the attention of researchers from economic, social policy and political science disciplines. Early studies tend to describe the MLG with no theoretical lens or explanation for the policy, or look at the MLG through a particular theoretical approach without explicitly seeking to explain it, or analyse the MLG from the perspective of poverty alleviation leading to critical conclusions. Descriptive studies of the MLG set out the programme and sometimes give an historical review until the time the work in question was published (Leung 2003, 2006; Leung and Wong 1999; Saunders and Shang 2001; Wong 1998, 2001). There is also work which uses the MLG as a tool that helps measure the difficult question of what constitutes poverty in the People's Republic (ADB 2004; Saunders and Sun 2006). Other studies discuss the MLG as part of the overall social policy provisions of the Chinese state highlighting its potential effectiveness in alleviating poverty in China's cities (Hussain 2003), noting recipients of the MLG as part of an emerging hierarchy of unemployed in China (Solinger 2001), highlighting China's increasing efforts to centralise the provision of social goods in the 2000s (Saich 2008), or analysing the regional differences in provisions for laid-off workers in the 1990s and 2000s (Hurst 2009). A number of studies reflect on the place the MLG has within the various measures introduced by the state to cope with increasing urban poverty and unemployment (Liu and Wu 2006; Qian and Wong 2000; Wong and Ngok 2006).

A growing body of work has addressed the MLG from a more empirical and quantitative perspective. The most comprehensive of these studies is Gao's *Welfare, Work, and Poverty* (Gao 2017). These studies have provided important insights into the changing make-up of *dibao* recipients (Gao 2013) – what factors may lead to a household receiving *dibao* (Gustafsson and Deng 2011), the relationship between how *dibao* is implemented and the wealth of the city in question (Solinger and Hu 2012) – and have provided empirical evidence to identify particular policy problems such as leakage, regressive redistribution and mistargeting (Gao 2013, 2017; Ravallion and Chen 2015; Wu and Ramesh 2014). The position that *dibao* should be judged as a poverty alleviation programme is often articulated in this body of work.

Recent contributions from Solinger (2008, 2011, 2013), Cho (2010, 2013), Zhang (2015, 2016a, 2016b) and Wong, Chen and Zeng (2014) have broadened our understanding of what it means to live on *dibao*. Recipients of *dibao* are often an invisible part of the picture. What is shown by this work is that those receiving *dibao* are a diverse group who have found themselves marginalised in China's post-Maoist development surge. Seen as either undesirable, at home caring for relatives, or the former champions of a system now discarded, MLG recipients often struggle to survive and to understand a world which seems intent on leaving them behind.

What is lacking in the extensive research on the MLG at present are studies which seek to explain the emergence and development of the policy. This is understandable given that the majority of studies on the MLG come from an economic, sociological or social work background. The concern of the authors is not to discuss theories of policy making or the origins of the MLG in particular, and it is therefore not the focus of their work. Implicit in existing studies is that the MLG was a political choice by the Chinese government that sought to cope with increasing urban poverty. For example, Leung (2003: 83) writes:

> To establish a last-resort welfare safety net in the cities, the government restructured the traditional social assistance programme in 1993, with the aim of extending their coverage, raising the level of benefits and securing financial commitments from the local governments.

The implicit suggestion in these studies is that the MLG was a rational response to increasing urban poverty.

The Chinese language studies and documents on the MLG also present the MLG as having followed a rational, coherent and consistent developmental path. I refer to this, because it is replicated by the Chinese government, as the MLG discourse. There are two clear themes to this discourse which form a dominant understanding of the MLG in the available Chinese sources, and which are reflected in the English language studies of the policy. The first theme is the historical development of the policy and the second is that the policy has served a consistent objective. This presents the programme as operating as intended throughout the 1990s and early 2000s as well as having followed the developmental path that is commonly associated with the Chinese policy process (Interview 5 (see the Appendix at the end of the book for a complete listing and details of each interviewee)). The outcomes of the MLG being presented as intended is also part of this discourse. The MLG discourse is a manifestation of the state presenting policy as a coherent process that follows the scientific principles that have been popularised by the CCP leadership throughout the reform period.

Historically the MLG is presented as having a very straightforward developmental history. The policy is consistently described as having emerged in Shanghai in 1993, having been implemented nationally in 1997 and having gone on to achieve the present-day number of recipients and funding without any of the underlying complexity of the process being discussed. This presents the MLG as having followed a smooth development from initial emergence through to national implementation. It also lends the policy a coherence of development which reflects the ideal policy process in the PRC where policy is first rolled out as local experiments before realising national implementation. This official history of the policy is pervasive throughout the political system and across China. For example, a speech by a senior Ministry of Civil Affairs (MCA) official in Beijing which I witnessed during fieldwork in 2006 presented the policy in such a way as did interviews with local-level officials in the city of Anqing, Anhui Province (Interviews 5 and 6).

The second theme is that the targets of the MLG are consistent throughout the various periods of development. The target group is represented as the urban poor (*chengshi jumin pinkun*) or those with livelihood difficulties (*kunnan shenghuo*), who are sometimes presented as the new poverty (*xin pinkun*) (Tang 1998). This group is left relatively undefined, leaving the MLG as a programme that can be presented as having been smoothly developed by the state with the explicit goal of helping urban residents to cope with urban poverty. This version of events surrounding the MLG can be found in academic and research-focused materials (Chang and Lü 2005; Tang 1998, 2001a, 2001b, 2003, 2004,), media published for officials' consumption such as the *Zhongguo Minzheng* (*ZGMZ*) (China Civil Affairs) magazine (*Weiyuanhui* 2005; Zhu, Ren and Zhao 2002), the wider print media (Beijing-Youthdaily 2002) and speeches and writings by officials (Li 2002b). The story of the MLG as presented is pervasive and it lends coherence to what is a much more complex series of events.

The strength of such a discourse is that it presents a common story with coherent objectives. It makes explaining the policy much easier. This was reflected during interviews examining the development of the MLG where officials and researchers present a standard explanation of events and objectives surrounding the policy (Interviews 5 and 6). The dominant and implicitly rational explanation of the MLG – presented as: there were urban poor, the government recognised this, and the MLG was the response – sits easily with a history of the policy that passes through all the stages associated with the policy process in the PRC. This presentation of a simplified version of events and a straightforward explanation of a policy is comforting because it is a simple, clean and parsimonious explanation. Such a presentation of the MLG lends itself to a stages explanation of policy, but the problem with this type of explanation, as detailed in many studies of public policy (John 1998; Sabatier 1991, 1999; Sabatier and Jenkins-Smith 1993, 1994), is that it presents policy with little actual explanation. The problem with the MLG discourse is that the story presented raises an enormous number of questions as well as not holding up under closer examination. If the current explanatory discourse on the MLG is inadequate, then what explanation is satisfactory?

Table I.1 presents three iterations of the MLG from different points during the development of the policy. What should be immediately apparent is that the MLG has gone through three iterations during a period when the policy is typically presented as being fundamentally the same. This is not enough in itself to suggest that the discourse is misleading but the difference between each of the iterations does raise doubts. Shanghai is used as the starting model of the MLG because it is the first documented social assistance programme which uses the name MLG despite the later policy having closer resemblance to measures

Table I.1 Comparison of MLG iterations

Features/ MLG iteration	Shanghai 1993	National 1997	National 2002
Target group	The *San Buguan*	The *San Wu* and New Poor	1997 MLG targets plus *Xiagang* and unemployed
Funding mechanism	Local government and local enterprises	Local government	Local government plus National government subsidy
Administration mechanism	Local administrative units and *Danwei*	Local administrative units	Local administrative units

introduced in Dalian. The MLG as it initially appeared in 1993 was a local-level policy and was not an experiment in terms of the phases presented in some of the Chinese literature (Tang 1998). An experimental policy would be explicit, it would be named as such in official documents, whereas in the case of Shanghai's MLG no such documentation was found. The MLG aimed to address a very particular gap in the urban social assistance and social security apparatus as it appeared to the Shanghai Bureau of Civil Affairs and the Bureau of Labour in the early 1990s. The MLG was also administered and funded in a manner different from either the 1997 or 2002 versions, with the mechanisms combining both local government and local enterprises.

The 1997 iteration of the MLG removed enterprise involvement and expanded the target group beyond the limitations of what were labelled the Three Non-managed (*san bu guan*) (see Chapter 1) to a more general target group of traditional social assistance targets, and any household where the income fell below the MLG line – the 'new poverty' (Tang 2003). Funding was to be the responsibility of only the local government and the programme was also to be administered exclusively by local government.

By the early 2000s the MLG had changed again, with funding and administrative interventions from central government becoming standard practice. Central government became the main source of funding for the MLG in 2002, marking a significant change in the programme from its earlier design. In addition, there was a reintroduction of categorical requirements to the programme in an effort to resolve the challenge presented by laid-off workers (*xiagang*) and the exclusion of particular groups who were eligible for, but not receiving, the MLG.

Not only has the policy been through a number of technical iterations but there is also a noticeable difference and incoherence in the presentation of why the policy was being carried out. The rationale for the changes in social assistance as set out by different actors who took an active interest in the MLG has not been coherent beyond the objective of providing some form of basic income guarantee. This is clearly demonstrated when comparing the speeches and language used by Minister for Civil Affairs Duoji Cairang and Premier Li Peng in the 1990s, indicating incoherence in the presentation of why the policy was being carried out. Although the idea of a single coherent policy development with a single driving rationale is attractive, at a most basic level the development of the MLG is not this straightforward.

Finally, the discourse does not address the transition of the MLG from a local innovation to a national policy or the expansion into rural areas. The time between 1993 and 1997 is left empty except in some work where it is referred to as an experimental phase (Tang, 2003). Similarly, there has been no real discussion beyond short descriptions of what occurred in the lead-up to 2007 and the introduction of the rural *dibao*, or after.

A major failing in the discourse surrounding the MLG is in the story of its origins, or the lack of such a story. Although the initial emergence and development of the policy do get covered in English language materials, the coverage is often cursory and used for context and background before dealing with more contemporary research issues. An exception would be Chen et al. (2013) and Wong, Chen and Zeng (2014). In the majority of the Chinese-language material, both academic and official, the origins of the MLG range from a passing sentence or comment (Beijing-Youthdaily 2002; Li 2002b; Wang 2006; Zhong 2005) to no more than a paragraph (He and Hua 2005; Tang 1998; *Weiyuanhui* 2005). All contain the same basic information: that in June 1993 the city of Shanghai was the first city to implement an MLG system which had an initial level of 120 RMB per person per month.

This lack of information was further demonstrated during time in the field where the origins of the MLG were seen to be not relevant to the state of social assistance as it was in twenty-first-century China. This point of view appears flawed because not only are the origins of the MLG fundamentally important to how the policy developed, but they are also not clearly understood outside of the Chinese policy community concerned with social assistance.

The current body of work does not explain why the MLG took the form it did. For example, although it is presented as a poverty alleviation measure (Liu and Wu 2006), it excludes many urban poor and provides a very basic subsistence benefit. Finally, a rational approach does not explain the development of the policy from its initial emergence through to implementation and beyond. The question of why a policy which fundamentally transformed the most basic urban social provisions emerged, and what explained its subsequent development, is, arguably, as important as understanding how effective the policy has been in attaining its objectives. This is because by understanding the development of the MLG we can better understand and explain why the policy has the objectives it does, and why they may not be wider or more ambitious, as well as a better understanding of the outcomes of the policy. If we consider the recurring criticism that the MLG does not help in pulling people out of poverty the answer is to be found in the origins, development and implementation of the policy. In order to address these issues we need first to understand the programme.

The current literature does not provide a convincing explanation for the emergence and development of the MLG, instead focusing on description of the policy, and this is the gap that this book will address. This book makes a contribution to the China studies and policy studies disciplines by explaining a particular policy, the MLG, in the context of previous research and theoretical contributions made in the China studies, political science and public policy disciplines. The case of the MLG has, from a political perspective, received scant attention, and this book will redress that gap by examining the emergence and development of the policy from 1992 to 2014, with some discussion of announcements in 2016 in Chapter 5. In doing so this book will not only provide an in-depth explanation of the processes and influences surrounding this particular policy, it will also contribute to wider debates on policy in China and policy in general. The question this book will answer, therefore, is what explains the emergence and development of the MLG in China?

Explaining policy in China

Although explanations of the MLG as a policy are lacking, explanations of other policy developments in China have developed theoretical contributions that can help form the basis of an understanding of the MLG. Early studies of policy making in pre-reform China reflected the limitations of studying an authoritarian regime and the hierarchical nature of the Chinese state. These studies focused on the role played by the elite leadership of China. Ideology and policy objectives informed elite leaders who then made decisions that set policy for the country as a whole (Doak Barnett 1974; Harding 1981). This explanation for policy did not view elites as atomised but saw them as groupings or factions with the conflicts between factions influencing policy outcomes (Nathan 1973, 1976; Tsou 1976). While China went on to change radically – and this has informed later explanations of the policy process – it is important to remember the significant role elite leaders have in an authoritarian system like China.

While it is authoritarian, reform era China is not a totalitarian society, and the openness of the reform period helped researchers understand this more than had been possible before the 1980s. Goodman (1984) explored the idea that groups existed and might influence the policy process, suggesting that any understanding of policy needs to look beyond the role of the state and elite leaders. Harding noted the increasingly consultative nature of the Chinese state in the 1980s, which suggests that any policy explanation needs to be open to possible interactions between the state and non-state policy actors (Harding 1987).

The means by which the state made policy, both as an internal bureaucratic process and with external actors,[1] was further developed in work on Chinese bureaucracy and the later development of the Fragmented Authoritarianism model (hereafter, FA) (Lampton 1987b, 1987a, 1992, 2014; Lieberthal 1992; Lieberthal and Oksenberg 1988). As it is typically understood, this body of work argued that policy in China could be explained by understanding that the complex hierarchy and fragmentation of state institutions compelled policy actors, who are conceived of as bounded rational bureaucratic actors, to negotiate and bargain over policy (Lieberthal and Oksenberg 1988). The approach was refined further in later work by both Lieberthal (1992) and Lampton (2014).

While the term model was frequently deployed to discuss the explanation outlined by Liberthal and Oksenberg, this is problematic. Using the term suggests a particular type of methodological approach which is more rigid than FA. It is more helpful to think of FA as a heuristic or framework which allows those interested in Chinese policy processes to explain outcomes. Viewed in such a way FA is one of the most influential if misinterpreted explanations of Chinese policy making to date. As will be detailed below, the framework which FA establishes is specific enough to the Chinese case to explain policy developments but flexible enough to cover the scope of policy activities the Chinese state and society are involved in. It can explain why policy might be successfully implemented, and also explains policy failure, an area often overlooked by policy scholars.

As is typical of many approaches which seek to explain policy FA addresses both institutions and actors. Institutions are understood here in the broad sense ranging from organisational manifestations through to informal rules of the game as per the new institutionalism (Hall and Taylor 1996; March and Olsen 1984). There are three institutional elements to FA: values, political structure, decision making and implementation (Lieberthal 1992: 6–8). Lampton has also recently contributed six propositions regarding FA which can be integrated into the earlier articulations of FA (Lampton 2014: 84–87). Dealing with each of the three institutional elements of FA in turn, values are perhaps the least well-developed aspect of FA. Lieberthal emphasises that they need to be integrated or shared among those who are deciding and implementing policy. The importance here is that shared values reduce the need for leaders to use or develop other resources in order to achieve particular policy goals (Lieberthal 1992: 6). What might these values be? This is where there is less detail, but they can be tied to the dominant political ideology, the goals of particular leaders, or the guiding principles underpinning a particular organisation. For those not at the very top of the system these values would be framed by the leadership of the Chinese state and the CCP – this could be understood as the outcome of so-called speech spaces by Yan Jiaqi (Yan 1995). As will be shown in this book, leaders and bureaucrats frequently appealed to specific values when seeking to effect policy change. As the values of key leaders and the bureaucracy serving them changed so did the development of the MLG. When the values of different actors did not chime with each other there was a significant impact on the MLG system.

The second institutional element is the political structure of the Chinese state, or as Lieberthal puts it the 'formal allocation of decision-making authority' (1992: 7–8). The complex vertical and horizontal relationships between different parts of the Chinese state lead to layers of fragmentation which start with the State Council and permeate all the way down to the basic levels of local administration. Who holds resources – the key ones being information, money and personnel – and who decides how they are used can have a profound impact on a policy programme. An important element here is rank, which determines whether an actor can order or compel another to carry out an action. If two actors share rank, they cancel each other out. The structure of the state is where the first four of Lampton's propositions can be integrated into a general understanding of FA: first, the 'Chinese system is a complex grid' which has 'tens of thousands of nodes' around which different bodies must cooperate; that 'governance, policy-making and implementation problems stem from so many nodes operating in a diverse, populous, and far-flung country'; that 'many officials in the territory hold ranks equivalent to those of officials in the vertical systems'; and that 'most disputes are addressed in an environment in which financial resources are insufficient' (2014: 84–85). In the case of the MLG the structure of the Chinese state has had a profound impact on how the policy emerged, was implemented, and has subsequently developed.

The third institutional element is decision making and implementation (Lieberthal 1992: 8) and this can perhaps be best understood as the formal and informal rules of the game which come into play when policy is being made in China. Lieberthal suggests that in instances where resources are high there is a tendency towards bargaining; whereas when resources are low we might see 'groping' and a tendency to implement policy in a flexible manner which achieves some basic objectives (1992: 8, 17; see also Paine 1992). Lampton's fifth and sixth propositions support these observations, suggesting that 'politicians and bureaucrats in China have just three means by which to make decisions and coordinate behavior'; these being to use command hierarchies, use markets and bargaining, or use voting systems – with bargaining being the default choice as command is frequently ineffective and voting does not match the values of the system; and 'when neither bargaining nor command is sufficient ... disputes are kicked up the hierarchy' (2014: 86). Lower-level officials can resist policy or use policy initiatives to seek particular outcomes through 'ignoring or circumventing' decisions which are vague, taking advantage of the leeway often provided in reform-oriented policies by leaders; and, because coercion is expensive and undesirable, bargain with higher-level authorities for resources in order to see policy carried out (Lieberthal 1992: 21). While it is recognised that China is a state where considerable power is invested in the elite leadership and organisations, the structure of the state means that individuals and agencies lower down the hierarchy do find the space and means to innovate, obstruct, interpret and manipulate policy. At the same time, as will be demonstrated in the case of the MLG, the structure of the state can also constrain.

What explanation does FA have for how actors behave? This is another aspect of FA which has often been overlooked and under-developed but there are three explanations that have emerged. First, Lieberthal and Oksenberg (1988) conceive actors as bounded rational bureaucrats. Individuals within the system therefore make rational decisions based on the flows of information available to them. This emphasises the significance of information as a resource as it can have an impact on the decisions made by individuals. Second, both Lieberthal and Oksenberg (1988) and Lieberthal (1992) note that actors can tend towards ministry building when it comes to making decisions. This might not always appear the best option when it comes to policy in terms of outcomes but, for the bureaucrat, the collection of responsibilities and resources for their ministry can motivate decisions. Finally, recent work has used the concept of the policy entrepreneur (PE) to explain the behaviour of key individuals in the policy process (Hammond 2013; Mertha 2009; Teets 2015; Zhu, X. 2008, 2016; Zhu, Y. 2013; Zhu and Xiao 2015). The advantage is that this offers explanations for how actors behave and the decisions they make which goes beyond state actors and motivations driven by access to resources. This is important when considering some of the criticisms of FA.

FA suggests that the policy process in China is a convoluted, incremental and slow process dominated by competing bureaucratic actors framed in an institutional setting which encourages negotiation. This leads to bargaining, incremental change and a tendency to kick problems up the system until they reach a level where the problem can be resolved. Within the state, access to and distribution of information, money and personnel is extremely important when it comes to making and implementing resources. However, there is also space afforded within the system for actors to push particular policy agendas and in particular circumstances for policy decisions to be made and implemented with striking rapidity when values, resources and authority align.

The FA framework has proved influential, but it has also been recognised as flawed, not least by both its original authors. Lieberthal argues that while it excels at explaining the complex bargaining over resources in economic and major infrastructure projects it is less successful when explaining outcomes for less resource-rich policy. This is because without resources to bargain and negotiate over one of the driving rationales for policy actor behaviour is removed (Lieberthal 1992). In a second criticism Oksenberg suggests that it may be flawed in coping with the increasingly plural nature of the Chinese policy-making process (Oksenberg 2002). Although still dominated by the state, there is an increasing role for actors outside of the bureaucracy when it comes to policy that moves away from the focus of the FA model on rational bureaucrats as the sole actor. These may be domestic non-governmental organisations (NGOs) or international NGOs, reflecting an increasing role for consultation by policy makers with actors outside the government. Guo (2013) argues that FA is an ineffective means to explain policy and politics in China because it is static, echoing Oksenberg's criticisms. Furthermore it 'cannot distinguish a communist regime from a regular authoritarian regime' (Guo 2013:19).

These criticisms can be dealt with in turn. First, there have been studies which address policy areas beyond the traditional strength of FA including education (Paine 1992), health (Li 2013), foreign policy (Lampton 2014) and social policy (Ngok 2016). This has led to further refinement of the approach, such as the 'groping' outcome in under-resourced areas (Lieberthal 1992; Paine 1992) and the refinements of Lampton's propositions (2014: 84), and in multiple case studies Mertha introduces a means to integrate non-state actors (2009). Second, the argument that FA is not specific to China does not bear much scrutiny. This is because FA was developed specifically to explain observations of the Chinese policy-making process which built on the established understanding (Lieberthal and Oksenberg 1988). Furthermore, if one is to dismiss an approach the alternative needs to stand up to similar scrutiny. In the case of Guo's alternative, the Leninist Party-state, this is not the case. If anything, the points raised by Guo, focusing in particular on the dominant ideology regarding governance of the CCP, can be integrated into FA as part of the values that inform decision makers (Guo 2013). Additionally, the Leninist organisational principles followed by the CCP find articulation in the structure of the state, and the outcomes of this are what FA is describing and using to explain policy outcomes. Third, as has already been noted recent studies have shown that the concept of the PE can be used to explain policy developments in China and, as both Mertha (2009) and Lampton (2014) argue, this can be integrated into the FA approach.

The strength of FA as an approach lies in its specificity to China but also in that it takes a broad view of how the state – through values, structure, decision making, implementation, and the role of actors – interacts to influence policy outcomes. To view it in the narrow sense, which is often interpreted as only referring to state structure, is a mistake which is often made. For example, a recent discussion of social policy highlighted the significance of FA but went on to note the importance of centre-local and state-society relations as separate elements when they should be interpreted as part of the FA explanation (Ngok 2016). FA works best when understood as a flexible framework within which established and new observations of the Chinese policy-making system can be integrated. For example, as the nature of policy actors has changed this can be reflected in FA, as Mertha (2009) and Li (2013) have demonstrated. Another notable example would be the policy experimentation China frequently uses as articulated in Heilmann's work. This can be understood in the context of FA rather than as an explanation which requires one or other to be dismissed (Heilmann 2008a, 2008b). A final point to note is that FA has persisted since it emerged in the late 1980s as the main explanation for policy making in the PRC which suggests that it cannot be so easily dismissed.

Theoretical approach of the book

This study will explain the emergence and development of the MLG while acknowledging the extensive empirical and theoretical work that has preceded it. What the body of work discussed above has demonstrated is that China, although authoritarian, is not a homogenous entity in terms of policy making. Policy decisions and outcomes cannot be explained simply by looking at the actions of the elite. Differences can manifest for example as competing groups trying to attain political supremacy as described by Nathan (1973, 1976) and Tsou (1976); or the distinctions between specialists and generalists outlined by Liberthal and Oksenberg (1988). What the studies above do suggest is that explaining policy requires acknowledging the influence of individual policy actors (state and non-state), the influence of previous decisions, and the influence of the structure of the state and hierarchy of state institutions.

I argue, based on my study of the MLG, that an adapted form of FA provides the answer to the question of what explains the emergence, implementation and subsequent development of the MLG between 1992 and 2014. This also helps to explain the answer to the question of what *dibao* is for, because the process of forming, implementing and managing a policy over years defines its objectives and the realities within which it operates. The interaction between the three institutional aspects of FA, the broad conception of policy actors, and some additional elements borrowed from the new institutionalism (Hall and Taylor 1996; Lowndes 1996; March and Olsen 1984; Peters 2005; Solinger 2005), explains the origins, implementation and development of the MLG. This also helps address some of the challenges which emerge in the literature discussed above: the mismatch between the discourse on the MLG and what really happened; and the mismatch between what the MLG was implemented to do and what the MLG is interpreted as being for.

The framework for analysis follows the structure articulated in the preceding discussion of FA. The key points and periods will be addressed through a discussion of the various elements and their impact on particular outcomes. This leads to the overall argument that the story of the MLG's origins, implementation and subsequent development has been shaped not by the goal of poverty alleviation but the changing priorities of a number of key bureaucrats and leaders – who in large part are focused on social stability as a policy goal rather than any moral or rights-based desire to address the problem of poverty. The manner in which these developments played out were shaped by the structures of the state, which both facilitated and constrained the decisions and actions of particular actors. All of this was framed by the context of previous decisions and the general ideological (or value) trends of the CCP and the state at a given point in time. FA, with a few embellishments from the PE and new institutionalist literature, provides a framework within which the origins, implementation and subsequent development of the MLG can be understood.

In each of the chapters which follow the explanation for different developments in *dibao* will be based on the core points of the FA framework as follows. First, the difficult concept of values. These are broadly understood as covering two general areas leading to one specific outcome significant to policy actors. The ideological climate of the particular period in question forms the general value context within which policy actors operate, and is therefore significant. Observers of China, as is the case with other political systems, will recognise that the governing ideology generated by the CCP and state influence the context and discussion of policy. In some instances it will rule out certain possibilities, and in others it will create opportunities. The goals of particular policy actors, both leaders and those further down the system, will also establish a set of values that different policy actors will need to address, engage with and acknowledge when seeking to develop and implement policy. These two elements together help form the 'speech space' within which policy actors operate. The idea of speech spaces is that the utterances of leaders in China constrains what those below them are able to discuss, and how they might frame policy options (Yan 1995). Values are something which frame what leaders and bureaucrats might seek to do, and so act as constraints; but they can also be exploited, and for some policy actors the framing of a particular policy so that it matches the values of their leaders or subordinates is a strategy for getting a policy implemented or adjusted.

As Lieberthal (1992) notes, the identification, unpacking and attribution of values within the Chinese political system is problematic due to the closed nature of Chinese politics and policy making. Arguably this is true of any system where values encapsulate a set of unknowables which can only to some extent be determined through anthropological and survey work. How then do we navigate this issue in the Chinese context? There are two factors to consider here. First, what we might consider to be the true values of individuals which are to some extent unknowable and can only be pieced together through interviews and observation where the opportunity presents itself. Second, what we can consider to be the values which individuals say matter to them. These values are much easier for us to observe as they manifest in the numerous documents and speeches that China's bureaucracy and bureaucrats produce. It is the second set of values which are accessible and observable in the Chinese context and can form the foundation for discussion. We might question whether or not these espoused values are true, but at the same time we can question the extent to which this matters. As noted, the top leader in China's system sets the speech spaces available to Party cadres and state bureaucrats who are then constrained by what has been said by those above them. Officials in China who want to get things done will match their objectives with those of the day, meld them to the dominant ideas and values espoused by their superiors, and through this exploit the constraints placed on them by the hierarchy of the speech space.

In the same way that values both constrain and provide opportunities for policy actors to exploit, the structures of decision making and resource allocation are a similar set of obstacles and spaces for China's policy actors to work with and around. The complex mesh of vertical and horizontal relationships does provide ample opportunities for disagreement or lack of resources to manifest in non-implementation or incomplete implementation of policy handed down from Beijing. This can lead to a range of outcomes depending on the particular circumstances, such as policy getting stuck, decisions getting kicked up to higher levels of authority, innovations occurring in the spaces and gaps, or policy getting implemented very quickly when elite leaders get involved.

As noted by previous explanations of FA, there are two elements of the Chinese political structure to consider when seeking to understand policy developments: rank and resources. The policy process runs into difficulties when actors or organisations with the same rank disagree or when there is a mismatch in the resources available and those required. In the worst case, both factors come into play. As will be shown, lower-rank actors and organisations can find their goals completely frustrated without higher-level support; similarly, higher-level actors can see their objectives unravel when a lack of resources leads to the phenomenon of groping or non-implementation.

The dynamics of political structure do not just occur in the centre. As has already been alluded to, a common point of friction is between organisations of the same rank. In the Chinese system this is particularly important when looking at the relationship between line ministries and the provincial government, both of which share the same rank. At the local level the dynamic is further complicated because, in the case of the MLG and the MCA for example, a local department will find itself equal in rank to its local counterparts in other areas (for example health, human resources and social security) as well as subordinate to the higher tiers of local government and the ministry in Beijing. It is this complex mesh of relationships which both constrains policy options and provides opportunities in particular circumstances.

This brings us to the final element of FA – decision making and implementation. Unlike the preceding two elements this brings together, or manifests, the complexities of values, structure and also the behaviour of actors involved in the policy process. However, it is also institutional in that it is a series of rules of the game which we might expect actors to follow. Decisions are informed by both the values and policy objectives of particular actors, as well as their place within the political structure. As will be shown, it is important who someone is, what their values are or how they engage with the dominant values of the time, but also where they are in the political system. This informs the kind of decisions which can be made. It is the same when we consider implementation. As Paine (1992) and Lieberthal (1992) noted, when structures are 'mushy' and resources are low we can expect to see 'groping' by lower-level bureaucracies as they seek to achieve a form of good-enough implementation. At the same time, the space in the system allows this 'groping' for implementation to manifest in different types of implementation or different models. These can be both advantageous, providing new means to achieve goals with reduced resources, or problematic, as adjustments are made to policies that lead to undesirable outcomes. In order to achieve the desired implementation type or policy goals, a significant part of the policy process in China is attempting to navigate around these outcomes. This can lead to commands, pleading and bargaining, the use of *guanxi* or political capital, and the injection of resources. These efforts are in turn subject to the values and political structure of the PRC – in some cases such efforts are enough to overcomes the problems and achieve a satisfactory implementation, in others the efforts fall short and problems continue. In most cases a middle ground is found, where the problem might be addressed to some extent but the underlying issue persists. In the case of the MLG, issues such as the extent the MLG reaches its target group, the adjustment of the MLG when prices change, and the overall purpose of the programme are all examples where the desires of the policy makers have run into the problem of political structures and the preferences of different decision makers resulting in unsatisfactory implementation. This has then had to be dealt with through a mixture of appealing to values, infusions of resources, and the use of the additional authority of higher level actors.

Key to this policy process are the policy actors who make the decisions on the form a policy might take, how it is designed, and ultimately how it is implemented. Policy actors are subject to a series of constraints which can determine the cases of action available to them and also the strategies that might be used to achieve particular outcomes. The values of the political system and its structures are two constraints, others are the previous decisions that form the historical context within which developments occur – so-called path dependence which has been used to help explain certain development in China (Solinger 2005).

How an actor or group of actors respond to these constraints helps to explain how a policy subsequently develops. The default is for the actor to make decisions, based on the information and other resources available, which best serve their interests. This can be understood as the bounded rational actor as described by Libertahal and Oksenberg in their original work articulating FA (1988), the vested interests of Beland and Yu's (2004) study of pension reforms, and the bureaucratic interests of Duckett' study of healthcare reform (2001, 2003). Depending on the outcomes of this calculation these actors might comply with decisions from above, 'grope' for an implementation of best fit, or in some cases obstruct the policy process using the means articulated in the preceding sections.

However, actors can also seek to pursue particular policies which benefit their organisation beyond simple ministry building, or support a set of values and goals that they want to see implemented. This is where the PE becomes a useful explanatory tool to help explain why some actors behave in the way they do and how they achieve particular outcomes. PEs can inhabit any part of the state structure or, indeed, can be non-state actors. What distinguishes them is exploiting the spaces in the state, actively pursuing changes in policy to fit their particular goals, and when circumstances allow it exploiting so-called policy windows – often a crisis or political event – that provide the opportunity of getting a particular policy onto the agenda and eventually implemented (Kingdon 1984). In both cases the role of policy actors is to decide and implement within the constraints and opportunities of China's FA.

The case of the MLG is an example of a low resource policy in a 'mushy' policy sector which has led to opportunities for PEs to shape the agenda but also for implementation to be subject to extensive 'groping' type outcomes. The MLG has been subject to and shaped by the values of the time, with actors exploiting these values in order to pursue different developments at different times. This helps explain the changing forms of priorities regarding the MLG, including explosive growth, direction of resources and legislative activity giving way to drift and business as usual. At the same time the decisions and activities of actors, shaped by the political structures they occupy, have shaped the MLG. The decisions made, and possible means of implementation, are defined by the authority and resources available to particular positions in the political structure. The MLG is highly susceptible to this as it is a responsibility of the relatively low-resource MCA which at times has struggled to see the programme implemented, leading to 'groping' outcomes as the original policy was sacrificed in order to achieve some form of good-enough implementation.

Overall, the MLG is subject to the FA which characterises the Chinese system of politics and policy making. It is a product of the changing values of China's political and bureaucratic actors operating within the constraints and opportunities of the political structure. What the MLG is for, how it was implemented, the features of its design, and how it operates day to day are all defined by these features. This explains why the MLG faces the challenges it does, why its future is arguably ambiguous, and why the Chinese government is still in the process of tweaking how the programme operates.

A note on methods

To explain why and how the MLG emerged, was implemented and subsequently developed, a mixture of methods were used. This section will briefly discuss the different approaches I used. The project is an exploratory qualitative case study which uses descriptive statistics where appropriate. The primary source base for the project is a combination of contemporary documents in the Chinese language which include government reports, circulars, regulations, speeches by officials, and also magazine and newspaper articles; and, second, interviews conducted with a range of policy actors and researchers who were involved in or who observed closely the policy process surrounding the development of the MLG. Materials were collected, and interviews were conducted, during a series of fieldwork trips between 2005 and 2015. During these field trips I spent time in Tianjin, Beijing, Anqing (Anhui Province), and Hong Kong where I made use of the Universities Service Center at the Chinese University of Hong Kong. On two of these field trips I was hosted by the Zhou Enlai School of Government, Nankai University, and the Social Policy Research Center, Chinese Academy of Social Sciences. Ethical approval was granted for all of these field trips by either the University of Glasgow or the University of Edinburgh.

Having gathered the materials I adopted a grounded approach to building an explanation which addressed the question of why and how the MLG emerged, was implemented, and subsequently developed the way it did. This included reading all documents and interview notes/transcripts before coding them according to a frame which I built up over time and expanded/reconfigured as new documents and interviews were coded. These coded materials then allowed me to ask questions of the materials and get answers informed by the evidence. For example, the relationship between key phrases, particular actors and their significance at a given point in time could be deduced from the documents by looking for a particular combination of codes. Once an explanation had been developed it was then compared to the existing theoretical contributions on the policy process in the China studies, political science and policy studies disciplines. It was this process which led to the conclusion that a mixture of FA and policy entrepreneurship best explains why and how the MLG developed the way it did. Throughout the text I refer to the relevant documents directly and use a number system for interviews. Each interview number corresponds to the list in the Appendix at the end of the book, so readers can see the place where the interview was conducted and the position of the interviewee. For more details on methodological matters please refer to previous works which formed the foundation for this book (Hammond 2010, 2011a, 2011b, 2013).

Structure of the book

To show how FA explains the origins, implementation and development of the MLG this book will be structured as follows. Chapter 1 will provide a historical background for the reader detailing the development of social assistance in China from before 1992 and the emergence of the MLG through to 2014; and it will discuss developments in the structure of poverty in China during the reform era. This will provide the reader with a detailed account of the MLG which will serve as the foundation for the arguments that follow and will also situate social assistance in China within the larger context of poverty and the alleviation of poverty.

Chapters 2 and 3 deal with the urban incarnation of *dibao* covering a number of developments between 1992 and 2003. Chapter 2 addresses the emergence and development of the MLG from local innovation to national policy. The chapter then discusses two key processes of the period 1992–1999. First, the spread of the MLG; and, second, the efforts to achieve national implementation. In these examples we see the importance of particular policy actors as they interact with the dominant values of the time and struggle or exploit the constraints imposed by the structure of the state. This results in a compromise in some instances leading to a diversity of MLG models implemented across China's cities; but it also leads to innovative resource use to ensure implementation is achieved, notably through the use of information to cajole uncooperative local government to comply with the centre's demands.

In Chapter 3 the book discusses how the efforts made to get the MLG implemented resulted in a number of unintended and unwanted consequences – not least the proliferation of local variations and the exclusion of particular target groups from the programme. In seeking to deal with these issues the MCA's desires collided, fortuitously, with the political agenda of a powerful policy actor in the form of Zhu Rongji, Premier of China from 1998 to 2003. In seeking to resolve the crisis in China's SOEs and the failing support system developed for laid-off (*xiagang*) workers the MLG was presented as a ready-made programme which could resolve the issues – matching the goals of a powerful policy actor and the dominant values of the CCP and state at the time. This resulted in the programme being infused with resources it had previously lacked, the nature of the programme being altered to reflect its new purpose, and the original underlying problems being (temporarily) addressed.

In Chapter 4 the rural MLG programme is addressed. Nationally implemented in 2007, ten years after its urban predecessor, the rural programme has experienced similar challenges when it came to implementation in spite of significant changes being made on the basis of previous experience with the urban *dibao* system. Again, the confluence of changing values, hindering and enabling political structures, and the different roles of actors help to explain these developments. In this chapter the book will first address the regulatory framework around which rural *dibao* is structured. This will highlight differences and similarities in relation to the urban programme. The chapter then addresses why the rural MLG was implemented when it was. It will be argued that the changing value priorities of the time, initiated by the accession of Hu Jintao and Wen Jiabao, meant that an opportunity for the MCA to push the programme into rural areas emerged, building on the perceived success of the urban programme; it also provided the MCA with a further foothold in rural social policy in addition to its traditional provision of the Five Guarantees (*wubao*). Politically, the rural MLG matched the changing values of the time and was presented as being useful for the new leadership regime. However, as the chapter will go on to show, the implementation of the rural MLG ran into problems similar to the urban programme. Local capacity is limited and priorities are mismatched to the programme, leading to misdirection of funds and the use of the rural MLG in rural areas as a resource for local officials to use as they see fit rather than a means to providing families with a minimum standard of living. These problems highlight the particular problems caused by centre-local fragmentation in the Chinese system with local rural administrations a long way from the decision makers, underfunded, understaffed and interpreting policy within a particular local context leading to groping outcomes.

Chapter 5 is a critical discussion of developments between 2007 and 2016 and whether or not further institutionalisation of the MLG would help. Based on Fewsmith's (2013) discussion of institutionalisation the chapter will address two key goals, making reform last and making reform matter, and asks what is the answer regarding *dibao*? To do this, three developments are discussed: the stalled Social Relief Law; the responsiveness problem; and changes in the *dibao* in 2014 and 2016. It will be argued that in each case the challenges facing *dibao* are a consequence of the fragmented nature of the system. Can institutionalisation resolve fragmentation and what form might this take? The idea of indexation and automatic government will be brought in to serve as a basis for this discussion (Weaver 1988). Such an approach might resolve a number of the issues regarding the impasse of actor obstruction and structural blocks deployed due to a lack of funding; but it would also change the MLG from what it is now – a useful tool that can be adapted and moulded to serve the rapidly changing environment and values in which China's policy making takes place. As Weaver notes in his discussion of indexation in American politics, overcoming various interests is at the centre of indexation as a policy and while it might appear to resolve certain problems it can also have undesirable outcomes for policy makers and those at the receiving end of policy outcomes (Weaver 1988). The challenge of what to do about the problems the MLG faces is that the proposed fixes do not take into account what the intended goals of the policy are, and how this is always related to the established values of the time. It may be possible to address the problems the MLG faces through addressing elements related to the structural aspects of China's system, for example by automating resource allocation, but what this chapter will make clear is that the underlying values within which decisions are being made are not necessarily favourable to such outcomes. The MLG serves particular objectives and these are not necessarily to benefit those most in need.

The book concludes by revisiting the arguments presented in the preceding chapters. It then returns to the central question of the book: what explains the origins, implementation and development of the MLG? It will be argued that FA with some additional embellishment from the literature on policy entrepreneurship and new institutionalism provides all the tools necessary to address the question. The urban and rural MLG are a product of China's political system. They were conceived as ideas and implemented as policies within the complex hierarchy of vertical and horizontal structures and married to the dominant values of the time as different actors sought to see the MLG first implemented and subsequently adjusted to fit their particular agendas. Differences between actors in the structure of the state, in particular between the central and local government, meant that the implemented programme frequently did not match that initially envisaged, and a continuing theme of *dibao*'s development is the efforts made to ensure that the programme in practice matched that desired by the decision makers at the very top. But, in order to understand all of this we have start with the historical foundations of social assistance in China and the emergence of the MLG.

Note

1. In the discussion of energy policy in Lieberthal and Oksenberg (1988) the focus is on intra-bureaucratic agents, but external actors were included. These actors were transnational companies or government actors providing the theoretical basis for the model could be stretched to encompass INGOs or NGOs, see Oksenberg's comment below.

Chapter 1

Historical Background to Dibao and the Question of Poverty in China

Introduction

As with any policy area, social assistance in China does not develop in a historical vacuum. The weight of precedent, established vested interests and the emergence of particular policy paths are all consequences of a policy's history. In addition, how a policy's story is told and later relayed can go a long way to shaping how it is responded to and the extent to which it is deemed successful. The MLG system in China has been heavily influenced by its own history as well as the preceding history of social assistance.[1] A final point to consider is the way in which the problem that a particular policy is addressing is defined or measured and the ways in which this has developed over time. The following discussion has three main aims. First, the chapter will introduce the historical background to social assistance in China. This will not be a comprehensive history of social assistance in China before the 1990s, but it will provide readers with a background to developments which have, to varying degrees, influenced the more contemporary developments of *dibao*. Second, the chapter will provide a review of the development of *dibao* from 1992 to approximately 2014. The intention of this part of the chapter is to provide readers with a broad understanding of the developmental events which occurred during this period regarding both urban and rural *dibao* but not to provide the details and argument which subsequent chapters will explore. Instead, this section will provide readers with the context in which to situate the subsequent discussion. The third and final part of the chapter takes a different tack and will discuss the ways that poverty is defined and the ways in which the problem has developed during the period that *dibao* has been practised. The chapter therefore follows a straightforward structure addressing, first, the history of social assistance prior to the reform era, which is then followed by a more detailed discussion of the development of the *dibao* from 1992 through to 2014. Third, and finally, the chapter will discuss how poverty has changed in China during the reform era.

Social assistance before 1992

While the primary concern of this book is the period after 1992 and the MLG policy it is impossible to address this without first discussing what preceded it. The reason for this is twofold. First, in some Chinese texts it is noted that there has been something practised or an ideal articulated which might be described as social assistance for the last 2,000 years. Having said this, with the exception of the Ming and Qing periods, there is little evidence presented to support this beyond a fairly generic set of principles which might be associated with an ideal of Chinese dynastic governance (Zhong 2005). It is also important to remember that China went through a number of different regimes and the practice of government in dynastic China changed within and between dynasties. Having said this by the time of the Qing (1644–1912) dynasty there was a system in place that broadly speaking might be understood as providing the Chinese populace with a system of social assistance with critical contributions by both state and society.

The system which formed the traditional provision of social assistance in pre-Republican era China was primarily cantered on dealing with two problems that could impact the population and by extension the dynastic government: seasonal population movements and hunger, and movements of people and starvation brought about by natural disasters. Seasonal assistance was provided through a mixture of state and societal efforts in Beijing which, as noted by (Chen 2012), would provide the annual influx of hungry rural workers with food and clothing during the winter months. In other areas it would depend on local capacity but a mixture of in-kind services would be offered by benevolent halls and associations so that the poor could access medical care, winter clothing, food and burials (Rowe 1990). When disaster struck, Wong (1982) notes the importance of the nationwide system of granaries which acted as a means for the government to redirect food in times of crisis, such as a flood or earthquake, and alleviate the increase in food prices and hunger which might then lead to social instability.

Towards the end of the nineteenth century attitudes towards poverty and the instruments that could be used began to change in China. This resulted in a radical reconfiguration of how the state approached those in need and extensive experimentation with new ideas. Chen (2012: 24) argues that from as early as 1903 there had been a significant shift in attitudes towards the poor in China. Rather than viewing poverty as an unfortunate but natural part of society it was viewed as an illness at the root of China's failings versus the Western and Japanese colonial powers. Chen (2012) and Lipkin (2006) both note that, in response to encroachment by Western powers and defeat to Japan in the 1890s, the question of the nation's poverty became a key area of concern. China was viewed by its own intellectuals as a nation of poverty, and turning the poor into productive citizens was viewed as a crucial part of reviving the nation. In order to do this, ideas were borrowed and adapted from outside of China. In 1905 workhouses were introduced in Beijing and spread to other cities like Chengdu (Stapleton 2000). These workhouses were designed with the intention of reforming individuals into productive citizens through a regime of work and training. The penal influence of Japan's workhouses is notable in that the Chinese workhouses would often mix both the impoverished and those who had been accused or convicted of a crime (Chen 2012: 31). In order for the poor to become productive they must be able to work, not just to consume, and this was to be achieved through training and if necessary coercion (Chen 2012; Lipkin 2005, 2006; Stapleton 2000).

After the Qing collapsed following the revolution of 1911 social assistance continued across China in different forms, although the link to productive citizenship was typically maintained. Between 1911 and the 1930s the idea that poverty was a social illness, and like all diseases should be treated, became more embedded in efforts to address China's national predicament (Lipkin 2006: 50). At the same time the country faced unprecedented challenges as it fragmented internally and was then invaded by Japan in the 1930s. Zhong (2005) notes that in spite of these challenges the early Republic enacted a 'poor law' in 1915 and this was subsequently followed by legislation in 1929, 1930, 1943 and 1944, although the specifics are not elaborated on. Studies which cover the Nanjing decade (1928–1937) do note that social assistance was increasingly viewed as a priority of the state not just because of the conflation of China's weakness internationally and domestic impoverishment but also as a means to exert social control, maintain regime legitimacy, and ultimately achieve long-sought-for modernity (Lin 2004; Lipkin 2005, 2006). It is also apparent through recent scholarship that in spite of the fragmentation of the Chinese state and the excesses of warlordism social assistance and more broadly defined social welfare efforts were established and maintained in various cities, these might be through the state as in Guangzhou under Chen Jitang (Lin 2004) or through charitable efforts driven by individuals such as Li Yuanxin in Shanghai (Fitzgerald and Kuo 2017). It is important not to forget those who were at the receiving end of these developments and as Dryburgh (2016) notes in her study of 1930s Beijing the notion of the poor as a passive population that the state and charities imposed themselves on needs to be challenged – people in China, much as elsewhere, navigate and assert themselves in the face of the demands of the social welfare regime. Ultimately, however, the coming of war undid many efforts to address China's impoverished population as state institutions failed or collapsed in the face of conflict or the movement of refugees.

The period following the collapse of the Nationalist regime and the establishment of the PRC after 1949 saw a number of significant changes in how social assistance was managed that have subsequently influenced the options and choices available to policy makers in the 1990s. These are perhaps best summed up as two divisions which were imposed on the population. Perhaps the most significant was the introduction of the household registration system or *hukou*. This divided the population into those who had agricultural (*nongye*) and non-agricultural or urban (*fei-nongye*) status. The policies which were subsequently implemented to address areas like social assistance were predicated on this rural-urban divide. The introduction of the *hukou* therefore had a profound long-term impact and would dictate where an individual might live, work, and what services they could access (for a detailed discussion of the motivations and working of the hukou see Wallace 2014).

The population was further divided on the basis of an individual's ability to work. Broadly speaking, this was the same in both rural and urban areas although the specific policies were different. By the early 1960s a system had emerged where the foundations of social security, welfare and assistance were all in place. Through urban SOEs, collective enterprises and rural collectives the PRC sought to absorb excess labour and achieve a situation where the majority of those who might previously have been deemed poor, a vagrant or in some other way deviant were absorbed into the working population. Because they were working, for either an enterprise or a collective, individuals could access social security and welfare provisions, such as subsidised food and housing, or basic medical care. It is important to keep in mind that these provisions were heavily dependent on the enterprise or collective and therefore did not provide a universal standard of provision.

The problem remained, however, of those who could not earn their social security or welfare through the contribution of their labour. The state developed an obligation to provide assistance for those who were deemed 'without' or as it has become known the 'Three No's' or 'Three Withouts' (*sanwu*). The Three No's were no ability to work, no income and no carer nor guardian. This covered a select group of people who fell into one or more categories who would then be eligible for some form of separate support – typically the orphaned, the old and the disabled (*gulaoyoucan*) (Wong 1998; Zhong 2005). The kind of support provided would depend on where the person falling into these categories resided. In rural areas the provision of social assistance was delegated to the collective organisation, and this did mean that the support given varied a great deal between different areas. The common marker though was the 'Five Guarantees' or *wubao* which ensured that the poor received food and fuel, housing, clothes, medical care and burial (Leung and Nann 1995; Saich 2008). These were provided *in kind* to a household rather than in cash and to the individual. In urban areas things worked a bit differently, reflecting the organisational differences and also the greater significance afforded to cities by China's leaders. Individuals would have to fall into one of the Three No's categories and would then receive a cash pay-out through the local government and neighbourhood offices and administered by the MCA. Funding for social assistance was dictated by the Ministry of Finance (MoF), and by all accounts the amount received by those who qualified was meagre (Leung and Nann 1995; Wong 1998).

The period of PRC history under Mao is typically viewed as being tumultuous, but remarkably it appears that the system of social assistance was maintained throughout, with the exception of the most chaotic period of the Cultural Revolution in the late 1960s when the idea of social assistance and poverty became politically unacceptable. With the return of relatively stable govern-

ment in the early to mid-1970s an essentially unchanged system was reintroduced (Zhong 2005). The changes which ultimately became the twin policies of
Reform and Opening began in the mid- to late 1970s but at this point in time
the impact on social assistance was minimal. Dixon (1981; Dixon and Macarov
1992) notes that in spite of the state system in place there remained an emphasis
on local responsibility and the role of the family during the Mao era, and this, to
some extent, facilitated patchy provision and local variation across the country
which is borne out by subsequent studies that have placed an emphasis on the
role of the family in social assistance (Gao 2017; Leung and Nann 1995).

The redrafted constitution for the PRC made it clear that the state, on paper
at least, continued to be committed to the idea of providing social assistance to
its populace. Article 45 of the 1982 Constitution notes that:

> Citizens of the People's Republic of China have the right material assistance from
> the state and society when they are old, ill, or disabled. The state develops social
> insurance, social relief, and medical and health services that are required for citizens
> to enjoy this right. (NPC 1999)

There are two points which are worth noting here before moving on. First, the
1954, 1975 and 1978 Constitutions all had similar or exactly the same wording so
the commitment to social assistance can be viewed as being deeply rooted in the
conception of state responsibility. Second, the article follows, or arguably helps
establish, the narrow terms of the Three No's and does not commit the Chinese
state to providing for anyone who does not fall into a particular category.

While social assistance continued without much change in the 1980s the
forces that were ultimately going to drive significant policy change had already
been unleashed. It was in rural areas where reform first took hold and began
to reconfigure the Chinese economy, and as a consequence social and political
relations. The introduction of the household responsibility contracts formalised the de-collectivisation of agriculture that had occurred in some areas and
forced the issue in others (Dikötter 2016; Unger 1985–1986). This ultimately
led to the collapse of the collective provisions established through the traditional
structures of agricultural production, and led to a crisis in welfare which, as
will be discussed, took decades to resolve. In urban areas the challenges reform
presented to the social assistance system took longer to become apparent. By the
early 1990s the decision that some kind of reform to the system was necessary
had taken hold within certain parts of the state. This has been tied to three
developments by Chinese scholars: first, the introduction of the market and
changes in the state-owned sector created a new group of workers who could
work but were either underpaid or underemployed, the so-called new poverty
or *xin pinkun*; second, provisions which traditionally were the responsibility
of SOEs were not being delivered, in particular the non-payment of pensions
began to become a critical problem; third, and finally, once the state did begin
to seek a resolution to the problem of the state-owned sector it created a new

problem in the form of unemployed or laid-off (*xiagang*) workers (Guan 2000; Tang 1998, 2003, 2005). Further, it should not be forgotten that the late 1980s and early 1990s were also a period of significant political and social instability due to the protests in 1989 and subsequent crackdown.

A history of *dibao*

The MLG system was first implemented during a period when China was re-emerging from a period of political and economic crisis and introspection. As will be shown in subsequent chapters the context in which *dibao* developed was critically important. The narrative which subsequently developed regarding *dibao* in both the Chinese and English languages has mirrored to some extent the notion that the policy was implemented in a manner that reflects the kind of scientific and rational principles that the Chinese government itself has articulated regarding the policy. This is not the case, and as I have argued elsewhere this does not stand up to scrutiny (Hammond 2010). While it is not the purpose of this book to provide a blow-by-blow account of developments regarding the MLG it is useful to have a brief chronological review of developments, and for the purposes of clarity this is presented as a series of discrete time periods.

Emergence 1992–1993

The first *dibao* system appeared in Shanghai in 1993. This followed investigations and discussions of policy changes which had started in 1992. The policy was introduced as part of a multifaceted effort to deal with concerns about increasing social instability as a consequence of reforms in local industries. The MLG was one branch of two which were implemented at the same time. The other was a minimum wage which would serve to protect those who were in work. The MLG was implemented on 1 June 1993, and had the means test and locally set *dibao* line that has defined the policy in subsequent years. The line was set at an initial 120 RMB per household member per month. If a household could demonstrate that its total income fell below the *dibao* line then it would receive a payment that would bring its income up to the line. Funds were raised by the local government and payments received from local enterprises (Shi 2002).

The process which ultimately led to the MLG being implemented was kick-started by the then Mayor of Shanghai, Huang Ju – when in late 1992 he ordered a report from the city's Bureau for Civil Affairs and for Labour – who worked with the Bureaux for Industry, Commerce, as well as the local branches of the Trades Union, Women's Federation, and district governments on what particular problems forthcoming enterprise reforms might present. Crucially, the report was also to present possible government responses regarding how to deal with those affected and for whom the Civil Affairs and Labour bureaucracy was responsible (Shi 2002; Yang 2003). The report was presented in January 1993.

With the title 'Views Regarding Resolving Livelihood Difficulties Faced by Elderly Residents' three groups were identified as being inadequately supported by the current system – the elderly who were poor but had children, workers who were unemployed without means of support, and finally dependants of deceased workers. Collectively these groups were identified as falling outside of existing remits and were given the label of Three Non-managed (*san bu guan*) (Shi 2002; Tang 1998; Yang 2003).

The MLG emerged in the subsequent discussion of the report and through the Social Security Committee which was formed in January 1993, with the Bureau of Civil Affairs taking the lead; it was given the remit to prepare a policy plan. In April 1993 the Shanghai City Government and related bureaux met and the fundamentals of what became the MLG were decided. There were two important decisions made here. First, any new policy programme needed to be able to deal with changes in prices, something which the Three No's was deemed unable to do. Second, the response should be a single, city-wide policy which was not an addition to the existing systems. The meeting decided that the response should be a two-branch policy. The first was to be the minimum wage, set initially at 210 RMB a month. This would ensure that those who were working would have a guaranteed income. The second branch was to be the MLG. On 7 May 1993 the Shanghai Bureaux of Civil Affairs, Finance, Labour, Social Insurance, Personnel Department, and Trades Union produced the 'Circular regarding establishing a local urban resident Minimum Livelihood Guarantee line' (Shi 2002). Once it was implemented on 1 June 1993 the MLG was awarded to an initial 7,680 recipients (Shanghai-BCA 1997).

Transition 1994–1997

Following implementation in Shanghai the next significant development occurred in April 1994 when the National Conference of Civil Affairs took place in Beijing. In two speeches the then Minister for Civil Affairs, Duoji Cairang, and Premier Li Peng both endorsed the adoption of the MLG (Duoji 1995a; Li 1995). While neither of the speeches was an announcement requiring national implementation, they did suggest that local government should adopt MLG systems and address the problems affecting certain groups such as pensioners experiencing non-payment of pensions. The content of the speeches was spread beyond the meeting itself when they were written into the MCA's circular regarding the conference (MCA 1995).

The focus of activity shifted slightly in 1995 as the MLG became a topic discussed at meetings within the Civil Affairs bureaucracy. In May 1995 the MCA held two meetings that appear to have been critical for spreading ideas regarding the implementation and practice of the MLG; a northern meeting taking place in Qingdao and a southern meeting which was hosted by Xiamen. This was followed by the MCA hosting a meeting in July regarding theoretical and research work on *dibao* (Hong 2004). In August, Duoji spoke at a

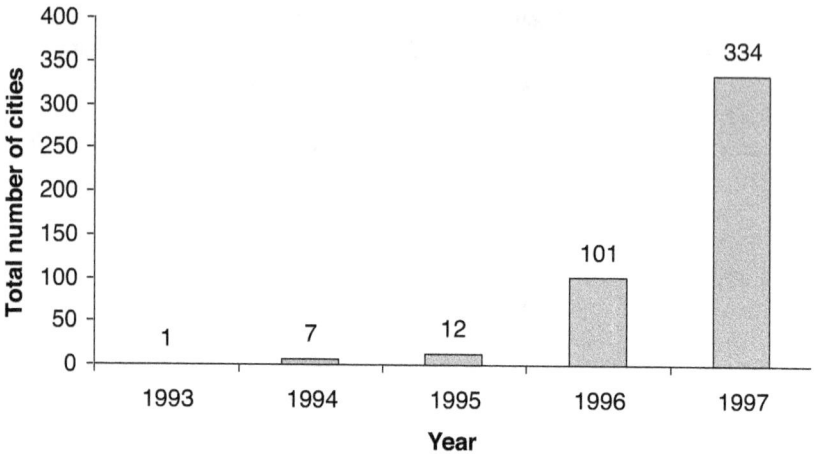

Figure 1.1 Total number of cities implementing the MLG 1993–1997

Source: see Hammond (2010: 251–254) for details on sources and calculation of city numbers.

symposium of provincial, city and district Civil Affairs department heads and addressed problems in the adoption of the MLG (Duoji 1998a). These exhortations to adopt *dibao* were responded to with a number of cities implementing their own MLG systems (Hong 2004; Leung 2006; Tang 2005). In 1994 this included Shanghai, Xiamen, and Qingdao adopting the system. In 1995, Fuzhou, Dalian, Shengyang, and Haikou implemented systems in January, Wuxi in April, Guangzhou in July, and Nanning in September (Tang 2005). This left approximately twenty Municipalities and provincial capitals in addition to several hundred smaller cities without MLG systems; the spread of the system was, at this point, fairly limited and slow.

The following year saw a significant shift in the kind of activity associated with the MLG. In January 1996 the then Vice-Minister of Civil Affairs Xi Ruixin made it clear that national implementation of the MLG was an objective (Xi 1998). Following this, the MLG was incorporated into the Ninth Five Year Plan (1996–2000) and the 2010 Long-Term Development Goals (Li 1998e; NPC 1998). This meant that the MLG had moved from being something the MCA was promoting to part of the long-term planning of the central government. There was also, during this period, an uptick in the number of cities implementing *dibao* systems with the number breaking 100 as shown in Figure 1.1 above.

National Implementation 1997–1999

For *dibao* 1997 is the year the policy moved from being the concern of plans and a small part of the Chinese state machinery to a policy of national significance. The publication of the 'State Council circular regarding the establishing of a national urban resident Minimum Livelihood Guarantee system' (State Council 1997; 1997 Circular hereafter) meant that, for the first time, there was a centrally endorsed set of goals and design elements for the MLG that local government would need to follow in order to achieve the explicit objective of national implementation in China's cities. Surrounding the publication of the 1997 Circular were a series of meetings hosted by the MCA including work report meetings for eastern and western areas, these were held in May and August respectively (Duoji 1998d, 1998e). Following these meetings and the publication of the 1997 Circular, MCA officials promoted the policy and articulated plans for *dibao* in November and December (Duoji 1998c; Fan 1998a; Li 1998a). *Dibao* also received national attention, with Minister Duoji writing an editorial for the *People's Daily* in August (Duoji 1998f). Outside of the MCA there were also high-level leaders involved in the run-up to and announcement of the 1997 Circular. These included Li Peng at a meeting regarding pensions in July (Li 1998f), State Councillor Li Guixian at the launch of the MLG and a meeting with MCA officials in December (Li 1998b, 1998c), Vice-Premier Zou Jiahua at the policy launch (Zou 1998), and in Party General Secretary and President of China Jiang Zemin's report to the National Party Congress in September (Jiang 1998). However, as Figure 1.1 shows, by the end of the year only 334 cities had a *dibao* system – this amounted to just below 14.5 per cent of the 2,310 cities in China that would ultimately have to implement the policy (Fan 2000a).

While 1997 was a landmark year, 1998 was much quieter with fewer high-profile announcements, events or publications. Behind the scenes a great deal of work was occurring with research reports conducted by the MCA into the implementation of *dibao* systems in the cities of Shanghai and Chongqing, and the provinces of Jilin, Shaanxi and Sichuan. Officials in the MCA also began drafting what would become the regulations governing the urban MLG (Interview 11). Finally, efforts were being made to cajole more cities into implementation as will be discussed in the next chapter. The number of cities implementing an MLG system increased by almost 1,500 to 1,801 by the end of the year. This was a significant jump and meant that implementation had increased to 78 per cent of cities.

Following the deceptive quiet preceding it 1999 saw three major events occur. First, officials in the MCA began to discuss problems with how *dibao* was being implemented and managed. In particular, the exclusion of certain eligible households became a cause for concern. Second, in August the MCA, the MoF and Ministry of Labour and Social Security (MoLSS) jointly announced a blanket national 30 per cent increase in the level of the urban *dibao*, basic pensions and the laid-off workers basic livelihood guarantee (MoF 2000a). As will be noted in Chapter 4, this set a significant precedent for central government interventions in the administration and financing of the MLG. Finally, on 28 September the State Council published the 'Urban Resident Minimum Livelihood Guarantee

Regulations' (State Council 1999; 1999 Regulations hereafter). As with the 1997 Circular preceding it the 1999 Regulations set out why the urban MLG should be implemented, what its goals were, how it should be set up, and who was responsible for what at various levels of government. It also included a final deadline for implementation, requiring that all cities adopt a *dibao* system by October 1999. On 26 November then Vice-Minister Fan Baojun announced that the deadline had been achieved (Fan 2000a).

Expansion, Part One, 2000–2002

Having established the urban *dibao* successfully, in the sense that every city had implemented a system, the period immediately following 1999 was characterised by three expansions of social assistance in China. The first of these roughly fits the period 2000 to 2002 and saw massive expansion in the numbers receiving urban *dibao* and the spending on the programme. In addition, it saw a fundamental change in the nature of how the *dibao* was funded. As Figure 1.2 shows, during this period there was a substantial increase in the number of people receiving *dibao*, jumping by over 15 million people between 2001 and 2002. Figure 1.3 shows that this increase in the number receiving urban MLG payments was paid for by a corresponding substantial increase in spending. Finally, Figure 1.4 shows that the period after 2000 saw a sustained shift in the way the urban MLG was funded as the central government took on increasing responsibilities for the costs of the programme. What events drove this dramatic change in the scope and cost of the urban *dibao* programme?

As Chapter 4 will show, the expansion detailed above was due to a complex combination of concerns and efforts to address the so-called 'Ought to protect, not protecting' (*yingbao weibao*) problem and concerns from other parts of government about the problem of laid-off workers (*xiagang zhigong*). In 2000, four speeches by leaders in the MCA and one circular produced by the ministry addressed the problem of the *dibao* not reaching everyone who was entitled to it (Duoji 2001b, 2001c, 2001d; Fan 2001b; Li 2001a). In April 2000, then Premier Zhu Rongji visited the coastal city of Dalian and announced that the urban MLG would serve as an effective policy to break the ties between China's SOEs and the provision of subsidies to laid-off workers (Interview 10). This was the beginning of what would become known as the 'Ought to protect, fully protect' (*yingbao jinbao*) campaign (Tang 2003). While the campaign was not explicitly tied to the concerns of the MCA regarding those not receiving the *dibao* the two issues essentially merged when it came to outcomes. During 2001, work on the MLG focused on a substantial increase in numbers with a number of work reports and circulars from the MCA all discussing the issue (MCA 2001a, 2001b, 2001e, 2001f). A target of 23 million people was set for June 2002 (MCA 2001e) and in October 2002 then Vice-Minister Yang Yanyin announced this had been achieved (Yang 2002b). By the end of 2002 the numbers had fallen back to 20.64 million (see Figure 1.2).

Finally, from 2002 MCA documents began to reflect a new focus on expanding the scope and subsidies delivered through the MLG. The first mention of this change appears in Vice-Minister Yang Yanyin's speech of October 2002 which highlighted the work of Shanghai, Beijing and Guangdong in establishing medical relief, with other unnamed areas providing subsidies for children in education and rent relief as well (Yang 2002b). These measures, which went

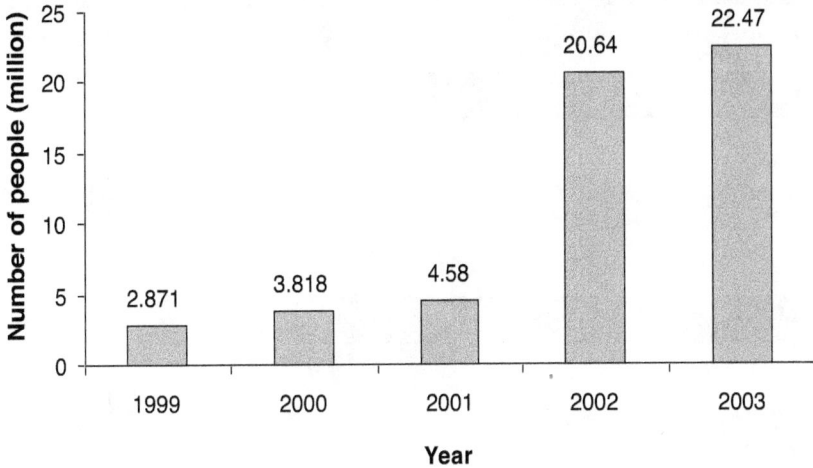

Figure 1.2 Total number of MLG recipients 1999–2003

Source: Hammond (2010).

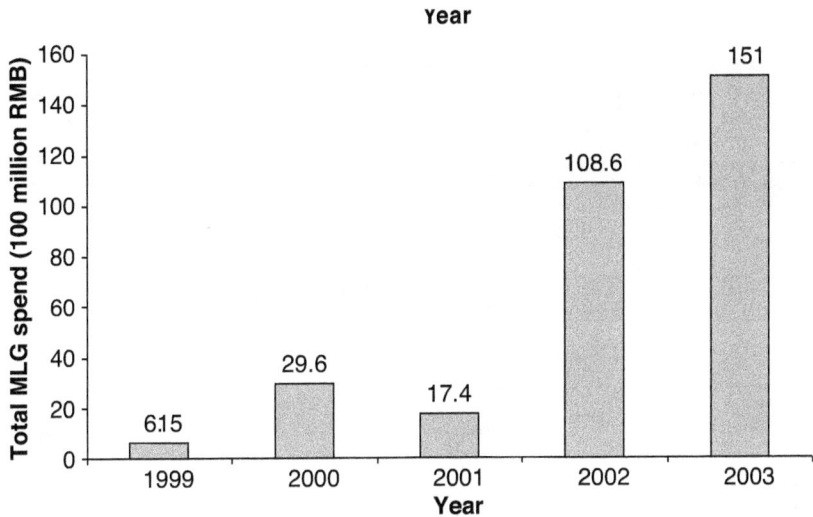

Figure 1.3 Total annual MLG spend 1999–2003

Source: Hammond (2010).

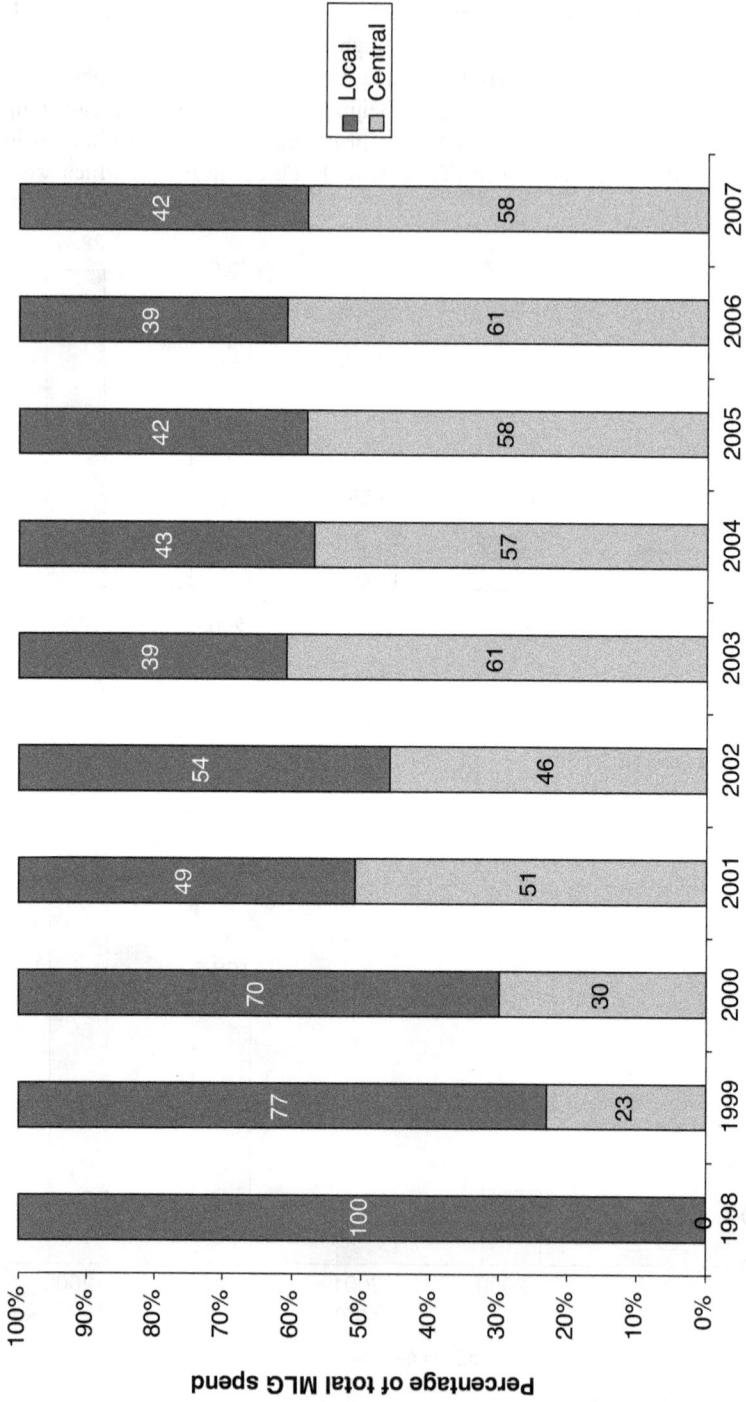

Figure 1.4 Proportion of MLG financing 1998–2007

Source: MoF (2005, 2007).

on to be collectively referred to as the 'classification guarantee measures' (*fenlei baozhang cuoshi*) reflecting developments in the city of Daqing, were developed further by the MCA during 2003.

Expansion, Part Two, 2003–2007

Following the numerical and fiscal expansion of the urban MLG the period from 2003 to 2007 was marked by two further expansions which were of a different nature. The first of these, discussed in more detail in Chapter 4, was the series of developments which eventually led to the national implementation of the rural MLG. While it has been noted that as early as 1992 an MLG type system was practised in Shanxi Province (Guan and Xu 2011; Social Relief Department 2013) the implementation of a national rural MLG system did not move onto the national agenda until the 2000s. Around 2002 the MCA committed to a national implementation of a rural *dibao*, and both academic and official sources suggest that at this point around 80 per cent of counties had implemented *dibao* systems. From 2003 to 2007 the implementation of a national rural MLG system became a goal for the state and culminated in the publication of State Council circular number 19 'State Council circular regarding the establishing of a national rural minimum livelihood guarantee system' on 11 July 2007 (State Council 2007).

The second development was that other social assistance programmes which used *dibao* as a gateway were implemented nationally. This reflected to some extent what had been localised practice in some areas as noted in the previous section, but it also reflected concerns regarding the complex nature of poverty and that those receiving social assistance might face problems beyond just subsistence costs. These affected roughly three areas. First, assistance with the MCA, together with the Ministry of Health and MoF, addressed the costs of medical care through a system of basic medical cost relief (MCA 2003c, 2003d). Second, the problem of housing was addressed through the introduction of subsidies for rent (Gao 2017: 6; Wang and Murie 2011). Third and finally, concerns regarding education were addressed with the introduction of subsidised costs for *dibao* recipients' children in 2004 (Gao 2017: 6). This was in addition to the use of the MLG as a temporary relief measure for high school graduates which was introduced in 2003 (MCA 2003b). It is at this point that the delivery of the MLG begins to transform again from a basic subsistence policy to a means that might deliver comprehensive social assistance. However, the fundamentals of the *dibao* remained the same, with access to additional support predicated on being a recipient of MLG payments.

A Crisis in Prices? 2007–2008

In October 2007 a great deal of media attention in China and also abroad focused on the question of how food prices were affecting Chinese citizens. The question

'Recently, can you afford meat?' being asked by then Premier Wen Jiabao caused a sensation and also elicited a series of online comments regarding the cost of living across China (Global Voices 2007). Concerns regarding the cost of living were not limited to just the elites of China's leadership or online discussion fora. The MCA ordered an investigation on 1 June 2007 into the impact that the increase in prices was having on those receiving payments from it (MCA 2007a), and later in the same month demanded that the local government increase subsidies in response to rising prices. This was followed by a national intervention by the central government on 5 September 2007 which ordered an increase of 15 RMB in the MLG line nationwide, effective from 31 August. This was then followed in 2008 by a follow-up intervention led by the State Council, the MCA and the MoF providing further details regarding the increase (MCA and MoF 2008). Interviews noted the significance of not just the increase in prices but also the intervention by the central government (Interviews 1 and 16). In terms of prices, the crisis highlighted the extent to which those receiving *dibao* were disproportionately exposed to increases in food prices – the cost of food made up a substantial amount of the costs the *dibao* was supposed to cover. It also highlighted the challenge of getting local government to respond in a timely manner to food price increases, one of the main areas where the MLG has continued not to function as intended. These issues will be further discussed in Chapter 5. A final point regarding these interventions is that they appear to have been a turning point, unknown at the time, where attitudes towards the MLG began to harden. As will be shown, subsequent developments have been about consolidating how *dibao* works and to some extent moving away from the expansion in scope and generosity which characterised the early 2000s.

Refinement or Retrenchment? 2009–2014

The period from 2009 until 2014 has largely been characterised by three developments which have had a dramatic effect on the direction and operation of both the rural and urban MLG systems. They have also had a significant impact on how the MLG might be viewed at this point – some have suggested that the programme has now institutionalised (Leung and Xiao 2016), others that the policy has consolidated (Gao 2017), and, finally, some view recent developments as encompassing a marked hardening in attitudes towards those receiving the MLG (Solinger 2017). The first of these developments was the MCA's attempt to draft a Social Relief Law which was subsequently rejected in 2010. This could have led to the full institutionalisation of the system, but it was by no means a perfect piece of legislation and would have embedded a number of problems which would have plagued the system. The rejection of the draft law was quickly followed in 2011 by the MCA's 'Guidance on the further regulation of the urban and rural resident MLG standard system and adjustment work' (MCA 2011). These guidelines focused primarily on how the MLG line was calculated and subsequently readjusted – although, as noted in Chapter 5, the focus was on the calculation of the initial line rather than the arguably more pressing problem of readjustment. Finally, in 2014, the State Council published the 'Social Relief Temporary Measures' (State Council 2014). The measures did fill the gap left by the lack of a Social Relief Law and went a long way to explaining and consolidating understanding of the social assistance system, including but not limited to *dibao*. The measures, as discussed in Chapter 5, outline the administrative structures surrounding the system encompassing social assistance and relief. The measures also dedicate a significant amount of space to new requirements regarding applicants' living status, what constitutes income, addressing new sources of income and how these should be factored in, and notably an entire section addressing what constitutes malpractice and how this should be punished. The 2014 Measures in particular – but also the focus of the 2011 Guidance on the question of the initial MLG line rather than the problems of the lack of readjustment mechanisms – suggest a shift in priority regarding the MLG that reflects both the reality on the ground and the way the policy has served the political priorities of leadership at a given time. On the one hand social assistance is as comprehensive as it ever has been in China; but on the other there appears to be a stark hardening in attitudes regarding who merits support from the state.

To what extent have these developments had an impact on the numbers receiving rural and urban *dibao*? Figures 1.5 to 1.8 present a somewhat contradictory picture regarding the two systems. On the one hand Figures 1.5 and 1.7 show a differing trend regarding the numbers receiving *dibao* in rural and urba China. In rural areas, the numbers up until 2014 have been largely stable but from late 2014 onwards there is an observable drop in the number of individuals and households receiving *dibao*. For urban areas, the fall in numbers predates the 2014 Temporary Measures and appears to have started as early as 2011. Overall, therefore, there is a downward trend in the numbers receiving the MLG, but the point at which the decline began appears to be different. In contrast to the falling numbers receiving the MLG, Figures 1.6 and 1.8 show that the amount spent, either per capita or overall, is on the rise and has increased each quarter for average per capita spend and each year for the annual cumulative spend. Therefore, this suggests that while it might be harder to get onto *dibao*, or indeed to stay on the programme, the amount spent continues to increase each year.

The history of social assistance in China and the *dibao* programme specifically is, therefore, more complex than that of a state or society responding to the challenges presented by poverty in a systematic or rational manner. Rather the history of social assistance reflects how ideas, both domestic and international, are adopted and adapted in response to social problems. Sometimes these ideas are put into practice and how the state functions (or not) determines how this implementation pans out. *Dibao* marked a moment of significance because it was, first, a departure from the previous system of basing eligibility on whether or not one fell into a particular category. Second, it saw a significant commitment of

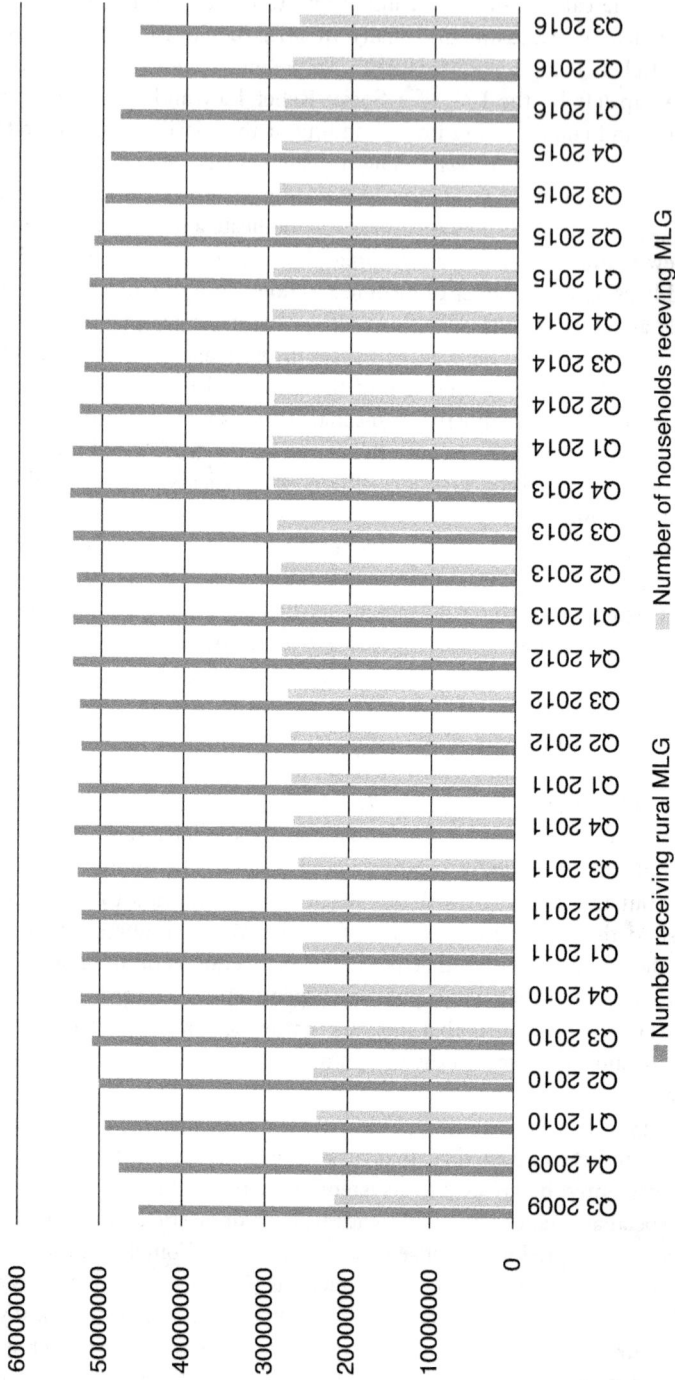

Figure 1.5 Number of individuals and households receiving rural MLG

Source: MCA (2016).

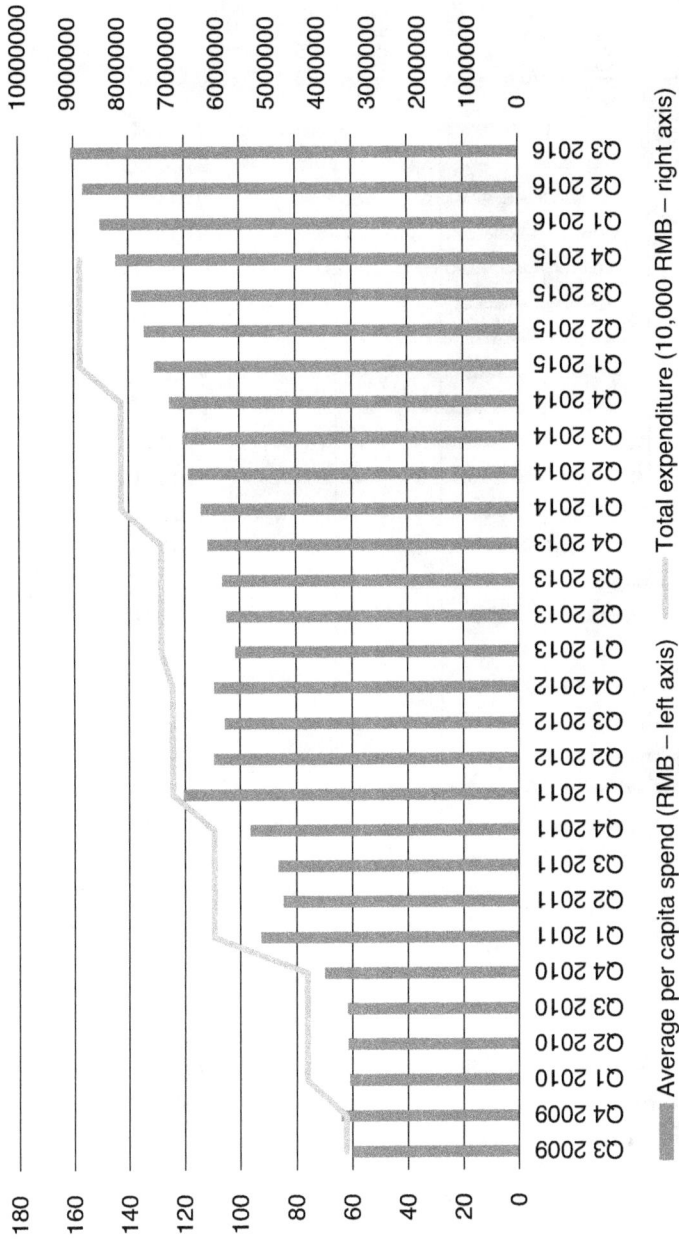

Figure 1.6 Average per capita spend and total cumulative expenditure for rural MLG

Source: MCA (2016).

Legend:
- Average per capita spend (RMB – left axis)
- Total expenditure (10,000 RMB – right axis)

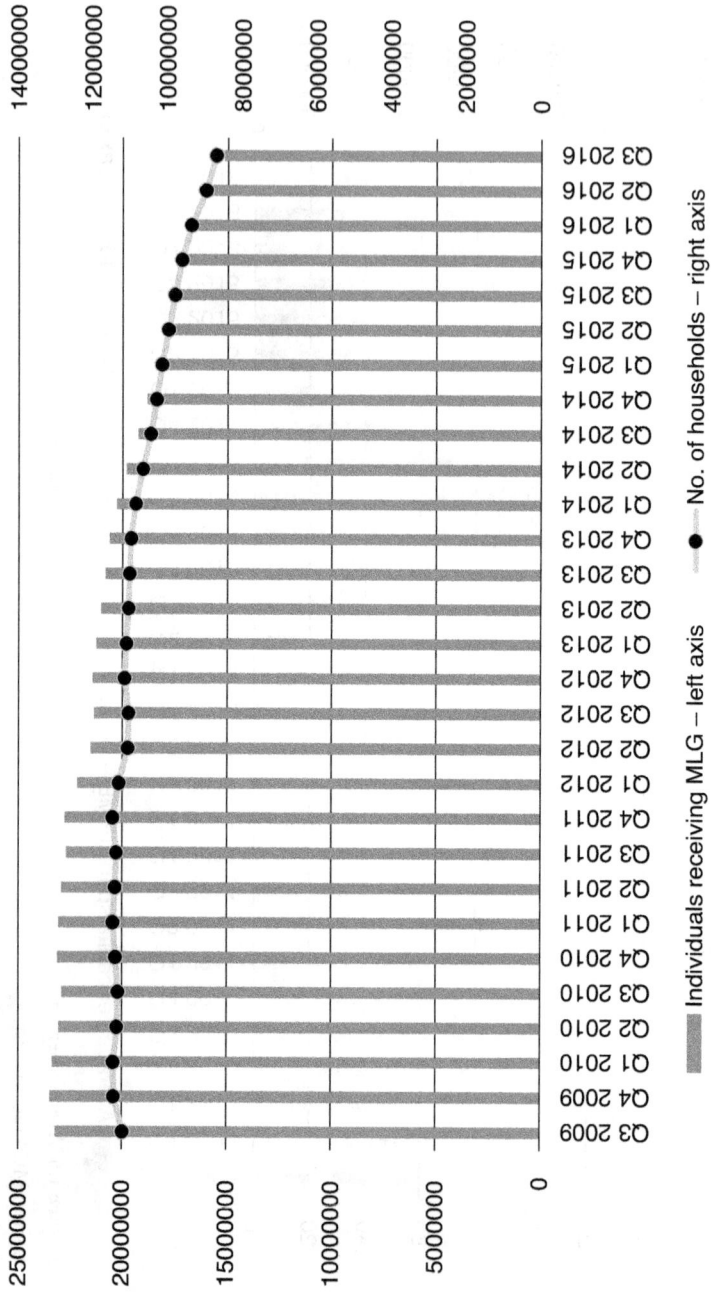

Figure 1.7 Number of individuals and households receiving Urban MLG

Source: MCA (2016).

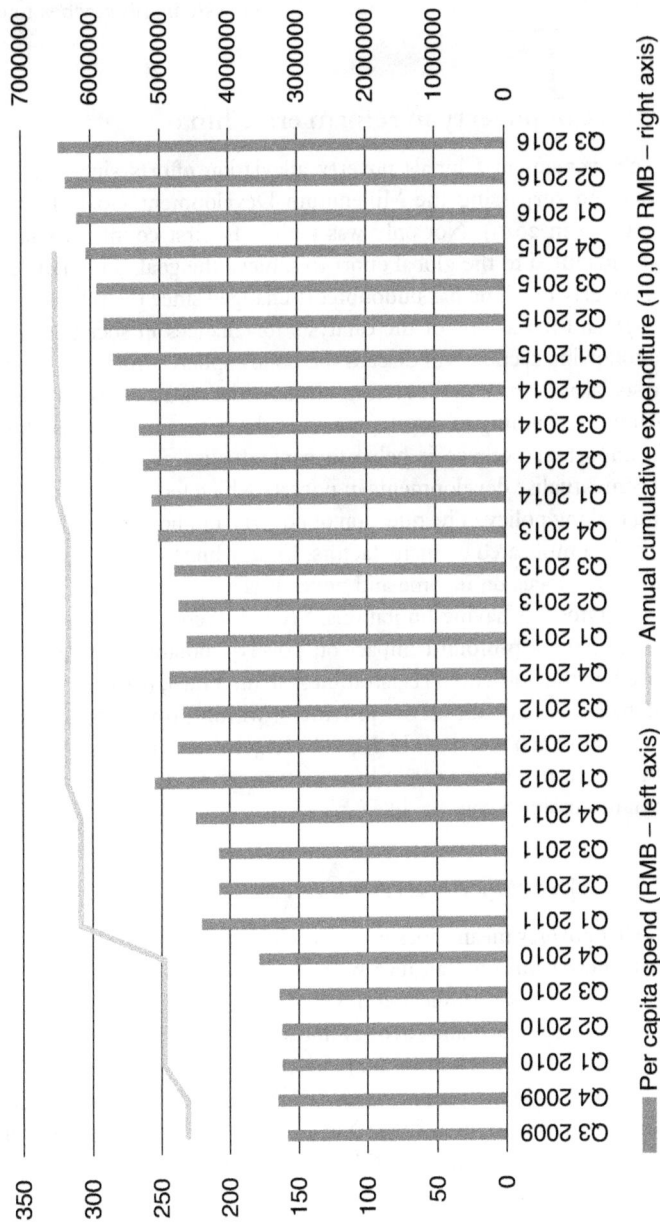

Figure 1.8 Total expenditure and per capita expenditure on urban MLG

Source: MCA (2016).

Legend: Per capita spend (RMB – left axis) — Annual cumulative expenditure (10,000 RMB – right axis)

Left axis: 0, 50, 100, 150, 200, 250, 300, 350

Right axis: 0, 1000000, 2000000, 3000000, 4000000, 5000000, 6000000, 7000000

Categories: Q3 2009, Q4 2009, Q1 2010, Q2 2010, Q3 2010, Q4 2010, Q1 2011, Q2 2011, Q3 2011, Q4 2011, Q1 2012, Q2 2012, Q3 2012, Q4 2012, Q1 2013, Q2 2013, Q3 2013, Q4 2013, Q1 2014, Q2 2014, Q3 2014, Q4 2014, Q1 2015, Q2 2015, Q3 2015, Q4 2015, Q1 2016, Q2 2016, Q3 2016 resources over a prolonged period of time, which saw millions brought into the Chinese state's social assistance coverage. Third, despite changes in the years since roughly 2011, and a notable dip in the numbers receiving *dibao* in both rural and urban systems since 2014, the MLG system still reaches tens of millions of people.

Nature of poverty in reform era China

The main achievement in China's poverty alleviation efforts since 1978 has been reaching and surpassing the Millennium Development Goal of halving its poverty rate (Yan 2016). Not only was China the first country to achieve this, it also contributed to the global effort to achieve the goal. The nature and incidence of poverty in China has undoubtedly changed since the reform period started in 1978 and it was one of the catalysts for changes in social assistance policy. The following section will discuss the policy sphere which incorporates poverty and social assistance as the setting within which *dibao* as a policy change occurred. An understanding of developments in the nature of impoverishment in China is important because it helps to contextualise developments. This section will contextualise developments in poverty which fed into the process of changing and making policy. The question of poverty and how it has changed in the reform era is complicated by many factors. First, while there are many large-scale studies which focus on income and poverty as a subset of questions these need to be understood as having limitations. Second, there are structural issues in China which have a profound impact on poverty, notably the rural–urban divide imposed by the household registration system. Third, because of China's size these imbalances play out across provinces, within provinces, and within sub-provincial units such as cities which can be larger than some countries. This does limit the extent to which a generalised picture can be drawn but this is not unusual when discussing a country like China.

What is Meant by Poverty in Contemporary China?

The idea of what poverty means does not vary within China from the definitions which most readers would be familiar with. There is, however, an important political aspect which has complicated how the problem is addressed in China up until the reform era. As Yan (2016: 2) notes, ideologically socialism sought to eliminate poverty, and during the more extreme periods before 1978 it was not politically acceptable for poverty to exist – because if socialism was being achieved this could not be. Under Deng Xiaoping the more pragmatic approach to running China under the guidance of the CCP meant that eliminating poverty remained the goal of socialism. The significance of poverty ideologically does help to understand why issues of its continued existence, especially in China's countryside, can result in large-scale policy efforts. This is doubly so if the importance of social stability to the ruling regime is also factored in.

The definition of poverty itself is contested because it reflects much of how an individual or an organisation views society, politics and economics. Generally speaking, poverty means having less than is necessary to meet a minimum standard of living. The Joseph Rowntree Foundation defines poverty as: 'when your resources are well below your minimum needs' (JRF 2017). Absolute poverty is when resources are below minimum material needs and cannot maintain a subsistence standard of living. This, ordinarily, extends to having access to basic requirements such as food and clothing, and to where working becomes difficult. Relative poverty is lacking resources relative to the rest of a population. This is normally an arbitrary measure set by an individual, organisation or state. Relative poverty reflects that even in wealthy societies there will be those who are not as well-off and who suffer socially and mentally, as well as materially, as a consequence.

International measures of absolute and relative poverty are not fixed but it is common for World Bank measures to be referred to. For absolute poverty this has most famously included the USD/day measurement, which moved from 1 USD/day to 1.25 USD/day in 2008, and most recently was revised to 1.90 USD/day in 2015 (World Bank 2015). The boundary for relative poverty is much more fluid and contested. It is normally a percentage of average income in a country. Internationally this is often measured as 60 per cent of the median national income (Feng and Nguyen 2014).

In China, when poverty is discussed it is typically absolute poverty that is being referred to. As Yan (2016) notes the definitions of poverty used by China's state organs broadly follow the definitions of absolute and relative poverty discussed above. What is important is that absolute poverty is generally treated as a rural problem and the Chinese state sets its own poverty lines. From 2010 China's rural poverty line has been fixed at 2,300 RMB/year (approximately 343 USD/year) (Wang, Xu and Hao 2015), prior to this it had been fixed at 1,274 RMB. Relative poverty was suggested, by two study groups, as the bottom 5 per cent of income in the population (Yan 2016: 6). There has not been a fixed urban poverty measurement announced by the central government in China. It is therefore apparent that while the different definitions of poverty are part of the discussion in China, it is absolute rural poverty which is the focus of definitions and, as a quick reading of Chinese texts on poverty alleviation will illustrate, it is rural poverty which has been the focus of state efforts.

How has the Nature of Poverty Changed?

Poverty has changed in four ways during the reform era. The first is perhaps the most straightforward and that is the overall reduction in the incidence of poverty in China. It is claimed that somewhere between 700 and 800 million people have been lifted out of poverty in the years since 1978 (Qu 2017: 79). The causes of this development are contested, and this will be discussed in the last part of this section. However, the fact remains that China has seen a major shift in the numbers who experience poverty, and as previously noted this has made a global contribution. Second, as the numbers who are classed as poor have fallen there has been a recognition within China that poverty does not just affect some who are in particular categories but that it extends beyond just those who are unable to work. The so-called 'new poverty' or *xin pinkun*, which was recognised in the 1990s encompassed those who needed support but were not being catered for by the existing system, the *san bu guan* in Shanghai, discussed above, is an example of this recognition (Tang 2003). This was a shift in how poverty was viewed, from absolute poverty defined by categories to relative poverty determined by income and eventually access to services. The idea that a household could be in work but still experience poverty was a major change in China and did lead to a shift in attitudes and policy by the government. This shift also reflected the changes in employment in the 1980s and 1990s where the traditional boundaries of rural and urban, state and collective began to break down. The introduction of private employment and the stratification of different forms of employment and unemployment (as noted by Solinger (2001)) meant that work, especially in urban areas, was no longer a guarantee of a minimum standard of living or of access to essential services.

Third, as noted by Cho (Cho 2010, 2013), is the move towards poverty as something which is measurable as well as something which is experienced. The quantification of poverty, a by-product of the shift away from the categorisation of poverty, has meant that its treatment and eradication has also become more statistically oriented. As Cho shows in her study of one urban district this helps explain why, in some instances, those who are eligible for help are ruled out – their living conditions and lived experience do not match the way that poverty has been defined and quantified by the local government. Fourth, and finally, in rural areas alleviating poverty has garnered the most attention from the state, which has led to a series of programmes spread out over the decades of the reform era, but which have faced a number of challenges. As Rogers (2014) notes, the literature suggests that there are some villages or counties which have proven almost immune to the interventions of the state and its reforms; while other studies have shown that poverty in rural areas is more complex and that there can be significant variation within a village. What remains is that in spite of significant state efforts rural poverty has persisted. One thing that has not changed during the reform era, however, has been the linking of poverty with work and the view that poverty as a social illness can in some way be cured.

What Makes Explaining Poverty and Poverty Alleviation Complex in China?

As alluded to above, the question of poverty and poverty alleviation in China is complicated by a number of factors that other countries have not necessarily experienced. While it is relatively easy to note that by various measures China has experienced an unprecedented change in the lived experience of hundreds of millions of its citizens, how and why are much more difficult to understand and explain. There are three reasons why explaining poverty and poverty alleviation are complex. First, the system of household registration is still a significant factor which has a profound impact on those who have one residence status or the other. For the purposes of this study the divide imparted by the *hukou* is the classic rural–urban divide that the system was originally set up to establish. It is worth noting that recent changes mean that while rural–urban is becoming less important, where someone is registered remains critical in understanding the kind of policies and services a citizen might have access to. Second, analysis has shown that China is divided along geographical and administrative lines, especially when it comes to inequality and by extension poverty. Studies which have used the China Household Income Project dataset have clearly illustrated divisions not just along rural–urban and coastal–inland lines but also increasingly intra-region and also intra-city. Between 1995 and 2002 inequality remained stable but high, with an increasing gap between rural and urban areas (Gustafsson, Li and Sicular 2008). However, between 2002 and 2007 the situation changed – inequality increased but poverty fell, regional differences narrowed but within regions inequality increased (Li, Luo and Sicular 2013; Li, Sato and Sicular 2013; Li and Sicular 2014). One way to understand what has happened in China is that while the lowest incomes are rising, and therefore the floor has risen in China, there are more highly paid jobs and non-income assets available which means that the highest incomes are increasing faster than the lowest (Li and Sicular 2014; Zhang 2016c). While the poorest might be better off than ever before in China, the wealthy are doing even better. Third, and finally, notions of poverty and how China addresses it are further complicated by ideals that the foundations of Chinese society are in some way fundamentally different to other human societies because of Confucian models regarding societal and kin networks providing care (Gao 2017). This is an influence that does need to be factored in, but it needs to be understood within the context of decades of Marxist-Leninist thinking and policy as well as the relatively recent introduction of market principles. This creates a complex mixture of influences when it comes to poverty and how to deal with it. Dai's (2014) study of care for the elderly illustrates this starkly with privately funded residents articulating reasons that mix traditional notions of Confucian obligations of the child to their parents and individual value mediated through successful engagement with the nascent market economy.

Was Social Assistance Peripheral to Success in Alleviating Poverty?

Finally, it is worth considering the extent to which state efforts within social assistance have had a discernible impact on the bigger picture when it comes to poverty alleviation and, at the opposite end of the spectrum, on people's day-to-day lives. In both urban and rural areas poverty alleviation has been achieved primarily through the impact of reforms. As China's economy began to grow, new opportunities and the increased earnings that came with this helped to shift hundreds of millions out of poverty. At the other extreme, as Solinger and Cho have shown, an existence on *dibao* does not necessarily lead to a high quality of life, nor does it respect people's dignity (Cho 2013; Solinger 2011). *Dibao* does affect some 60 million Chinese citizens every year and this is a significant number of people meriting an understanding and discussion of the policy.

The question of how the changes to social assistance have contributed to China's success in poverty alleviation depends, to a large extent, how the question is framed. If the MLG system had the goal of only lessening the effects of poverty, while also ensuring that those on the programme do not become trapped in a dependent relationship with the subsidy, then it has made a moderate contribution (Deng and Gustafsson 2013; Gao 2013; Ravallion and Chen 2015). If the question is changed a little and the effectiveness in addressing relative poverty becomes the focus, then *dibao* has not been effective (Gao 2013; Gustafsson and Deng 2011). The impact of the social assistance system on the question of poverty is perhaps best summed up by Li, Sato and Sicular (2013: 9–12) who state that: 'the minimum livelihood guarantee programs in urban and rural China have had only a moderate effect on absolute poverty, and they have not substantially reduced relative poverty and income inequality'. One of the points which will emerge from the argument that follows is that when it comes to *dibao* this outcome should surprise no one. It was never the intention of officials when implementing the programme that it would have such an impact; its purpose is somewhat different.

The nature of poverty in China, and how it has changed in the reform era, can be summed up along the following lines. China has moved from being a predominantly equal but poor and rural society to an unequal middle income and predominantly urban society. As a consequence of this development, 500 million people were lifted out of poverty between 1981 and 2004 (Yan 2016: 1), with the figure reaching over 700 million by 2016 (Qu 2017: 79). Yet in rural areas absolute poverty is perceived as persisting and relative poverty is now recognised as a problem by the central government. Social assistance measures have largely been tangential to these developments as the heavy lifting has been the success of the reforms. Finally, and perhaps most importantly, the perception of poverty has changed. Whereas before 1978, and arguably before 1992, poverty was something that only affected certain categories and was inextricably linked to the ability to work, the emergence and recognition of the 'new' poverty has led to alternative policy formulations being deemed necessary. Explaining the emergence and development of this response – the *dibao* – is the focus of the next chapters in this book.

Note

1. This is something that I have discussed extensively elsewhere and that has also been discussed by other scholars (for further reading see Hammond 2010, 2017; Solinger 2015).

Chapter 2

Urban Dibao: *Emergence and Transition to National Policy,* 1992–1999

Introduction

As the historical description of the development of *dibao* in the previous chapter has shown, the emergence and implementation of the urban MLG was a process that does not necessarily fit with the established discourse on social assistance policy in China. Rather the process was messy and involved numerous actors at central and local levels who interacted over an extended period of time, seeking particular outcomes and being enabled or frustrated by the structure of the state. The process of the urban MLG's national implementation was not just the announcement of the 1997 Circular or the 1999 Regulations but also the process leading up to these documents being published and enforced. This took place in the context of China's fragmented authoritarian political structure and this, together with the actions of certain key actors, had a profound impact on the shape of the MLG as well as establishing a number of problems that subsequently would need to be dealt with. Two processes need to be addressed in order to understand the problems which developed later. These are the spread of the MLG between 1994 and 1997 and the implementation of the MLG between 1997 and 1999. Both these processes were subject to the FA of China's politics and exhibited outcomes that would be expected for a policy that emerged in a bureaucratic structure lacking in political authority and fiscal resources.

This chapter sets out the case that in order to understand what the MLG is now it is essential to understand where it came from, what political values it was attached to and that underpin it, and how its implementation was brought about. Initially, when it emerged in Shanghai the urban MLG was a product of the space that exists within the Chinese system to innovate and experiment when the higher levels of authority allow it. As it moved from being a local innovation to a national policy the way the MLG was discussed changed, and the state structure that had fostered its development became a challenge to its spread. The explicit linking of the MLG to the cause of reform and social stability suggest that the policy had different goals to alleviating poverty. The constraints on some of the urban MLG's champions, and the compromises and groping these imposed, meant that from the beginning of the MLG's spread the traits that some have highlighted for criticism, notably variation and exclusion, were accepted as a means to get the policy implemented. Higher-level policy actors with greater authority were able to work around these issues in terms of making decisions that were in effect binding for those lower down the system, but the lack of resources initially allocated for the MLG meant that, while the policy eventually got pushed through, from 1997 the compromises that had been struck earlier remained. In seeking national implementation the lack of resources manifested again, as the MCA struggled to get local government to implement the programme and ultimately relied on a mixture of innovative uses of information resources, the authority of higher-level legislation, and finally the redirection of fiscal resources. These circumstances meant that while the MLG travelled from local innovation to national implementation in the space of only six years, the foundations for many years of implementation problems had also been set.

Emergence and spread of the MLG

The emergence and spread of the MLG is an area which is not addressed at present in existing studies of the policy. However, the process is an interesting example of the tensions between the space to innovate and the constraints imposed by established values and political structures inherent to the Chinese state. This means that it is possible to innovate at the local level and to spread a policy within a policy sphere such as social assistance, but, at the same time, this has to be done within the constraints of the established values and political structures of the state. This means that actors, when pursuing entrepreneurial agendas, need to be creative and achieve compromise in order to get things done.

Emergence of the MLG: Shanghai 1992–1993

The emergence of the MLG is significant because it highlights three aspects of how FA helps explain local innovations in Chinese policy. First, the structure of the state facilitated innovation with local government in a position to exploit available spaces when the opportunity arose. Second, the importance of policy matching the dominant values and the established speech space of the time is illustrated. Third, local actors can behave in an entrepreneurial manner to facilitate developments. The higher the authority of particular actors, the more influence they can wield over the process. Of particular significance is the role played by the Mayor of Shanghai, Huang Ju, and the local Bureau of Civil Affairs.

Huang Ju was active throughout the period leading up to the implementation of the MLG in 1993. Responding to opportunities created by the establishment of a speech space supporting reform of social assistance in the Eighth Five Year Plan he initiated the investigation process which eventually led to the MLG. Huang was also active in responding to the reports from the Bureau of Civil Affairs and other bureaux, giving orders regarding the formation of committees, and providing comments on proposals that contributed to the design of the two-branch approach agreed upon (Interview 16). The key feature of Huang's influence is that he oversaw the whole process, which involved a large number of organisations and individuals from various branches of government.

The relatively smooth development of the policy and the provision of funding was due to Huang's involvement. The relatively quick development and implementation of the MLG is one of its noted features among Chinese academics, and the role played by Mayor Huang helps explain this (Interview 8). Without a central figure with authority who superseded all the other involved individuals and organisations the process would have been subsumed by negotiation and consensus building resulting in a slow and incremental process (Lieberthal and Oksenberg 1988). In addition, the mayor had the authority to direct funds and influence the city budget.

What motivated Huang? There are political reasons for why he acted as he did. Shanghai had seen unrest in 1989 and afterwards. In the case of the Shanghai MLG the reform of state-owned textile and steel production enterprises in 1993 combined with the relaxation of price controls to create a possible threat to social stability. Although it is apparent that concerns over growing urban poverty did exist, it was the potential shock to the system that reform could bring that pushed the problem onto the agenda. The potential social instability which these changes would bring about, witnessed in the late 1980s, was such that these concerns were acted upon (Interview 16). The significance of the reforms in terms of creating an environment where a policy like the MLG was necessary is so great that one interviewee cited the decision to reform in the 1980s when responding to questions on the origin of the MLG (Interview 3). It is also notable that the MLG fitted with the pursuit of social stability during the reform process – it therefore matched closely the values of the time.

The actions of Huang would have amounted to little if it had not been for the investigative and development capacity of the line bureaux, especially that of the Bureau of Civil Affairs. Although acting on orders from above, the identification of problems and proposed solutions was the work of the Bureau. As well as providing information for reports and meetings the Bureau also acted as a filter through which information passed. The identification of the *san bu guan* would have been influenced by the Bureau which, as an institution, focused on the Three No's. In addition, if the Bureau of Civil Affairs had not put forward a subsidy type proposal which was administered by the Bureau at the basic level of urban government, then it would not have been on the agenda to discuss.

Was Huang Ju a PE? The mayor, through his actions, straddled the gap between the PE and the rational bureaucrat by being an agenda setter, a supporter of particular ideas and, finally, a decision maker; in this sense, by supporting a policy from the agenda setting stage through the developmental process to implementation using the resources available (mostly the authority granted by his position), suggesting entrepreneurship. Huang's support of the process and early MLG was significant because it brought authority, rank and the ability to direct resources to the process. If any of these had been absent the result might have been various similarly ranked branches of the city government involved in the process cancelling each other out.

What explanations are there for the MLG emerging as it did? The roles of historical precedents and policy feedback are significant because they act as invisible walls and doors in the policy process, constraining and facilitating the choices that can be made by individual and collective actors. The Three No's policy was both a problem and an influence on the emergence and design of the MLG.

The problems with the Three No's were based in what it was conceived to achieve and how it was operated. In terms of policy design the Three No's sought to provide for a limited group of people who would have fallen out of work-based provisions established through the work unit. The problem was when operational, as identified in the work report presented in Shanghai, the policy was inflexible. If a household or individual was outside the work unit system and impoverished, but was not one of the Three No's, then they were not entitled to relief. In the period leading up to reform, and for a great deal of the 1980s, this was a problem in theory only as the system acted in concert with the work-based provisions of the work unit.

The design of the Three No's became an issue only when the reforms of enterprises and employment began to deepen in the late 1980s and were reinstated in the post-Southern Tour climate of 1992. At this point, there were impoverished groups which the system did not cater for, such as the *san bu guan* identified in Shanghai. The Three No's was not only failing to accommodate the emergence of non-state employees, urban poverty and residents falling outside of the traditional welfare and assistance structures, but also funding limitations meant that it was failing to offer adequate provisions to the groups it did target (Tang 1998, 2001b). The Three No's was a failing policy in the early 1990s because it could no longer provide the social relief that the state was obligated to provide through Article 45 of the Constitution (NPC 1999).

The Three No's acted as a constraint on what policy makers could choose as an alternative policy once the decision to change had been made. The MLG also reflects the Three No's. The Shanghai MLG included categories alongside the means tested policy open to anyone who fits the requirements. The category element was not a requirement but was redefined as a target for the policy and was set out as those who are the traditional Three No's and households where income falls below the MLG line (Shanghai-RenminZhengfu 1996). This is a conflict at the heart of the MLG: a means tested policy with target categories. The categories fit with the previous Three No's and one interviewee explained this as a necessary requirement because the MLG had to account for both those identified as new and the traditional poor (Interview 16).

Although categories do exist in the Shanghai MLG, they are not the means by which benefit entitlement is decided. The mechanism for deciding if subsidies will be paid is a means test based on the total household income falling below a predetermined MLG line. The means test was put in place because it would, in theory, remedy the major problems of inflexibility that the Three No's presented. By having a means tested mechanism the MLG would be open to everyone who fell within its definition of poor, rather than only those who fell into certain categories. This made the MLG very inclusive in comparison to the Three No's, which was exclusive in its provisions (Shanghai-BCA 1997; Shanghai-RenminZhengfu 1996).

The funding and administration of the MLG also reflected the influence of the Three No's and previous patterns of institutional practice. Problems with the Three No's subsidy were reflected in the inclusion of local funding and adjustment mechanisms that would respond to local price changes reflected in the MLG. The lack of funding increases and the lack of adjustment for subsidies during the reform period were identified as issues in the Three No's, which had had the knock-on effect of stagnating the actual subsidy available to recipients (Duoji 2001a; Tang 1998). The introduction of local funding provisions and price-related adjustment mechanisms in the MLG meant that the new policy could in theory be more responsive than its predecessor.

The legacy of the work unit in the local government structure is the final element of feedback to discuss. Unlike the later iterations of the MLG, the Shanghai model had a role for the work units and their enterprises in both administering and financing. These requirements were set out in Articles 6 and 25 of the 1996 Methods (Shanghai-RenminZhengfu 1996). In the iteration of the MLG which was rolled out nationwide in 1997 the work units were not involved in the policy at all. The decision to use the work unit was explained in one interview as being an efficient choice at the time (Interview 1). As a unit of social and economic control the work units were still a useful administrative tool in the early 1990s. They were capable of providing administrative and financial assistance when there were few alternatives. The *shequ* (community or sub-district) which would be used later to administer the MLG was still being established as an informal administrative unit of the state, and the street and resident's committees were being used – but as part of the overall administrative structure for the policy. The use of the work unit as a means by which to provide funds would have been as pragmatic as their use as administrative mechanisms. A local initiative would have to be funded locally, and local enterprises provided a means to raise revenue.

A final point highlighted by the emergence of the MLG in Shanghai is that of the structure of the Chinese state facilitating innovation. The fragmented structure of the Chinese state and the increasing decentralisation of political and fiscal decision making during the reform period was significant in the development of the MLG and exacerbated elements of FA. The city of Shanghai is classed as a Municipality (*zhixiashi*)[1] for administrative purposes. This administrative classification and the structure of local government had a number of significant impacts on the Shanghai MLG. Before assessing the impact that Shanghai's classification had on the MLG there are three characteristics of the relationship between central and local government which should be restated. First, the administrative rank that a Municipality carries means it has parity with ministry-level institutions and the provinces. Second, the bureaux at local level are responsible to the Municipal (in the case of Shanghai) city government in addition to the higher tiers of their ministry. This is based on rank, but also reflects the local government responsibility for local appointments and control over the budget. Third, the Municipality has extensive control over its own finances. As noted above, the Municipalities like Shanghai carry the same rank as a province or a ministry and this meant, especially prior to the tax reforms of 1994, that Shanghai had extensive control over gathering and negotiating its share of the city's tax (Lieberthal 1995). These factors meant that Shanghai had space to innovate in terms of policy making. Obviously, this does not mean that the city makes policy without any links to the central government's policy goals or decisions, but it does mean that the city can, and frequently does, make decisions that create policy that is innovative and new in comparison to other areas.

In interviews, four different points were raised which supported the idea of Shanghai innovating within the confines of the Chinese state. First, there is the point that Shanghai acted because it was one of the more advanced cities in China and was facing the social pressures of reform before other areas. Because the city had advanced further along the reform path it had become exposed to the negative outcomes like new urban poverty sooner (Interview 12). Second, the proactive actions of policy makers in Shanghai were highlighted (Interview 16). Third, the idea that Shanghai could act with a degree of independence because of its status and fiscal strength as a Municipality was highlighted (Interview 3). Finally, it was argued that the reason for Shanghai's ability to act was because it had the political status to do as it pleased due to connections with the national ruling elites (Interview 15). The idea that Shanghai was, as an administrative unit, in a position to innovate in the early 1990s is clear, although the reasons given are varied. In addition, as noted above, the speech space had been established for reforms of social assistance to occur through the Eighth Five Year Plan. This emphasises that the Chinese state should not be treated as a centrally administered unit with little space for variation. It is clear in the case of Shanghai and the MLG that local innovation was both possible and allowed.

Spread of the MLG: Nationally 1994–1997

The journey from local innovation to national-level implementation took place between 1993 and 1997. In 1994 the MCA held its tenth national conference in Beijing and during his speech the then Minister of Civil Affairs Duoji Cairang suggested that cities across China should adopt the MLG. This was indirectly supported by then Premier Li Peng (Duoji 1995a; Li 1995). The speech was widely reported and marked the beginning of a significant effort on the part of Minister Duoji to see the MLG implemented nationwide. Between 1994 and 1996 the spread of the MLG was slow but steady, with an ever-increasing number of cities adopting the measure. In 1996 the MLG was incorporated in the Ninth Five Year Plan and the 2010 Long-Term Development Goals. In line with the plan and the increasing challenge of unemployment and layoffs from failing SOEs the MLG was implemented nationwide in September 1997 through a State Council circular (State Council 1997).

There are three points regarding the spread of the MLG raised by an analysis of materials published by provincial-level Civil Affairs units in a book series called *Trans-Century China Civil Affairs 1994–2002* which addressed all aspects of Civil Affairs work during the period (*Kuashiji de Zhongguo Minzheng Shiye 1994–2002*, see Li 2002b). First, the year of adoption. At provincial level it was observed that there was a clustering of implementation which occurred in 1995–1996. The peak year for provinces adopting the MLG was 1995, with twelve, followed by 1996, with eleven. This suggests that the adoption of *dibao* was not limited to particular provinces, with the rest rushing to catch up later on in the development of the MLG, and the main body of adoption occurred in the middle of the time period. As shown in Chapter 1, for cities the situation was very different, with the majority of adoption clustered towards the end of the time period. This suggests that adoption by provinces (or a city within the province) led to adoption by the majority of cities.

Second, it might be assumed that the main actor in the spread of the MLG would be the local-level Civil Affairs department reflecting the role of the Civil Affairs bureaucracy as a conduit for Minister Duoji's support. Analysis of the *Kuashiji* series shows that only five different actors were mentioned: the provincial Civil Affairs department, the provincial Civil Affairs department plus other departments, a single person, a single city government, and the provincial government. Two provinces did not credit an actor with adopting the MLG (Fujian and Guangxi). Of these five actors, the highest instance was for the provincial Civil Affairs department (twelve) followed by the provincial government (seven), single city government (four), single person (three), and then the provincial Civil Affairs department plus other departments (three). Before drawing too many conclusions from these findings it needs to be noted that the documents used were written by local Civil Affairs officials promoting the development of Civil Affairs work between 1994 and 2002, and that there was a degree of self-serving in the writing. It is possible, however, to make two observations. First, it is the large (or comparatively large) bureaucracies/institutions which are credited with adopting the MLG. Of the twenty-eight entries, twenty-one are for the Civil Affairs bureaucracy, Civil Affairs plus others, or the provincial government. The instances of individuals or smaller units, or units lower down the hierarchy, being credited is much lower, the remaining seven instances. This finding suggests that the assumption regarding the proactive nature of the Civil Affairs bureaucracy regarding the MLG is valid.

A final point is from whom early and later adopters took their cue to implement *dibao* systems. Either specific meetings or the concept of 'reform and social stability' (*Gaige he shehui wending*) were the main reasons cited. As will be discussed, the linking of the MLG with the policy of further reform and ensuring social stability during the process was an important part of justifying the spread of the programme. These two points account for seventeen cases. The influence of other cities was limited to four cases. The local situation was limited to only one case (Hubei).

By breaking down the findings into those that were early adopters and those that can be considered late adopters a clearer picture emerges. Early adopters were defined as those who implemented the MLG between 1993 and 1995. Late adopters were those who implemented the programme from 1996 onwards. The rationale for this split is based on two factors. First, 1995/1996 is the tipping point in the adoption of the MLG at provincial level, marking the shift to over 50 per cent of provinces with an implemented MLG system. Second, from 1996 the central government began to take an active interest in the MLG, marking a change in the pressures on provinces to implement the programme. What this split shows is that, first, early adopters took their cues from the 1994 conference, 1995 meetings, 'reform and social stability', the local situation, 'national spirit' and other cities' example. In the case of the 1994 conference and 'reform and social stability', early adopters were the majority citing these reasons for adoption. In the case of the local situation, 'national spirit' and other cities' example, the early adopters were the *only* provinces to cite these reasons. The later adopters cited the 1995 meetings in Xiamen and Qingdao and the '10th conference and other cities' example' as much as the early adopters as the reason for adoption. This suggests that the 1995 meetings, which were set up as opportunities to learn from the experience of cities who adopted the MLG very early on, and the combination of the 10th conference with other cities' experience was equally influential on early and late adopters. It appears that provinces were willing to take a risk in early adoption based on others' experience but also held back until such experience was available to draw on.

The only instances of the Ninth Five Year Plan, the Party (CCP), the government (central) and the 1997 Circular being cited as the reason for adopting the MLG took place among the late adopters. They still account for less than 50 per cent of the reasons cited for adoption among those defined as late, but it does suggest that there is some strength in the argument that early adoption is based on local pressures or the suggestion of others (the 10th conference was not an order but a suggestion to implement); whereas late adoption brings in the influence of more institutional pressures from the hierarchy, plans and immediate policy plans. A final point to note is that the last province to adopt the MLG, Xinjiang, was also the only province to cite the 1997 Circular as the reason for implementing.

Of particular significance to the spread of the MLG were the actions of Minister of Civil Affairs Duoji Cairang and Premier Li Peng, who both supported the spread and implementation of the policy. Initially the MLG spread with the support of Duoji but he was limited by his role as a minister which meant that he relied on framing the MLG as matching existing values and using his position to influence the limited part of the bureaucracy he presided over. His role is entrepreneurial insofar as he invested his own resources and position in pursuing the spread of the policy beyond the initial areas of adoption in 1993 (Hammond 2013). It is notable that after 1996 the adoption of the programme gained legislative and political significance, and this has been closely associated with the intervention of Li Peng. In this instance an authority figure with the power to push policy nationally became involved and altered the status of the policy resulting in an implementation uptake.

Unlike the typical PE, Duoji's main role was not that of agenda setter. Rather, his most significant action was tailoring his presentation of *dibao* to a bureaucratic audience. In tailoring the presentation of the MLG, Duoji put forward a specific interpretation of the MLG policy to counter emerging obstruction from local government and incorrect implementation of the measure. The main means to manage problems with the MLG was to match the policy to existing values and tailor the spread and expectations surrounding the MLG so that the policy would better suit local circumstances. Resistance to implementation was highlighted in one interview with an MCA official (Interview 11) and was also addressed in speeches and editorials by Duoji at the time (Duoji 1995b, 1998a, 1998b).

There were four significant problems during the spread of the MLG. To address these, Duoji tailored discussion and development of the MLG so that it matched the established values of the time. The first problem was the perception by some in local Civil Affairs offices that the MLG was not the responsibility of the MCA. Second, the MLG was too much work and too troublesome to be a worthwhile investment of resources. Third, it was a new policy that had no guidelines, no regulations and was unfamiliar. Finally, the policy was viewed as being inappropriate to certain areas in terms of their development (Duoji 1998a). This was a financial concern because poorer areas would have populations that would be more likely to receive payments but would have fewer resources to distribute.

Duoji Cairang countered each of these points throughout 1995 in speeches to Civil Affairs bureaucrats. Directing his arguments at the Civil Affairs bureaucracy is an interesting tactic by Duoji as the real decisions on introducing new policy in local government would be in the People's Government and the Finance Bureau. Furthermore, Duoji could not order local governments to carry out any policy. The hope may have been that his arguments would be transferred by Civil Affairs officials or it may be that he was also facing intransigence within the MCA as well as from local government. Ultimately, the target audience of Duoji's speeches on these problems reflected the limitations of influence that came with his position as a minister.

Duoji used three approaches to counter challenges to getting the MLG implemented. First, he tied the MLG to three core aspects of the CCP-state's overall policy aims at the time. Duoji connected the MLG to the overall objective of ensuring continued social stability using the specific phrase 'maintaining social stability' (*baochi shehui wending*) on a number of occasions when outlining the benefits of the policy (Duoji 1995c, 1998e). He also presented the MLG as a policy of legitimisation that would benefit all involved as it would encourage positive perceptions of the government, arguing that: '... this work [the MLG] reflects the Party and government care for the masses and the superiority of the socialist system' (Duoji 1998b). Further, that:

> Carrying out the urban resident MLG line system is important to both our nation and to guaranteeing human rights, because the right to life and to development are the most basic human rights. Carrying out the MLG is a major initiative for guaranteeing the right to live, it will have extensive and far reaching impacts both internationally and domestically[.] (Duoji 1998a)

Finally, Duoji tied the MLG to the continuation of the reform project by providing social stability and, therefore, it was linked to arguably the core value of the period. The MLG was indicated as a policy that both guaranteed the continuation of the reform process and also was an indication of China's development. In a speech to a symposium on the MLG Duoji stated that: 'Establishing a complete social security system is an important project which complements the deepening of economic reforms and establishing a socialist market economic system' (Duoji 1998a). Using other countries' social assistance policies as the basis for this Duoji also made the point that MLG-type policies were a global standard among developed nations and something that China should aspire to (Duoji 1998a, 1995b). By configuring the debate surrounding the MLG in such a way Duoji ensured that resisting the MLG for whatever reason would be unlikely as it would be the equivalent of questioning core Party-state doctrine, therefore tying the policy to the dominant vales of the time and exploiting the established speech space that he, and those subordinate to him, had to operate in.

In addition to linking the MLG with the wider policy objectives of the Party-state Duoji took two further steps to counter local-level intransigence regarding the MLG. The arguments that the MLG was outside the responsibility of the MLG, was additional work and was troublesome were countered together. It was argued that the MCA already had responsibility for the poorest and most vulnerable in China's cities, and so the MLG was not an extension of responsibility but a continuity of it. In addition, the MLG was presented as a reform of the Three No's policy rather than as a new policy in its own right (Duoji 1995b, 1998a). In one speech Duoji presented this argument as: 'We can very clearly say this work [the MLG] is a functional responsibility of the Ministry of Civil Affairs. Because the MLG is a reform of the traditional social assistance system it is not a new or increased responsibility' (Duoji 1998a). In the same speech Duoji argues that carrying out the MLG was not without guidelines and should not be troublesome because: 'The practical experience of Shanghai, Dalian and other cities already answers the problem' (Duoji 1998d).

Finally, dealing with opposition from local government because of varied levels of development elicited a very practical response. Implementation was staggered nationally in order to allow under-developed areas time to adapt to implementing the MLG. Focus was put on those cities seen as developed – predominantly in the east and the Municipalities. Those cities labelled as under-developed, mainly in the central-west, were encouraged to follow later when circumstances would allow it (Duoji 1995b, 1998e; Xi 1998).

A final means by which Duoji exerted influence over the development of the MLG was by personal interventions in two cases. Duoji is cited as personally intervening in order to see the MLG implemented in Beijing. In this particular case it is implied that pressure was exerted on the government of Beijing to implement the MLG. Given the status of Beijing as the political heart of the Chinese state and one of the Municipalities it would have been of great significance for the city to implement the policy, and would have benefited the process of spreading *dibao*. It would have leant weight to the push for the policy to be established but it would also expand the experience, methods and support that could be drawn upon when other cities began to implement (Liu 1997).

Duoji is also cited by a report on the MLG in Liaoning as having intervened in the development of the policy in the province. In this example, Duoji suggested in 1995 that the city of Dalian establish an MLG system to provide an example to the other cities in the area on how to set up and manage such a system (Zhang 2002b). The local government in Dalian subsequently established an MLG system which was used as an example not only for cities in Liaoning but also in the rest of China (Interview 10).

Both of these cases suggest that although Duoji might have been limited in his ability to push the MLG in some areas, in others he was more successful. This raises two points. First, Duoji was capable of persuading cities which were under no obligation to follow his instructions to implement MLG systems. This implies that he was either persuasive or had significant political capital in these cities, wherein officials would listen to his suggestions. Second, Duoji may have been tapping into the particular agendas of these cities when he made his interventions. It is entirely possible that both Beijing and Dalian at the time were prepared to invest in establishing MLG systems because the cities were facing enterprise reforms and the potentially destabilising effects of increasing urban poverty, like Shanghai before them.

What impact did Minister Duoji's support have on the MLG? The main outcome – using non-confrontational persuasive means to negotiate implementation as well as accepting implementation based on local developmental circumstances – was a relatively broad but low volume of implementation by the end of 1995. The other outcome was uneven sub-provincial implementation and local variations in financing and coverage within the core concept of the MLG policy. Provided the core concept (a means tested locally administered and funded measure to provide subsistence subsidies to the urban poor) was followed, variations were allowed. This can be put down to the fairly relaxed response to concerns over a lack of regulations. In addition, it reflects that without a State Council or CCP Central Committee decision on a policy there was no real pressure on local governments to comply with the wishes of a minister. The MLG was allowed to spread with a main aim attached to it, but beyond this no methods were attached. This, in combination with the specifics of local circumstances, led to variations emerging in the MLG in different parts of the PRC. The methods and outcomes of Duoji's support of the MLG contrast sharply with that of Li Peng, and the discussion will now turn to his intervention in the policy.

From 1996 the MLG experienced rapid change, increased coverage and national implementation, and was dominated by the actions of Premier Li Peng. Li took an active part in overseeing the accelerated development of the MLG into a national policy and, therefore, his actions need to be considered. While it is difficult to qualify a lot of information regarding these elite-level leaders, texts on the subject (for example (Tang 2003)) make it clear he was fundamental to the process. The role of Li Peng was highlighted frequently in interviews and he was the most-mentioned individual leader brought up (Interviews 1, 3, 9, 11, 16 and 18).

Premier Li made four impacts on the development of the MLG: pressuring areas to implement the policy; consolidating justifications of the MLG; incorporating the MLG into the Ninth Five Year Plan and 2010 Development Goals; and, finally, working towards the publication of the 1997 State Council circular. Demands and pressure on areas, especially in the central-west, to catch up and implement the MLG appeared, and the language used by Li Peng on this issue was less than accommodating. At a meeting of the Office of the State Council in May 1997 Li made it explicitly clear that such delays were unacceptable and that it was the Council's intention to see national implementation:

> Currently still only comparatively developed areas have implemented [the MLG] the number of central-west areas which have carried out this system is small ... This measure does not spend a lot of money, its effectiveness is extremely good, it is a capable measure beneficial to social stability, and it ought to be carried out nationally. Please would the MCA investigate putting forward this plan. (Li 1998d)

The justifications for the MLG put forward by the state also consolidated into what are now familiar points of ensuring social stability through the protection of those who were formally Three No's and those who were impoverished through unemployment, through being laid off, or through non-receipt of pensions (Li 1998f). The international/developmental comparison and concerns over the Party-state legitimacy were no longer explicit when justifying the policy.

Following his work report to the National People's Congress (NPC) in March 1996 (Li 1998e) the policy was incorporated into the 2010 Development Goals and the Ninth Five Year Plan for 1996–2000 (NPC 1998); a marked difference from the preceding ministry-based push. Li's role here is inferred from his high profile in interview data and because the NPC is often seen, somewhat unfairly, as a conduit for decisions that have already been made. Because the MLG is mentioned at this time it indicates the policy is to be implemented, but it also indicates that the decision on the policy has already been made even if the specific timetable or regulatory documents have not been published. Li's association with the MLG in interviews, his support of the policy in 1994 and his speeches supporting the policy in the lead-up to 1997 suggest that Li was fundamental to getting the policy implemented nationally.

The final part of establishing the MLG as a national policy and completing the transition was the State Council publishing its 1997 Circular on the MLG and announcing that it was to be established nationally. Again, Li's role here is not clearly set out, but the significance attributed by interviewees and the fact that he was the head of the State Council at the time suggest a significant role. The 1997 State Council circular was published on 2 September and this had two important impacts on the policy development of the MLG. First, it provided a clear and centrally endorsed set of core values and implementation methods, such as administration of applications and funding, for the MLG. Second, it also provided a solid timetable for the national implementation of the MLG, which built on the 2010 Goals and Ninth Five Year Plan, that the policy should be implemented by the end of the century (State Council 1997).

The methods used to achieve the transition by Li are much the same as those utilised by Duoji Cairang. Speeches which made reference to the MLG (Jiang 1998; Li 1995, 1998e, 1998f), comments recorded in meetings (Duoji 1998d, 1998e; Li 1998d) and the additional use of legislative institutions such as the NPC (Li 1998b; MCA 1998; NPC 1998), as well as the eventual emergence of a State Council circular regarding the MLG (State Council 1997), all contributed to the change in focus regarding the MLG. However, this all came from an individual in the system with the authority to make decisions and the expectation that they would be adhered to. The language used to promote the MLG changed during Li's involvement, reflecting a shift towards a more demanding style of language. For example, in Premier Li's statement quoted above there is no accommodation of regional developmental disparities and an order that the issue be investigated and resolved (Li 1998d).

The decision to implement the MLG nationally was made during the 64th meeting of the State Council cited by Minister Duoji in a work briefing on the MLG (Duoji 1998e). It is notable that Premier Li was associated with the MLG and took action on the policy before this meeting took place, whereas in the case of General Secretary Jiang Zemin and other central leaders the only documented speeches were a long time after the meeting around the time of the publication of the 1997 State Council circular (Jiang 1998; Li 1998b; Zou 1998).

Comparison with the actions and outcomes of the MCA Minister Duoji Cairang allows some interesting conclusions to be drawn. Within the context of China's fragmented system, when assessing the potential impact that a policy actor can have the following points need to be considered. The institutional position occupied by the policy actor in question is important as this places them within the overall structure of government, which is a significant issue in terms of who can be influenced and addressed. It also determines the authority associated with the individual. As noted above the differences in using certain tools of government or the resources that are available will have an impact on a policy. An actor who reports to the State Council for example will have different issues to overcome and different objectives to an actor who presides over the State Council. The influence of a policy actor is not, however, bound entirely in their institutional position but also by their latent or inherited political power. Both of these can be used to influence those around them without having to rely on the mechanics of the state which may or may not be available. In the cases discussed above it is clear that Minister Duoji relied on a combination of the influence granted by being a minister as well as the persuasive motivations he could mobilise through ideological rhetoric and political abilities to manipulate the situation to best serve his interests. In the case of Premier Li the reverse is more apparent, with the position of state and the powers it granted being the primary source of influence.

National implementation of the MLG: 1997–1999

Once national implementation was committed to as a formal goal in 1997, the next stage of the urban MLG's story began. Between 1997 and 1999 the development of the MLG was dominated by the challenge of bringing up to speed the remaining cities that did not have a MLG system in place. In 1999 the State Council published regulations for the MLG which included a deadline of October 1999 for implementation (Li 2000b; State Council 1999). In late 1999 it was announced that the MLG had successfully been established nationwide (Li 2000b). Looking beyond the narrative which has emerged surrounding the MLG, the documentary evidence and interviews make it clear that achieving the 1999 goal was a challenge (Interviews 11 and 18).

Two interviews in particular suggested this, both with central government officials working at the MCA in Beijing. In one interview it was made clear that there had been difficulties in getting some areas, typically those which were fiscally poor and with a significant SOE sector, to implement a MLG programme. In particular, the Province of Gansu was highlighted as a problematic area (Interview 11). In the other interview the lack of resources was the highlighted challenge in achieving implementation. To this end local government was encouraged by the centre to implement and launch implementation campaigns, and ultimately the MCA's newspaper, the *China Society News*, was used to aid implementation through what was in effect a naming and shaming campaign (Interview 18). It is apparent, therefore, that although China did manage to get its cities to comply with the 1997 Circular and the 1999 Regulations it took a greater effort than might be immediately apparent.

What explains the difficulty in achieving implementation? There are three areas which are worthy of our attention here: political structure, finance, and other resources. Political structure can be split into two separate issues; first, the hierarchy and ranking inherent to the Chinese system of government and, second, the previous decisions made on the implementation of the MLG. Finance refers to the challenge of funding a new programme of social assistance which committed local governments to spending on what was always likely to be a larger number of people than had previously been captured by the Three No's system. Finally, other resources refer to the fact that money alone does not get things done. Policy implementation often needs additional resources, typically personnel, to help facilitate the process of designing and putting in a place a new programme. These issues were compounded by the MCA being a resource-poor institution.

The structure of Chinese government, the hierarchy of ranks which administrative agencies fall into, is a key point in understanding policy developments as noted in the Introduction. The sharing of rank by different agencies with different agendas was one of the areas where the implementation of the MLG fell into difficulties. Interviews with MCA officials highlighted two particular problems. First, provincial government resisting implementation of the MLG, and, second, lower tiers of government dragging out implementation (Interview 11). In the case of the former this was put down to poorer provinces seeking to extract resources from the central government in return for implementation; something which the MCA was not in a position to do given its relatively resource-poor status in the central government (Interview 11). The latter issue is typical of policy implementation in China where the distance between Beijing and the smaller administrative units of the state is so vast that, despite circulars and subsequent newspaper articles and ministerial publications extolling them to implement the MLG, there was significant drag.

The second political issue is the impact of previous pronouncements on the policy. A timetable for implementation, based on administrative rank, was part of the 1997 Circular. Notably there had been previous announcements on when and in what way differently ranked cities should implement MLG systems. These different announcements were similar, that lower-ranked cities can hold off, although Li Peng's instructions appear to counter this (Li 1998d). The decision to make such announcements would have prolonged implementation because if a delay is deemed acceptable then a delay will probably happen. This then raises the question of whether or not the delay in cities implementing the MLG was perceived as being dragged out or not. Given that the issue was raised in interviews as a difficulty the MCA faced, the question of whether this was intended, a natural response or neither is not relevant (Interview 11). What is relevant is that the MCA perceived the issue as a problem.

The second issue which became apparent in trying to understand the challenge of implementing the MLG programme is finance. Specifically, the design of the MLG, as set out in the 1997 Circular, means that the cost falls on local government (State Council 1997). It is also clearly stated in the 1997 Circular that local government should implement their MLG systems in line with local circumstances (State Council 1997). Although this is left to interpretation it is easy to understand this as meaning that poorer cities are anticipated to offer a more limited form of social assistance. The problem identified by some interviewees was that poorer cities, and in one case an entire province, used weak local finance to claim that they could not implement the MLG at all (Interview 11). This is not, in and of itself, a surprise. The parlous state of local finances has been a persistent part of the reform era narrative and is still a significant issue hanging over China's development (Fewsmith 2013).

Finally, the lack of access to other resources was an issue in achieving implementation. The implementation of the MLG and by extension the MCA was not just lacking in the fiscal resources which might have smoothed out the implementation process but was also lacking in other key areas. Personnel, in terms of numbers but also ability, appears to have been a significant issue which affected implementation (MCA 2000a). In addition, a lack of effective information management systems and computers to support implementation and running the MLG were raised as problems faced by the MLG in the early days (MCA 2000b). Taken together it is clear that the government, through the MCA, faced a number of issues when seeking to achieve the compliance of its cities.

What was the response of the central government to this challenge to implementation, perceived or otherwise? How did a resource-poor ministry achieve implementation when faced with the challenge of intransigent or incapable local government? Interviews and documentary resources suggest that there were at least three different strategies adopted by the MCA and other branches of government.

The first strategy adopted, and this is typical when administrative deadlock occurs, is to send an issue higher up the hierarchy. In the case of the MLG this move up the hierarchy took two forms. First, there was direct intervention in the impasse between the MCA and a particular province where the governor was eventually persuaded to comply with the wishes of the MCA by an unidentified member of the State Council (Interviews 11 and 18). In this instance, the province was viewed as 'playing games' (Interview 11) with the MCA over implementation in order to extract additional funding, which the MCA could not provide, and this therefore required the intervention of, in terms of rank, a more powerful actor.

Second, in interviews it was made very clear that the eventual move from the 1997 Circular to the 'Urban Resident MLG Regulations' in 1999 was carried out in order to force a number of cities that were dragging their feet to implement the MLG programme (Interview 18). The thinking behind this move was that while a circular from the State Council was not something a local official should ignore it was possible to prolong complying with its requirements. A regulation passed down by the State Council, however, was another matter entirely, and as the MLG programme moved closer to becoming statute it would be more difficult for local government to resist implementation (Interviews 8, 9, 11 and 18). It is notable that the differences between the 1997 Circular and 1999 Regulations were very small. The 1999 Regulations did however make it clear that implementation be achieved by 1 October 1999, on the fiftieth anniversary of the founding of the PRC. Both officials and researchers pointed out that this meant that cities who had been putting off implementing the MLG had no real choice but to comply (Interviews 9 and 11) and this is borne out by the discussion of the spread of *dibao* earlier in the chapter.

The second strategy was the newspaper campaign carried out through the *China Society News* and directed by the MCA. This was identified by a senior official involved in the MLG implementation effort at the time. The interviewee mentioned that the efforts to essentially name and shame cities and provinces which had not implemented the programme was the MCA's effort to push implementation when it was without additional fiscal resources but did have exploitable information as a resource (Interview 18). The MCA was, through the use of its newspaper, publicly identifying those who were failing to comply without spending extra funds in order to achieve the publicity.

The campaign to ensure implementation was as follows. The sole means was the *China Society News* – and the official who cited the campaign notes that it was an innovative use of the newspaper and publicity in order to achieve implementation. Based on the information provided in the interview the campaign took place between 1997 and 1999, the period when implementation was being sought in line with national announcements. The campaign consisted of the levels of implementation being published on a city-by-city basis so the areas that had not established the policy would be shown up publicly. This was seen as a way to ensure implementation (Interview 18). What follows is a discussion of the implementation effort based on an analysis of the *China Society News* during this period.

Before addressing the question of whether a campaign is visible, the first issue to address is that of frequency: how often were articles on the MLG published in the newspaper? There is a slight downward trend in the number of articles from 1997 to 1999: in 1997, sixty-one articles; in 1998, fifty articles; and in 1999, there were forty-seven articles published. There were also spikes in the number of stories. In 1997 this occurred in September when there were twenty-eight stories on the MLG published. In October 1998, twelve stories were published and in 1999, fourteen stories were published in February. These are the only months where the number of stories went into double figures. It should also be noted that there are no periods of time where there were no stories although there are a number of months where only one story was published.

In September 1997, the MLG was announced as a policy for national implementation so it is not surprising that there were significantly more news stories at this time. For the other two spikes, the explanation is less apparent. In the case of October 1998 there was a cluster of 'best practice' stories spread over a number of issues. Finally, in February 1999 there was again a cluster of best practice stories, numbering nine in total.

In terms of where articles were posted the only month in which there is a spike in stories on the front page is September 1997 which, as noted above, makes sense. The best practice stories were displayed on pages two and three of the newspaper in both of the spikes in this coding category.

Based on a reading of the articles there are three discernible series which focused on the MLG during the time period in question. The first of these is a series of stories focusing on the MLG during the immediate post-announcement implementation. They were distinguished by a special announcement regarding the story on page one of the 4 September 1997 issue, and a boxing of the stories when they subsequently appeared suggesting they were part of a series which appeared in each issue inclusive to 25 September 1997.

The second series of articles which stands out is the cluster on best practice, discussed above. There is no clear indication in either the newspaper or in interviews conducted on the MLG as to why these articles appeared, but they do fit a strategy by government to disseminate information and good practice which can be found in speeches and meetings as well as newspapers. In this instance the stories focused on Guangdong in ten page-two articles on 6 and 7 October 1998, and also multiple regions in ten page-two articles on 3 February 1999.

The final area of note is evidence of the actual campaign highlighted in the interview with MCA officials. The campaign took the form of bordered boxes which appeared on the front page of the newspaper. The box has a consistent format including a title 'Countdown to establishing the urban MLG system' (*jianli chengshi zuidi shenghuo baozhang zhidu, daoji shipai*) and an indication of the number of days left to the end of 1999, which then introduces the 'work schedules for provinces, autonomous regions, and Municipalities who have not established an urban MLG system'. The table then includes the name of the sub-national government unit, the number of cities that have not yet implemented the programme, the status of preparations for implementation, the planned dates for the policy being introduced, the date for comprehensive implementation, the numbers expected to be on the programme, and the initial MLG line being implemented.

The first of these boxes appeared on 1 April 1999 and continued through to 2 September 1999 after which no further boxes appeared. The boxes appeared on the front page of the newspaper on the first of the month or the date nearest to this. In the initial box from April 1999 a total of fifteen provinces were identified as not having completed implementation. These were: Shanxi, Inner Mongolia, Heilongjiang, Jiangxi, Hubei, Hunan, Hainan, Sichuan, Chongqing, Guizhou, Yunnan, Tibet, Shaanxi, Ningxia and Xinjiang. In total, 319 cities are noted as not having implemented a MLG system with a prospective 218,994 people to be brought into the system. In the last box, from September 1999, five provinces remained (Hunan, Hainan, Guizhou, Tibet and Xinjiang), with thirty-four cities still to implement. In the last box no numbers are referred to, with only the intended dates for implementation noted – a mixture of September and October 1999.

Based on the content of the boxes it is difficult to construct an argument which would support the idea that they were fundamental in terms of achieving the final completion of the urban MLG system. This conclusion is drawn for two reasons. First, at the time the first box was published it is clear that all of the provinces in question had plans in place for introducing and implementing the programme. Second, there was no apparent intensification in the introduction or implementation of the programme following the introduction of the text box. In essence, things appear to have followed the plans of the local government units in question without the public naming having any discernible effect. It might be considered that by publishing these plans the units in question were being held publicly to their timetable, but as no region or city went beyond the deadline impact or lack thereof is impossible to discern. Given that this information was the only apparent information resource the MCA had available to exploit it does suggest an innovative attempt by the ministry to work around the problem of ensuring local government did what it was told. By making such information public the MCA was ensuring that any failure to implement the MLG would have been widely publicised, which would have been very embarrassing for anyone involved.

The final strategy adopted was that of the central government quietly subsidising the MLG programme. While the MLG was originally designed as, and has remained until the present, a system which was supposed to be administered and funded by local government, according to local circumstances from 1999 this ceased to be the case. Transfers from the central government budget to local government, when recorded, began to grow in the late 1990s, and in 2001 the central government was funding the majority of the programme (Hammond 2011b, 2013).

Why would this have eased the implementation of the MLG? While more specific data are not available the implication drawn from the shift to central subsidies, and confirmed in an interview (Interview 11) and later documents that do detail central subsidies (MCA 2000a, MoF 2000a), is that the money coming from central government encouraged poorer provinces and cities to implement the programme. In short, the money provided by the centre bought the compliance of the localities. In some instances it is almost certain that the financial support would have been needed, as it does not take much to imagine that areas with high numbers of potential MLG claimants would also be areas that had faced significant shocks and fiscal tightening during the reform period. This subsidisation of the MLG did not end with implementation but has continued, as will be discussed in the next chapter.

On the back of these three strategies full implementation of the 1997 Circular and the subsequent 1999 Regulations was achieved ahead of time in late 1999 (Fan 2000a). The MLG had been implemented nationally against a backdrop of the MCA's struggle to coax local government into line initially without additional resources. In these circumstances, the strategies used are those which might be anticipated under FA. The MCA used the political structure where possible to invoke a higher authority and therefore work around the problem of the minis-try's place in the state hierarchy. The MCA also tried to use the resource it did have available – information – to its advantage through a newspaper campaign to ensure local government followed through on their commitment to the policy. However, it appears that ensuring implementation came down to resources the MCA did not have – money – and this was ultimately provided by the top tier of government to ensure implementation.

Conclusion

This chapter argued that the emergence, spread and implementation of the urban MLG was due to a number of factors. The political structure of the Chinese state provided the space for actors in Shanghai, constrained by the established speech space and values of the time, to develop a policy that addressed concerns regarding social stability and ongoing reform. Previous decisions and policy design further constrained the options available leading to the emergence of a locally funded and administered means test. Picked up by the Minister for Civil Affairs, Duoji Cairang, and supported by Premier Li Peng the policy was then promoted on the national stage. Operating from a position of limited means as head of a resource-poor ministry, Duoji invoked the values of the time to cajole local governments to implement their own MLG systems between 1994 and 1996. The spread of the policy accelerated when Li Peng, a figure with more authority and the means to put the MLG onto the legislative agenda, became involved. This supports the argument that under FA policies can get stuck in the bureaucratic impasse of rank and lack of resources, at which point only figures with the appropriate authority can break through. The move to implement the urban MLG nationally after the 1997 Circular was announced further reinforces this line of thinking. The MCA, lacking any resources other than information, struggled to keep implementation of the MLG on track and resorted to two strategies before a third strategy using influence higher up the system was employed. The first of these was to kick the problem to a higher authority and in the form of the 1999 Regulations hope this was enough to get implementation achieved. While this set a deadline it alone was not enough. Second, the MCA used its newspaper, the *China Society News*, to utilise the information it had available to hold local governments to their commitment to implement the MLG. Third, and finally, subsidisation of the MLG resolved the last problems facing local government and meant that implementation was achieved. The successful national implementation of the urban MLG did not, however, end the story of the government's struggle to get its vision of the MLG implemented in China's cities, and this will be discussed further in the next chapter.

Note

1. The term Municipality as used here is the term for referring to the cities in China that have this classification (Shanghai, Beijing, Tianjin and Chongqing). Other scholars use their own terms, such as 'named citiy' in Lieberthal (1995). The term Municipality will be used throughout, with the capital 'M', and will always refer to a city with the specific *zhixiashi* rank.

Chapter 3

Urban Dibao*: The Resolution of Unwanted and Unintended Outcomes, 1999–2003*

Introduction

The previous chapter noted how the emergence, spread and implementation of the urban MLG could be explained through the FA framework. It was shown that the space provided by the structure of the Chinese state facilitated innovation in social assistance policy in Shanghai when there were policy actors willing to exploit it. It was also shown that the structure of the state could serve to shape and constrain the choices available to particular actors, whereas those who wielded additional authority were in a position to force through decisions. In this chapter the development of the urban MLG in the period 1999 to 2003 will be discussed. This period is significant because, as noted in Chapter 1, there was significant expansion in the scope and spending on the urban MLG but the reasons for this go undiscussed. What is notable about this period is that it demonstrated that even during a period when the policy-making environment in China was changing the power of elite leaders was undiminished and could still be used to force through significant changes in policy. What is also notable is that the expansion of the urban MLG shows the MCA taking advantage of the situation in order to resolve a number of problems it was facing and also to expand its own capabilities.

The chapter will first discuss some of the challenges that the urban MLG was facing after national implementation was achieved – primarily a problem of variation although it manifested in different ways. It will be argued that the reasons for this variation are partly due to the design of the policy but also due to the process through which it came to be implemented nationally. The chapter then goes on to show how the intervention of a powerful policy actor, Premier Zhu Rongji, brought about a situation where various issues facing the MLG were temporarily resolved. This intervention demonstrates the key elements of the FA framework in action, namely the interaction of values, state structure and the relative authority of different actors in the system. The chapter will end with a discussion of how the MCA exploited both Zhu's intervention and the fragmented nature of the system in order to pursue its own agenda.

Unintended and unwanted outcomes

Variations in the MLG began to emerge as soon as it spread beyond Shanghai. Wong (1998) notes three early models of MLG finance. The Dalian Model was funded 100 per cent by the state. The Fuzhou Model was complex, with fragmented funding and administrative responsibility among multiple stakeholders. Finally, the Benxi Model relied on an initial fund set up by the city government which was then sustained through income tax and social insurance payments (Wong 1998). Tang Jun highlights variations between the Shanghai, Wuhan and Chongqing models. Shanghai was a mixed funding model with funds raised from the city budget and local enterprises and Wuhan used a model based entirely on government funding. The Chongqing Model was not distinguished by its funding, which appears to have been based initially on fees levied on enterprises, but by its inclusivity and generous provisions (Tang 2003).

The key variation which emerged was between the Dalian and Shanghai Models (Duoji 1998b). The Shanghai Model was characterised by a mixture of local government and local enterprise in the division of financial and administrative responsibilities. Dalian used the emerging sub-district (*shequ*) level of local government and full local government funding. The two models did impact on the eventual design of the MLG when it was rolled out nationally as they formed the basis for the policy design. Shanghai provided the core concept of means testing and local adjustment and Dalian provided the financing and administration model (Interviews 10 and 12). Although Shanghai is cited as the birthplace of the MLG and did set out the fundamentals of the policy, it was the Dalian Model which went on to become the national standard.

The initial implementation of the MLG was also characterised by the challenges of slow implementation and continued uneven administration throughout China's myriad localities, evident in official and semi-official documents (Li 2001c; Li and Zhu 2000; Lü, Y. 1998; Lü, Z. 2003; Ma 1998; Qiao 2003; Wang, Z. 1999; Wang and Wang 1998; Wu 1998; Zhang 2002a) and interviews (Interviews 3, 5, 8, 11 and 16).The initial focus on getting cities to first implement the MLG meant that ironing out inconsistencies in the administration was not addressed. Problems with administration primarily concerned the application and allocation procedures being varied, groups who should be receiving the MLG being excluded, and some concerns over the low level of the MLG line (Interviews 11 and 18).

These challenges for the policy were a result of the decentralisation of fiscal and political authority in China combined with the local focus of the MLG design. The lack of fiscal power in some parts of China, primarily areas in the centre and west, impacted on the MLG because it affected the ability to adequately fund the policy (Interview 11). The local basis of the 1997 MLG design meant that if an area faced tight fiscal constraints the ability to raise funds for new social assistance requirements would be a significant challenge. Because of the decentralised nature of policy implementation, the situation emerged where there was significant drag in terms of acceptable implementation. This was because if a certain area did not want to fund or could not fund *dibao* it could resist implementation by not establishing a system or by carrying out the policy with limited provisions. Such a stance was supported by the design of the MLG.

Concerns from officials began to appear in the *China Civil Affairs* (*ZGMZ*) magazine, a monthly publication of the MCA, regarding both lack of implementation and inconsistencies in implementation (Wang, Z. 1999; Wang and Wang 1998; Wu 1998). Concerns here focused on a lack of local funds resulting in some areas implementing *dibao* in a limited manner. This meant that certain areas made it standard practice to discourage applications from groups such as laid-off and unemployed workers even if their household income fell below the local MLG line. Other tactics included the rejection of applications made by these groups or the introduction of stricter criteria in awarding the MLG than had originally been envisaged by the government.

The initial response by the MCA regarding these problems was the issuing of the January 1999 'MCA Circular Regarding Accelerating the Establishing and Completion of the Urban Resident MLG System' (MCA 1999; 1999 MCA Circular hereafter), and in September 1999 the State Council 'Urban Resident Minimum Livelihood Guarantee Regulations' (State Council 1999; 1999 Regulations hereafter). The 1999 MCA Circular was addressed to authorities with responsibility for implementing and administering the MLG and highlighted problems with the MLG not being implemented at all in some areas or incorrectly in other areas. The main problem identified was the exclusion of certain categories of people from receiving the MLG when the system was supposed to be means tested and not category based – the 'Ought to protect, not protecting' problem (*yingbao weibao*). In addition, it dealt with the first significant post-1997 intervention in the MLG by the central government, but this will be discussed further below. The 1999 Regulations provided a reiteration of what had already been set out in the 1997 Circular (State Council 1997) and can be considered to be an effort to move the MLG onto a formal footing by making the guidelines for the MLG a legal document. As one MCA official reported, the functional differences between the MLG as set out in the 1997 Circular and the 1999 Regulations are negligible (Interview 11).

The important difference was how the MLG was referred to after the 1999 Regulations were announced and how the policy would be viewed by those who were tasked with carrying it out. In one interview with a group of Chinese researchers it was made clear that the difference between policy, regulation and law is an issue of considerable importance in the policy process (Interview 8). Another interviewee stated that the MCA had sought that the MLG become more closely tied to the 'force of law' during 1998–1999, and the State Council suggested that regulations were drafted in order to achieve this (Interview 18). The 1999 Regulations therefore served the purpose of moving the MLG further away from the 'request' it was perceived as being by some localities, and closer to a legal requirement of the state.

The problem of incorrect administration of the MLG continued beyond the promulgation of the 1999 Regulations. The exclusion of potential recipients and inconsistent application and screening procedures were a consistent concern in both circulated speeches and documents (Fan 1999a, 1999b, 2000a, 2000b, 2000c, 2001b; Li 2001a; MoLSS 2000) and articles published in *ZGMZ* (Li 2001c; Li and Zhu 2000; Lü, Y. 1998; Lü, Z. 2003; Ma 1998; Qiao 2003; Shu 2002; Wang, Z. 1999; Wang and Wang 1998; Wu 1998; Zhang 2002a). Second, the challenge of financing the MLG was not resolved by the 1999 Regulations, in fact the issue was sustained by continuing the locally funded design concept in spite of central government subsidies having begun earlier in the year, and this only began to get resolved with the intervention of the central government.

Overall, it can be argued that the unintended and unwanted outcomes affecting the MLG were rooted in the FA of the Chinese state. A combination of the methods used to spread the programme, the methods used to implement the programme, and the general context of the urban MLG operating in a mushy and resource-poor part of the bureaucracy all occurred in the context of a fragmented Chinese state, leading to the various outcomes noted above.

The urban MLG was affected by the spread promoted by Minister Duoji. Although Duoji occupied a position of authority relative to many parts of the Chinese state he was also constrained relative to the provinces and therefore the local government which was to implement the programme. This meant that he could use his position to promote the MLG and this is what he did. However, it also meant that he compromised in terms of the nature of the policy that was implemented. In order to achieve implementation a compromise was struck regarding how the MLG looked, which led to the emergence of various models that persisted after 1997. This variation was further compounded by the design of the MLG which both encouraged variation through adaptation to local circumstances and at the same time was vague enough to leave local government with little option but to grope for an implementation of some sort.

This affected both the funding mechanisms used and also the decision about calculating the MLG line. The MCA either did not provide guidance or left a number of options open. In the case of funding the MLG there were two dominant models which emerged between 1995 and 1997: Shanghai and Dalian. In May 1995 Minister Duoji made it clear that the choice of which model to follow was open (Duoji 1998b). How to finance the MLG was not clearly resolved until 1997 with the publication of the State Council circular on the policy.

The calculation of the MLG line is the other area where the handling of the issue led to variations, with different methods adopted by different cities. Various options emerged, from household surveys, 'scientific' methods like the Engels Index, shopping basket systems, or a vaguely defined 'rational' approach (Xi 1998). The calculation of the MLG line is extremely important because it determines the potential number of MLG recipients and what level of subsidy they would receive. The search for a calculation method is also significant because it is an area where local interests, such as how much money is available for the MLG, would become influential. What is of interest is that during the spread of the MLG the calculation method was never resolved but, as Xi's speech in 1996 suggests, the government was aware of and was disseminating ideas on the issue from local-level initiatives. This approach to the calculation method invites variation to occur because no clear path was set out by the MCA.

The efforts to implement the demand of the 1997 Circular and 1999 Regulations regarding national implementation also had an impact on the MLG. While the top tier of government supported the MLG being implemented this did not come with any additional support in the form of fiscal or personnel resources. As noted previously, this meant that the MCA was left to cajole local government into implementation of some form in order to meet its deadlines using the only resource it had available – information. The late infusion of limited fiscal subsidies appears to have ensured national implementation but by this point the policy had already been left as an unfunded mandate for local government to deal with, leading to the variable outcomes detailed above.

Finally, the MLG was being implemented and then managed in a system where at the centre the MCA was subordinate to the wishes of the State Council and Politburo, as well as the Finance Ministry, and was operating in parallel to other ministries and the provinces. At the local level the Civil Affairs units were subordinate to both the MCA and the local government units. This meant that although the MCA was aware of, and in some instances was trying to push through, changes regarding the MLG, without the necessary resources or authority it invariably ran up against China's fragmented system. In essence, there are various decision points within the system where different actors and goals regarding the MLG and the MCA are subordinate or equal to each other. This mushy bureaucracy led to groping for solutions, and the problems outlined above, and was further exacerbated by a lack of resources.

The initial phase of the MLG's State Council endorsed national implementation, essentially from the 1997 Circular's publication onwards, and was carried out with no additional personnel or fiscal resources provided by the central government. Because the MCA was a resource-poor institution (Wong 1998), by design it spends funds rather than raises them, and this had three impacts on implementation during the post-1997 period that had to be resolved later. First, the MCA struggled to get the MLG implemented in some areas. Second, the MLG was implemented in a non-standard way in some areas. Finally, the lack of resources meant that the MCA had to adapt its approach to getting the policy implemented.

The lack of specific resources for the MLG was due to two factors. The first was a result of the design of the policy, which was based around the decentralised fiscal and administrative system. The MLG as designed in 1997 relied on local-level financing and management as well as the residence- and street committee-level involvement for basic administration in order to operate. This was the Dalian Model which had emerged in the mid-1990s. Enterprises were being removed from the day-to-day provision of welfare and assistance to urban residents and the sub-district agencies were only just emerging in their stead. Using local government to both fund and administer the policy would therefore reflect the reality of Chinese local government, and the splitting of the state from enterprises, and the decline of the work unit.

The second factor contributing to a lack of resources for the implementation of the MLG was the MCA. As noted above, the MCA was a resource-poor institution but this was further exacerbated by the MCA being given the responsibility for overseeing the implementation of the MLG while not receiving additional resources for the purpose (Interview 18). This suggests a lack of willingness on the part of the central government to fund the MLG or, perhaps more likely, that the central government did not feel the need to fund a locally funded and administered policy. The MCA was, therefore, faced with getting the MLG implemented within a two-year time frame but with no additional resources to help. The previous chapter argued that Minister Duoji's support of the MLG was in part hampered by a lack of resources and this continued to be the case after the 1997 Circular and 1999 Regulations.

The extensive delegation of authority in overseeing and enforcing the implementation of the MLG combined with the lack of financing to create three major issues for the MLG. The first of these was the slow implementation of the MLG. Despite the clear objective for establishing the MLG nationally, available figures show that the extension of the policy did not achieve this until late 1999 (Fan 2000a), just achieving the objective of the 1997 Circular. The MCA did not have the incentives nor the political power to force areas to implement the MLG quickly and, as discussed previously, had to resort to public naming and shaming of cities in order to speed up implementation.

A second impact was the incorrect implementation of the MLG policy as set out in the 1997 Circular. The major problem in this instance was the consistent exclusion of groups which should have been receiving the MLG. The most frequently cited problems concerned those who had been entitled to other benefits, such as unemployment insurance, which had now expired, those who were receiving benefits or incomes that were below the MLG line, and laid-off workers applying for the benefit but being refused in spite of passing the means test (Interview 11; and Fan 1998b; Tang 2003). This incorrect implementation of the MLG was a result of the MCA lacking resources to either support the policy in areas that had decided they could not afford to implement the policy or to push the policy through in areas that decided they did not want to implement the policy (Interview 11). Guan and Xu's study of the difficult relationship between the central government and localities regarding getting a standard or correct form of the MLG implemented supports this conclusion (Guan and Xu 2011).

The delegation of policy responsibility to local government therefore allowed for deliberate and accidental delays in the policy being implemented as well as similar problems with interpretation of how the policy should be operated. A major sticking point which contributed to these problems was the lack of funding outside of what could be allocated at the local level. Due to some areas facing fiscal difficulties or being unwilling to contribute to required funds MLG lines were set low, groups were excluded and implementation was slowed through the policy existing on paper only (Interview 11; and Duoji 1998b; Fan 1998a; Li 1998a; Li 1998c).

The third impact is how the lack of resources determined the actions of the MCA. Due to restricted personnel and lack of funds the MCA relied on alternative means to work towards implementation. In some respects the MCA relied on similar methods to those which it had been using in the period preceding 1996. This consisted primarily of pressure being applied through repeated calls for implementation to be carried out in speeches and circulars on the subject (Li 1998a; Li 1998c; Fan 1998a; Duoji 1998b), as well as the innovation discussed in the previous chapter. The work of the Department for Disaster and Social Relief (*Jiuzai Jiuji Si)* in the MCA was important during this time as it was tasked within the MCA with overseeing the implementation. From first-hand observation the department is small and the task would have been a significant undertaking. The result of these issues as they developed was that there was a national implementation but it was limited and incomplete.

Interventions

Unlike the spread of the MLG and initial implementation efforts, the measures which contributed to resolving some of the problems the MLG had developed are more familiar to the FA framework. As noted above the problems were primarily a consequence of low resources and bureaucratic mushiness. These problems were resolved through the intervention of those with higher authority and the allocation of significant resources. This, to some extent, bypassed the formal state and reinforced the informal nature of politics and policy making in China noted by Lieberthal (1992). The urban MLG during this period highlights that at this point in time individuals in the Chinese system could still be vested with enough authority and the ability to direct resources to the extent that they could reshape a policy to fit their agenda.

Both the higher level of government and also the MCA learned early on that the MLG could be boosted with a direct infusion of resources as was demonstrated in the first direct intervention during 1999 which is the first element discussed in this part of the chapter. In order to really change how things were being done fiscal resources needed to be matched by political authority and the mobilisation of personnel. This is what happened in 2000–2003 when the MLG was expanded rapidly, not because that was what was necessarily best or intended for the policy, but because it suited the agenda of the Premier, Zhu Rongji.

It is worth quickly noting here that the expansion of the urban MLG is another aspect of the story of social assistance in reform era China which is taken for granted and fitted into the accepted discourse. The implication is that the expansion of the scope of the MLG just happened and was largely an intended outcome. This was not the case and the reality was much more complex in that the MLG changed because of the intervention of a powerful policy actor and the infusion of resources that followed and this was, as stated above, to suit the agenda of that actor rather than any inherent desire to make good on the commitments inherent in the design of the MLG.[1]

The First Central Government Intervention and Implications for the MLG

On 1 July 1999 the central government, through the State Council, MoF and Central Committee of the CCP, announced a 30 per cent increase in the MLG line nationwide as part of a general increase in social policy provisions (CCPCC 1999; MoF 2000a). Baumgartner and Jones argue significant changes in policy, so called punctuations, can have their origins in seemingly innocuous developments and I would argue that the first central intervention in the MLG would be an example of such a development (Baumgartner and Jones 1991, 1993). There are three important points resulting from this development: a break with MLG convention in administration and funding practices; the central government viewing the MLG as a policy it could and should intervene in; and the setting of precedent for central intervention.

This was a significant moment in terms of breaking with convention and setting a precedent for central government intervention in a locally administered policy. The 1999 MCA Circular dealt with funding of the MLG and also the specific direction of the policy marking a deviation from the primarily local nature of the initial MLG design. Regarding the direction of the policy the 1999 MCA Circular called for a blanket national 30 per cent rise in the MLG level. In addition, the *xiagang* basic livelihood guarantee (XGBLG) and unemployment insurance (UEI) benefits were also subject to a 30 per cent increase (MCA 1999; MoF 2000a). The central government committed to funding the increase. Funding for the increase was provided by allocations from the central government budget for areas that would be unable to fund the increase themselves. Areas which were to fund themselves were Beijing, Shanghai, Shandong, Jiangsu, Zhejiang, Fujian and Guangdong. For all other areas an application procedure and guidelines were outlined in material circulated throughout the bureaucracy, and the entire process and funds were to be administered by the MoF (MoF 2000a).[2]

The 1999 intervention is interesting because it implies that the higher echelons of the state were involved. Although it was suggested by an interviewee that this increase was an internal decision resulting from dissatisfaction with the levels that the MLG line was being set at, this does not appear to be the case for four reasons (Interview 12). First, the increases were announced for three different policies, with two falling under the remit of the MoLSS, the XGBLG and UEI, and only the MLG being a responsibility of the MCA. Cross-system cooperation can be difficult, so this implies that the higher echelons of the state were involved. Second, the funding and details on how to administer the increase came from the MoF, implying that they had a high degree of control over the projected increases rather than the line ministries that were to administer it (MoF 2000a). In addition, the MCA would not be able to issue such an increase even if it had wanted to because of its position in the state hierarchy. Third, both the State Council and the Central Committee of the CCP released a joint circular on the matter indicating they had a high degree of involvement beyond just the MCA being active (CCPCC 1999). This document is significant because it indicates that both the state and the Party were involved in the increases, whereas previous developments on the MLG had tended to come from the state only. The document justified the increases as a means to ensure social stability by increasing the income of poor workers and 'strengthen the confidence of urban residents regarding the outcomes of economic development' (CCPCC 1999: 14). Finally, the timing and reasoning given by the MCA, MoF, State Council and CCPCC for the increases shows that the increases were linked to the fiftieth anniversary of the People's Republic that year (Anonymous 2000; MCA 1999; MoF 2000b). While it is conceivable that the MCA could have secured funding independently for the increase, the involvement of three ministries, the State Council, the Party and the link with the anniversary of the founding of the PRC point to this being a clear intervention by central authorities further up the chain of command than the line ministries.

Why should this intervention be considered a significant event for the MLG? There are three reasons why the decision should be considered important. First, the decision to intervene was a major break with the initial convention established regarding the function of the MLG. The policy was supposed to be managed locally in all aspects but the decision to force a rise in the MLG line and also establish central funding broke with two of the core conventions regarding the policy.

Second, these actions show the influence that the central government can have over local processes if it so desires. This might be considered a point of interest and no more but the fact that the central government could, if it wanted to, break with the core conventions of a policy through the use of its political and fiscal resources is an important point to consider. This is because of the third reason as to why the intervention is important, that being that a precedent was set for intervention by the central government. The MLG has become subject to increasing central control, dependent on central resources, and hamstrung at times by an expectation of central interventions.[3] It is arguable that without the precedent set in 1999 for central interventions future interventions may not have occurred or may have been more difficult to bring about. The policy actor who will be discussed below, Zhu Rongji, would have been involved as Premier in this increase in the MLG and so the precedent would not have been lost on him either. At the very least, the idea of central government intervention has become part of how the MLG now operates, and this precedent paved the way for more significant interventions such as the one made by Premier Zhu Rongji in 2000.

Zhu Rongji's Intervention in the MLG

Before discussing the intervention of Premier Zhu two points need to be made regarding the context in which his intervention took place. First, the increase in the level of the MLG and the tighter regulatory framework provided by the 1999 Regulations did not successfully resolve the problems facing the MLG. This is because the main problems of funding and local administration practices were not effectively addressed. Second, the exacerbation of problems in policies outside of the MLG provided a driving force on the political agenda that eventually led to decisions being made with long-term implications for both the nature and funding of the MLG. This can be understood as exogenous feedback or at the very least the setting of a political context for understanding the motivations behind Premier Zhu's intervention in the MLG.

The 1990s were a period of uncertainty and change regarding the direction and success of China's reform project. The post-Tiananmen uncertainty of the early 1990s gave way to an unprecedented boom and massive restructuring of the state-owned sector. It was this dynamic of change which had contributed to the initial emergence of the MLG in the early 1990s. The continued repercussions of the Iron Rice Bowl's deconstruction and attempts at constructing a new social security system provided challenges which led to the MLG emerging as a major investment of the central government in the early 2000s, as noted in the early part of this chapter. The 'Ought to protect, fully protect' (yingbao jinbao) campaign which ran in two cycles from 2000–2003 saw unprecedented investment in the MLG and massive increases in numbers receiving the MLG and funding. This expansion was the result of political and fiscal interventions by the central government and notably Premier Zhu Rongji; but it was the challenges presented by the faltering attempts at social security reform and the continuation of deepening SOE reform, essentially the ending of state support for failing SOEs, which provided the need to bring about such a mobilisation of resources. In short, the failure of the laid-off worker XGBLG, UEI and other social security reforms within the context of continued SOE reform created a political agenda regarding the future direction of basic-level social welfare and the MLG.

What then were these failings and how did they present a challenge to the government? The reform of health insurance, the development of the unemployment insurance system, problems with pension provision and finally, perhaps most significantly, the twin failure of the XGBLG and the re-employment service centres all put pressure on the government. Taken together, the general failure of the government to adequately replace the previous system of social provision created a major challenge to the central leadership and especially to Zhu Rongji. The reasons for this were threefold. First, the reforms to enterprises were creating an increasingly impoverished and agitated urban group which was perceived as threatening to undermine social stability. Second, measures introduced to compensate for the disappearance of the Iron Rice Bowl had not proved effective at providing comprehensive coverage, leading to widespread discontent and uncertainty for the urban population regarding the social security system. Third, and finally, the two points above meant that Zhu Rongji risked seeing his efforts to introduce the market into the state-owned sector derail – a project Zhu was, from 1993, inextricably linked to (Gilley 2001; Naughton 2002).

The first area to be discussed is health. In terms of the MLG there was increasing recognition, especially among researchers and the MCA, that being sick might not only impoverish urban residents but also made the benefit provided by the MLG ineffective in terms of providing a minimum livelihood (Ken and Zhang 2002; MCA 2003c, 2003d; Wang 2003; Zhu 2003). Second, the MLG was affected by the state of the UEI because it soaked up the unemployed who were not provided for by the system, and it was intended that those with UEI who had exhausted their three years of benefits would move onto the MLG (Duoji 1998b). The MLG, however, had become a de facto unemployment provision to make up for the shortcomings of UEI (Interview 12). Third, pensioners who fell into poverty because of non-payment by their enterprise were supposed to have *dibao* act as a safety net to ensure that there was some provision. Non-payment of pensions was the result of major problems in getting a functional replacement to the original pension system working, with the main outcome being the non-provision of pensions by SOEs facing economic difficulties (Cai 2006; Li 1998f; Saich 2011). Saich (2004) notes that the problem had become critically important as early as 1995 with 70–80 per cent of pensions being unpaid and with Premier Li Peng raising the issue in 1996 (Li 1998f).

The biggest challenge presented to the state was that of laid-off workers and the failure of efforts designed to smooth over the transition from SOE employee. In order to make the transition easier the state provided a benefit in the *xiagang* basic livelihood guarantee and also the re-employment service centres (RSCs) to help find new jobs. The RSCs were an innovation adopted from Shanghai and were introduced nationally in 1998 with the idea that laid-off workers could sign up at a centre and then find work (Cai 2006). The RSCs and XGBLG were funded by the central government with the laid-off worker's enterprise acting as the administrator of the funds and managing the RSCs. The problem was that the scale of the laid-off problem was enormous, and the policies put in place failed. The number of laid-off workers in 2000 was estimated at 10–12 million urban workers (Interview 16; and Anonymous 2000; Cai 2006; Shu 2002; Zhao 2002) and the XGBLG and RSCs were designed to deal with their transition out of the state-owned sector.

There were two areas where these policies fell down severely, thereby leaving the problem of laid-off workers unresolved. First, the RSCs were not particularly successful in re-employing those laid-off workers in need of new work. The causes for the RSCs policy failure are complex but can be boiled down to a combination of inadequate funding, a lack of desire by laid-off workers to sever relations with their SOE to join an RSC, and finally the inability of the RSCs to actually find jobs for laid-off workers (Anonymous 2000; Cai 2006; Song 2001). Second, the XGBLG funds made available (ultimately by the central government from 1998 onwards, see Cai 2006: 20) were absorbed by SOEs facing financial difficulties. This created what Premier Zhu Rongji termed a 'debt conflict' which would form the basis of his choice to use the MLG (Interviews 11 and 12). The 'debt conflict', where an SOE would use funds provided by the government to service existing debts rather than social security and welfare commitments, resulted in either reduced or non-payment of benefits to laid-off workers.

Overall, the reforms of the social security system and the state-owned sector had three outcomes for the urban population that were not desirable for China's leaders. First, the emergence of unemployment combined with the deconstruction of the Iron Rice Bowl created a situation where urban residents, under certain circumstances such as being made unemployed, being laid-off or becoming sick, could find themselves substantially poorer as a result of changes brought about by the reform process. Second, failings in the state-owned sector meant that groups such as pensioners and laid-off workers were not receiving, or receiving sporadically or in reduced form, the benefits to which they were entitled. Finally, efforts to resolve some of these challenges, such as the implementation of the RSCs or the UEI system, were not successful due to issues with funding, coverage and design.

The situation meant that social stability was in danger of becoming a problem that the state could not cope with as urban social groups such as pensioners protested (Hurst and O'Brien 2002). The desire to see through the reform of the state-owned sector and ensure continued social stability during the process was the motivation for Premier Zhu when he began the 'Ought to protect, fully protect' campaign in 2000. This impact on the MLG can be viewed as feedback from policies external to the social assistance sphere. These policy outcomes, especially the failure of the XGBLG and RSC policies, impacted on the MLG by being the motivation for a massive increase in funding and scope for the policy. The MLG was attractive because of its capacity to deliver social assistance to groups that had previously been catered for by the SOE sector without the involvement of enterprises nor any 'debt conflict'.

It was against the backdrop of increasing concerns about the fate of the laid-off worker that the most significant central involvement in the MLG occurred through the intervention of Premier Zhu Rongji. As with the support of Duoji Cairang and Li Peng discussed previously, the intervention of Zhu is supported both by interviews (Interviews 1, 3, 4, 8, 9, 11, 13, 16 and 17) and also by documentary evidence (Benkanpinglunyuan 1998; Gu and Liu 2001; Shu 2002; Wang 1999). He is repeatedly cited by both as having a significant impact on the direction taken by the MLG from 1998 onwards. Zhu was also associated with the MLG and 'Ought to protect, fully protect' campaign of 2000–2002 in the official press (Li 2002a; Liu 2002; Zhu 2003). This support of the MLG was over a sustained period of time, of at least two years, and Zhu was closely involved in multiple stages of the policy process including problem identification, setting the agenda, developing a response and overseeing implementation.

Premier Zhu's role in the MLG is important for two reasons. First, he tried to incorporate the MLG into the wider social security provisions of the state with the concept of the three security lines. The MLG was to be the final security line for urban workers once the minimum wage, XGBLG and UEI had been exhausted (Anonymous 2000; Fan 2000a, 2000c; Li 2000a, 2001b; MoF 2000b). Second, the 'Ought to protect, fully protect' campaign was a result of his intervention in the policy both politically in calling for the establishing a social security system independent of enterprises (*duli yu qiye zhiwai de shehui baozhang zhidu*) during his Dalian visit in April 2000 (Fan 2001a; Song 2001) and financially by releasing funds for the MLG.

What did Zhu do? First, academics, government researchers and officials were very clear about Zhu's role in setting the agenda for expanding the numbers receiving the MLG. The impact which the trip to Dalian and comments made there had upon the policy community surrounding the MLG was very clear when discussing the development of the policy (Interviews 11 and 12). The MLG was put onto the agenda in a particular manner by Premier Zhu as he tied the policy with a particular policy outcome and the construction of a social assistance system with no 'debt conflict' nor ties to enterprises (Interviews 11 and 12), rather than just opening up the policy for discussion in a more general manner. Debt conflict was the term given by Zhu to the problem of funds for social benefits like the XGBLG being swallowed up by an enterprise's existing debts and/or financial commitments.

Premier Zhu supported the expansion and development of the MLG through a number of practical financial measures. As noted in Chapter 1 there was a massive injection of funds from the central budget for the MLG and the 'Ought to protect, fully protect' campaign from 2000 onwards. Not only was there an injection of funds but this money, fundamental to expanding and sustaining the MLG in many areas, was guaranteed by Zhu Rongji for the future. Interview 18 made it clear that it was understood that funds were guaranteed and would only increase, not decrease, in future. Finally, Zhu took an active role in the mobilisation campaign which surrounded this expansion of the MLG, the 'Ought to protect, fully protect' campaign that effectively ran twice (Interview 18). All of these actions by Zhu worked to consolidate the principle of central government intervention in the MLG as well as incorporating the policy into a general vision of how social security should work in the PRC.

Zhu was noted as a leader who tended to have one policy priority at a time which occupied his attention. The chosen policy would benefit not only in terms of being sustained on the agenda but also through a massive input of resources (Naughton 2002). The perceived uniqueness of how Zhu operated was highlighted by a departmental director in the MCA who noted it as 'interesting' because of the single-minded manner in which the Premier focused resources on the policy preference of the moment (Interview 18). This focus on an individual policy or problem is perhaps not that unique when one considers the distinction made by Lieberthal and Oksenberg (1988) between generalists and specialists within the elite ranks of China's leadership. For the Premier of the PRC to behave as a 'specialist' is of note because he occupies such a senior position in the government. Given the considerable political and financial resources associated with those in the elite levels of the state the active focused interest of a Premier in a policy would have a significant impact.

The first impact in the case of Premier Zhu and the MLG was the intense focus that was brought to bear on the laid-off worker problem and the decision to use the MLG as a means to provide increased state welfare provision. The release and guarantee of funds from the central budget would require a considerable amount of political authority given that agreement would be required from the State Council as well as compliance from the MoF. In addition, the money would need to be found from somewhere, which implies a degree of oversight and authority that not many within the national level of government would wield.

Information from interviews conducted implied that Zhu's intervention in the MLG occurred in a hands-off fashion, with funds being released with specifics attached leaving the MCA to get on with implementation. Zhu did continue to show an interest in the development of the 'Ought to protect, fully protect' campaign throughout the period, with communication and meetings between Zhu, the Minister of Civil Affairs and the MCA Department for Natural Disaster Relief and Social Assistance departmental director conducted to track progress (Interview 18). Given that the initial phase of the expansion faced some difficulties in 2001–2002, mainly due to concerns over funding, the continued impetus for the expansion through 2002 would have been in part due to the requirements of an elite leader being actively involved (Interview 18). Apart from the initial visit to Dalian which effectively kick-started the campaign Zhu did not take a particularly visible public role, only appearing to deliver speeches given at large scale Civil Affairs events (Li 2002a) or at meetings of involved participants (Li and Zhu 2000).

The reasons given for why Zhu acted on the MLG were consistent in interviews and documentation. The fundamental issue was securing a resolution to the laid-off worker problem – but why would this motivate Zhu Rongji specifically to take an active role in the MLG? In one interview the idea that the position of Premier required acting on the problems being faced by the social security system was put forward. The implication was, and was stated as such, that it did not matter who was Premier at this time, they would have had to act on the laid-off worker problem (Interview 8). The circumstance of increasing concern over social stability due to the continued problem of urban poverty in a multitude of groups does suggest that it was a problem that any leader would have had to address eventually. However, the issue of why Zhu became involved in the MLG is more complex than association through occupation.

The previous intervention in the MLG by the central government would have set a precedent that Zhu would have been able to follow. Although not a motivation as such, the significance of previous central-level interventions in the setting and funding of the MLG should not be underestimated. Zhu's actions can be better understood in a context where there was a precedent for central leaders to take actions which intervened in the operation of the MLG, even if this did go against the initial concept of the policy. It is also likely that because of his status Zhu would have been closely involved in the 1999 intervention in the MLG discussed earlier in the chapter. Zhu would therefore not have had too much of a problem with the idea of manipulating the MLG to a particular goal.

There is an implied personal motivation in Zhu's involvement because of his association with the reform of SOEs and resulting failure of the XGBLG through funds being swallowed up, forming a clear set of values which *dibao* was tied to. By this line of thinking Zhu needed to resolve the problem because otherwise he would be held responsible for any difficulties arising from the resulting social instability. Given the circumstances of Premier Zhu's association with the reform of SOEs throughout his time in office (Gilley 2001; Naughton 2002), the concerns he raised specifically on the problems of the XGBLG in the Dalian visit, wider concerns over the laid-off worker problem pervasive in the Chinese government and his previous incorporation of the MLG into the wider social security system through the three security lines concept where workers would be protected by the minimum wage, UEI and MLG systems (Anonymous 2000; Fan 2000a, 2000c; Li 2000a, 2001b; MoF 2000b), and the idea that in Jiang's China personal political security was tied to performance (Pye 2002), it is not unreasonable to infer such a motivation.

In addition to ensuring social stability the expansion of the MLG might also have served the purpose of allowing reform of the state-owned sector to continue. Zhu's close association with the economy and the reform of the SOE sector in particular would have provided a strong motivation to ensure the reforms were successful. Not only would failure have severely damaged China's reform era agenda but his legacy would be at risk. Three years from his retirement in 2000 Zhu would not have wanted his legacy to have been the collapse of China's state-owned sector under the weight of its obligations to former workers. Rather, he would have wanted to drive through marketisation successfully and secure his legacy as one of the 'architects of post-Deng' China (Naughton 2002).

Finally, the option to inject finances and increase coverage would not be possible without funds being available. The existence of sufficient funding or the ability to negotiate the release of funds could be a motivation for an elite leader. While it is not apparent where funds came from for the increases, the corresponding winding up of the XGBLG and RSCs would in theory have released those funds for reallocation. The reality may well be different, with the funds released from another part of the budget or from a central windfall resulting from the continued development of the economy.

The likelihood is that there was some combination of the three occurring, because the funding mechanisms for the 'Ought to protect, fully protect' campaign were similar to previous central interventions in the MLG and XGBLG/ RSC policies. In 1999 certain areas, well developed provinces and Municipalities such as Beijing, Shanghai, Shandong, Jiangsu, Zhejiang, Fujian, and Guangdong, were specifically named in relevant documents as being capable of funding increases themselves whereas all other areas would be able to seek allocations from the central government to cover any shortfall due to their own financial difficulties (MoF 2000a). Although not set out explicitly, it is likely that the increases in funding for the 'Ought to protect, fully protect' campaign were managed in a similar manner as the 1999 increases. This was combined with guarantees that the input would be sustained, suggesting money was perceived as being available in the budget both in the short and long term (Interview 18).

The activity of Zhu, therefore, covered actions such as managing the overall developments in the MLG during this time, as well as agenda setting through a high-profile political position and using his position to allocate and channel resources towards a particular end. These activities, particularly the ability to secure resources for a policy, can be closely associated with actors who occupy elite levels of the state. There is a question here as to what extent Zhu might be considered a PE, or whether his actions fit with the points made by Lieberthal that under FA individuals in elite positions have the power to forge policy change through direct interventions, informal political arrangements and the primacy of politics (Lieberthal 1992). On the one hand Zhu acts like a PE, taking advantage of opportunities that open up to him, and as Kingdon (1984) notes anyone occupying any position can be a PE; but at the same time Zhu used his position much as might be anticipated under the FA framework.

The Ministry of Civil Affairs during Zhu's intervention and after

It was the MCA that managed the day to day running of the 'Ought to protect, fully protect' campaign ensuring that it was a success. In addition, the MCA developed new means to manage the MLG and oversaw the emergence of a more dynamic version of assistance that could respond to the challenges facing the urban poor in reform era China, the 'classification guarantee measures' (fenlei baozhang cuoshi). Unlike early developments in the MLG which were closely associated with Duoji Cairang, during this period the MCA and the Department of Disaster Relief and Social Assistance as organisations came to the fore. This section of the chapter will therefore discuss the MCA's sponsorship of the MLG rather than that of a particular individual official.

Up to 2004 the MLG was administered through the MCA Department for Disaster Relief and Social Assistance (Minzhengbu Jiuzai Jiuji Si, JZJJ hereafter) and this continued until the Department for the Urban Resident MLG (Interview 18) was established for handling the MLG. The role of the MCA, and

JZJJ, as an organisation was noteworthy during this period because it had three significant impacts on the nature of the MLG. First, it administered the 'Ought to protect, fully protect' campaign, carrying out the orders of Zhu Rongji. Second, it facilitated the transfer of new variations in the MLG from local to national level, such as the 'classification guarantee measures', by supporting new ideas and encouraging their adoption. Finally, it established a centralised data collection network for managing the MLG, allocating resources from within the ministry and pushing the policy over a number of years. Although elite input was fundamental to the development of the MLG its success and further evolution was due to the work of the MCA. The behaviour of the MCA during this period therefore fulfilled two roles. First, it acted as the administrative arm of the central government in this policy sphere. Second, the MCA actively pursued its own agenda regarding the MLG and used the resources it had available to achieve these goals.

During the 'Ought to protect, fully protect' campaign the MCA was the primary implementer of the expansion of the MLG. This was mainly an administrative task of channelling households onto the MLG, and in the first year the method sought by the MCA was a low-level publicity campaign in factories where affected householders were thought to be working or had been laid-off from (Anonymous 2000, 2001; MCA 2002b; Yang 2002a, 2002b; Zhong 2002). The initially slow upturn in numbers meant that the MCA decided, or was ordered by Zhu, it is not entirely clear, to take a more active hand in the process. An interviewee reported that this resulted in the despatch of JZJJ section members and heads of other sections in the MCA to the provinces in order to oversee the implementation of the campaign during 2002 (Interview 18). This personal involvement meant that members of the MCA were actively operating as the relay between elite leaders and the local level of government in personal face-to-face meetings on the ground – something that had not occurred previously with the MLG; normally leaders met officials during work meetings or specific conferences. The same official reported that the goal of the 'Ought to protect, fully protect' campaign was very clearly tied to resolving the problem of laid-off workers, stating that in September 2001 the JZJJ section head informed officials that when on visits to the provinces they were to ensure that: 'If laid-off workers qualify for the MLG, as their income was low enough, then they must be covered, no excuses' (Interview 18). This focus was because Zhu had very clearly set out to the Minister for Civil Affairs that the MLG and subsidies for the MLG were to be used as a means to resolve the problem of laid-off workers, and this was reported to the JZJJ section head.

During these meetings, the main goal was to get the message across that households, especially those with laid-off workers, which fell into the remit of the MLG, *had* to be brought onto the benefit. These personal meetings were also used to convey reassurances and guarantees regarding the funding of the expansion. Essentially, the personnel involved were conveying the message that the funding was coming from the centre and was guaranteed over the long term;

local officials just had to get the required groups and numbers onto the MLG as quickly as possible (Interview 18). Local-level officials were also requested to go into factories and sign up householders who might be entitled to receive the MLG (Interview 18; and Anonymous 2001; Yang 2002a, 2002b; Zhong 2002) – a mechanism that had not been seen before or since given that the MLG was supposed to be a means tested benefit sought by the applicant.

The MCA exhibited more proactive entrepreneurial behaviour in the other two areas identified as significant during this period, especially after 2002 and the completion of the 'Ought to protect, fully protect' campaign (Interview 18). The development and implementation of the 'classification guarantee measures' for the MLG are worth discussing because this helps illustrate the proactive stance of the MCA during the period in question. The 'classification guarantee measures' are at their most basic level recognition that there are specific categories within the mass of MLG recipients who have specific needs that place additional financial pressures on their households. These groups included urban residents with long-term illnesses, pensioners, those with dependents such as disabled children, and those with children of school age (MCA 2003a, 2003d; Yang 2002b; Zhu 2003). The concept behind the 'classification guarantee measures' was that a household that falls into one of these groups would incur additional costs that would further impoverish them. The 'classification guarantee measures' would allow for additional benefits, determined at the local level, to be paid to these households if they were on the MLG. Examples of such a system in operation can be found in the cities of Dalian with its four-in-one system (Interview 17), Nanjing which supplemented MLG recipients who worked with a lunchtime subsidy, and Daqing which developed the actual concept of 'classification guarantee measures' (Interview 18).

The 'classification guarantee measures' are another example of the MCA working to counter perceived problems with the current system of the MLG, this time using the example of work carried out in Daqing City, Heilongjiang Province and promoting it through the work meeting system (Interview 18). The measures were to be supported on the ability to pay by region, so while supported as a national development it was more in principle than the sort of support the central government could provide, for example in the 'Ought to protect, fully protect' campaign. There are similarities to the early development of the MLG but the 'classification guarantee measures' occurred within the context of the MLG this time. The MLG had, by the early twenty-first century, become a policy sphere in its own right and subsumed the previous social assistance sphere.

The introduction of the 'classification guarantee measures' reintroduced a category element to the urban social assistance system that the MLG had originally been designed to work around because of the limits it placed on the provision of benefits. The 'classification guarantee measures' could be understood as feedback from the previous system of social assistance measures with local officials, who may well have been working under the old system prior to 1997, introducing these categories as an innovation when in fact they were nothing of the sort. There is a difference between the two periods though, with the Three No's determining who gets social assistance and the 'classification measures' determining who might be entitled to extra assistance. The interesting point is that there is an apparent continuity in the methods developed, categories in this case, through the Civil Affairs bureaucracy at the local level. The 'classification guarantee measures' were a development which demonstrated that the MCA was willing to back variations in local-level policy that were seen to benefit or resolve the challenges of coping with urban poverty.

The development and implementation of improved data collection and computer network systems to help administer the MLG began as early as 1999 (MCA 2000b) but it was during the 'Ought to protect, fully protect' campaign that the system was heavily pushed by the MCA (Interview 18). The implementation of routine data collection on the number of MLG recipients, spending on the MLG and the level of benefit paid out benefited the MCA in two ways. First, it helped collect figures on the MLG which were more accurate for reporting to the State Council and other government bodies. The collection of data also provided a means for the central government to make sure that the expansion required by the 'Ought to protect, fully protect' campaign was being met. Second, the implementation meant that there was greater oversight possible by those administering the MLG and would, in theory, make defrauding of MLG funds easier to detect (Interviews 11 and 18). The promotion of the computer network was pushed solely through the MCA in circulars distributed through the Civil Affairs system during the early 2000s (Anonymous 2000; MCA 2000b, 2001c, 2001d, 2002a; Song 2001; Zhao 2002). It is also apparent that the funds were made available for the system which suggests that the MCA had lobbied the State Council and MoF to release finance (MCA 2000b, 2001c, 2001d, 2002a). These funds would pay for the equipment (basic PCs and a software package distributed online by the MCA (MCA 2002a)) but also required training to use it. The push to computerise the MLG appears entirely to have been down to the MCA and reflects long-term concerns with the way the policy was being administered, the lack of oversight possible, and the actions of low-level administrators of the policy (Interviews 11 and 18; Ma 1998; MCA 2001d, 2002a; Yang 2002a, 2002b; Zhong 2002). Given the timing of the concerted push to improve data collection and network building, from 2000–2002, it can be inferred that the 'Ought to protect, fully protect' campaign was a key issue in why it was made then. However, the issues that the push resolved were part of concerns that the MCA had been trying to cope with since the inception of the MLG on a national scale and this would have been an additional motivation for the MCA.[4]

In the case of the MCA response to the 'Ought to protect, fully protect' campaign it made sense for the organisation collectively to follow directions from the higher tiers of government because that is its job. However, as has been discussed previously, there had been obstruction to various developments in the policy, so the question to ask is not only why did the MCA comply so willingly with the expansion requirements of Premier Zhu but also why did local government comply? For the MCA there are three reasons. First, the expansion of the MLG benefitted the MCA in general terms. The money and the successful implementation of the campaign would bring prestige to the ministry – both Premier Zhu and Hu Jintao were noted as having been impressed by the actions of the MCA regarding the 'Ought to protect, fully protect' campaign (Interview 18). Second, it secured the policy in the long term through the financial input from central government which guaranteed future central government funding subsidies. Finally, the 'Ought to protect, fully protect' campaign resolved challenges with the MLG that the MCA had been facing in funding and also provided an additional policy goal that was concrete and achievable – the incorporation of the ten million or so urban laid-off workers who were in need of subsidy from the government.

The reason for local government compliance would have been the 'Ought to protect, fully protect' campaign resolving both a policy problem and guaranteeing long-term funding. As one MCA official noted, because the campaign would help resolve what could be career-ending social instability it was popular with local officials (Interview 12). What the campaign also brought, which would have ensured compliance, was the guarantee of central subsidies for the MLG in areas that were finding it difficult to fund the policy. This was something the MCA had not been able to provide previously and as a result the MCA had faced severe difficulties in securing local compliance on the MLG as demonstrated throughout the 1990s.

There is another possible motivation for the MCA further developing the MLG during this time. There was a change in thinking within the MCA and the research community associated with the MLG. Additional developments in the MLG such as the construction of a computer network, improved data collection, and developments such as the 'classification guarantee measures' reflected debates taking place in the MCA and official publications during 1999–2003 that addressed issues of MLG administration (financial sources, personnel training and behaviour) and aims (who to provide for and to what end). It was argued that the policy needed to move beyond the 'food only' concept as poverty was more complex than this, the actual well-being of people was felt to be significant, and in addition there was a view in the MCA that the MLG could be used as a means to boost domestic consumption (Interview 11). There were repeated concerns regarding the administrative capacity of those at the basic level of the implementation of the MLG that had concerned the MCA for a prolonged period (Gong 2000; Lü 2003; Luo 2003; Ken and Zhang 2002; Qiao 2003; Zhao 2002; Zhu and Sun 2002), and the computerisation of the MLG was felt to help resolve this problem (Ma 1998; Zhao 2002; Zhong 2002). The 'classification guarantee measures' and 'Ought to protect, fully protect' campaign helped the MCA meet the challenge of defining what the MLG was supposed to be achieving in terms of objectives, provided resources to achieve these goals, and provided a means for local-level officials to resolve the potential social stability crisis that laid-off workers and increasingly varied urban poverty presented. The actions of the MCA in supporting the expansion, administrative development and evolution of the MLG are, therefore, understandable in the wider context of the challenges that the MLG had been presenting, the structure of the Chinese state, and the ideas being discussed at the time.

Conclusion

This chapter has argued that the unintended and unwanted outcomes associated with the MLG and highlighted by both the Chinese state and researchers actively working on the policy in the late 1990s can be explained by FA. The outcomes, in particular the extensive variation in policy and the exclusion of those eligible for support, were a result of previous practices coming to the fore, the compromises struck during the spread of the MLG resulting from the limited authority of the minister supporting the policy, the unfunded mandate and compromised national implementation post-1997, the mushy bureaucratic context which the urban MLG occupied with a resource-poor ministry sitting subordinate or parallel to central government organisations, and local Civil Affairs offices subordinate to both local and central government demands. These outcomes were resolved to the satisfaction of the MCA through the intervention of Premier Zhu Rongji. Zhu's intervention, based on the failures of social security and SOE reform, closely match expectations under the FA framework where a powerful elite leader brings significant authority and resources into play that bypass the bureaucratic impasse inherent to the Chinese system. While his attention was focused on the MLG Zhu's authority and the resources he brought into play meant that the MLG was transformed rapidly into a policy affecting tens of millions of residents. At the same time, the MCA reverted to more expected behaviour taking advantage of the situation to build capacity and to expand the scope of the MLG into new areas, securing the urban MLGs significance while at the same time playing the role of subordinate ministry to the Premier.

Notes

1. As Cho (2010) shows, recipients of the MLG under the expansion were in some areas quickly removed and forgotten about once the campaign was over, in spite of total numbers remaining broadly steady.
2. The formula for increases in funding was set out by the MoF (2000a) as:
   (MLG Line at end of June 1999 * 1.3) * (MLG Target Numbers at end of June 1999 *1.2) * 6
   = Six months funding allocation.
3. An example of this precedent affecting future policy developments was the protracted response to rises in pork prices and other foodstuff inflation during 2007, as discussed

in Chapter 5. Ultimately the MLG was adjusted by a central government intervention but only after price increases had undermined the benefit for the first seven months of 2007 (Interview 16).

4. It is noticeable that the volume, quantity and consistency of statistical data regarding *dibao* improved from 2003 onwards.

Chapter 4

Rural Dibao: The Countryside and Fragmentation

Introduction

The previous two chapters focused on explaining the development of the urban *dibao* programme between 1992 and 2003. It was argued that a combination of the opportunities and limits of China's fragmented authoritarian system and the actions of particular actors had a profound impact on the form and function of the urban *dibao* system. While developments did not cease to occur in urban *dibao* – notably the introduction of a more comprehensive (*quanmian*) system which provided *dibao* recipients with relief for medical, housing and education costs – the major development during the period after 2003 was the introduction of the rural *dibao* system as a nationwide policy. This marked a significant change in the focus of social assistance in China which had previously been centred on urban areas and the problem of the new urban poverty, and saw the spread of ideas and practice from the cities into the countryside. Notably the promotion, spread and implementation of the rural *dibao* system also saw the emergence of similar practices and challenges that had characterised the urban programme. Not everything was the same, however, and the rural *dibao* system which was eventually implemented also shows slight differences which suggest that lessons may have been learned from the previous experiences implementing the MLG in China's cities.

This chapter will focus on explaining why the rural *dibao* system was implemented at the time, and in the way, it was. While interviews with Civil Affairs officials suggested that the MCA had learned from the experience of the urban *dibao* system this is not entirely borne out by a critical analysis of the documents and events leading up to implementation of the rural system and its aftermath. For example, implementation ran along similar lines, with a spread of implementation by local government which was encouraged by the MCA, but not wholeheartedly supported until a higher authority became involved and drove national implementation. Similarly, while some concessions based on the problems of the urban programme were worked into the design of rural *dibao*, such as guaranteed funding, other problematic areas were left alone, such as calculating the minimum income line for the MLG (the *dibao xian*). Perhaps most critically, the rural *dibao* system appears to be a policy which is in search of a problem to solve whereas its urban counterpart has always been clearly matched to the problem of new urban poverty. As will be argued later in the chapter the rural *dibao* programme appears to have been implemented because it matched the values of the time, as established by Hu Jintao and Wen Jiabao, but it exists alongside the established Five Guarantees rural social assistance programme and a plethora of rural anti-poverty measures. A critical question to answer when considering rural *dibao* is, in addition to how it was implemented, what was it implemented for?

The chapter will be structured as follows. First, the timeline of implementation, design and function of the rural *dibao* system will be compared with that of the urban system. This will highlight similarities and differences between the two systems. It will support the assertion by MCA officials that lessons were learnt from the urban *dibao* experience (Interview 21) but it will also highlight similarities between the two systems that have caused problems up to and including the present day. Second, the chapter will highlight the areas where the rural system can be considered a success and also areas where it is facing challenges. This will lead into the third section, where the features of the FA framework and role of policy actors developed earlier in this book will be used to answer and explain why rural *dibao* was implemented when it was and why it faces the challenges it does. In turn, this provides an answer to the question of what the rural *dibao* system is for. Finally, the arguments set out in this chapter will be summed up. However, before setting out the argument of how the fragmented nature of China's policy process shaped the rural *dibao* system we first need to understand the timeline and design of the policy.

The timeline, design and function of rural *Dibao*

As the historical discussion in Chapter 1 showed, the developmental timeline of rural *dibao* followed a very similar path to the urban programme. It was lengthier and arguably subject to less support and longer pauses before key decisions but the pattern is broadly the same. As early as 1992, at around the same time that the idea of an MLG was being discussed in Shanghai, Guan and Xu note that Zuoyun County, Shanxi Province, was implementing its own *dibao* type system for its poor (Guan and Xu 2011). They go on to argue that rural *dibao* had a much longer gestation period than the urban programme and only emerged as something of national significance in 2004, although it had been supported by the MCA throughout the 1990s (Guan and Xu 2011). Documentary and interview evidence broadly support these assertions although there are some important differences to highlight.

First, early mentions of rural *dibao* systems are sparse in official documents and the MCA's newspaper *China Society News*. There are MCA documents which established the basis for the early adoption of the rural MLG in 1996 (Zhang, Xu and Wang 2012). A newspaper article from June 1996 discussing the establishment of a rural social security system does address social assistance but only goes so far as to state that social assistance is the most basic level of the social security system, and the focus here is on disaster assistance, with social insurance and social welfare schemes operating above this (Anonymous 1996). Examples in the press were also notably absent until 1996 when *China Society News* mentions adaptations of *dibao* systems to accommodate those with rural registrations (*nongmin*) (Chao 1996; Commentary 1996). Stories explicitly discussing the establishing of specifically rural *dibao* systems did not start appearing until 1997, covering Hubei, Shaanxi and Xiamen (Dong 1997; Jiang 1997; Lai 1997). It is worth noting that these followed comments made on a visit to Henan Province by Minister of Civil Affairs Duoji Cairang which encouraged the establishment of urban and rural *dibao* systems (Zhao 1997). Furthermore, the provinces of Jilin, Gansu, Guangxi, Henan and Qinghai were all noted for their work on rural *dibao* (Li 2008: 65). These are all provinces which are distant from the booming coastal areas and are noted for instances of rural poverty. This broadly supports the assertion by Guan and Xu (2011) that while the MCA might have supported rural *dibao* early on, it was not promoting implementation as much as the urban version. In fact, early change to rural social assistance was focused on changes being made to the Five Guarantees system (Commentary 1994; Fan 1994; Wang et al. 1994).

Second, analysis of official documents and materials in *China Civil Affairs* and *China Society News* do show that interest and support for rural *dibao* picked up in the early 2000s, but it can be argued that this began to peak earlier than 2004 as stated by Guan and Xu (2011) or indeed 2003 as stated by MCA officials during interview (Interview 21). The MCA committed to the implementation of the rural MLG in its 2002 work report, predating both these points (Zhang, Xu and Wang 2012). The MCA started to promote adoption of rural *dibao* around 1997 with Minister Duoji explicitly encouraging adoption (Zhao 1997) and follow-up articles highlighting implementation (Dong 1997; Jiang 1997; Lai 1997). Sporadic support for the implementation of rural *dibao* continued in *China Society News* after 1997.

In 1998 a single article discussed the implementation of rural *dibao* in thirteen counties under the administration of Yantai city (Tong et al. 1998). In 1999 one article outlined the general introduction of a rural MLG system in the Province of Jilin which, by December of 1998, covered 24,034 households and 69,311 individuals – approximately 0.5 per cent of the rural population (Qi 1999). Following this in 2000 there was a single article which provided the main headline on the front page announcing that over 1,600 counties had already started work on rural *dibao* systems and 3.1 million people were now enjoying payments. The article noted that this action had been in response to the MCA's call for rural *dibao* work to be carried out in areas where 'conditions permitted' (Anonymous 2000). In 2001 a Civil Affairs official from Linhai in Zhejiang Province wrote on three issues affecting rural MLG work. Two are notable in that funding issues were creating an 'Ought to protect, not protecting' (*yingbao weibao*) effect for rural *dibao*, and also it was argued that the minimum number who were supposed to be receiving the payments was unclear – echoing issues that the urban programme had experienced (Wu 2001). At the end of 2001 a headline story noted that over 3 million people were receiving *dibao* and that RMB 7 million had been spent. The story also explicitly noted that in eastern areas the majority received rural *dibao*, in central areas many could, and in western regions the majority of counties had started to experiment with rural *dibao* systems. The article went to some lengths to explain why a different system in rural areas was required, noting different levels of development between rural and urban areas, that assistance in the countryside consisted of in-kind and cash support, and that the rural *dibao* level was set lower than the urban system (Anonymous 2001). Zhang, Xu and Wang note that by the end of 2001 80 per cent of counties had implemented rural *dibao* systems (2012: 154) and according to Li (2008: 65) 4.04 million were receiving rural MLG payments. This suggests that five years before the rural MLG was officially implemented nationally it was part of the MCA's planning and was being promoted heavily in much the same way as the urban programme had been.

After 2003 the way implementation of rural *dibao* was handled followed a similar pattern to that of the urban system, with a steady number of stories including front-page banner headlines exhorting implementation. Provinces which were ahead of the pack in terms of complete implementation featured as lead stories, following a similar pattern to how reporting of implementation of the urban system was handled, for example Jiangxi (Anonymous 2003a) and Ningxia (Anonymous 2003b) in 2003, and Fujian (Liu 2004) and Liaoning (Anonymous 2004) in 2004. A significant difference is that it appears the MCA did not have to revert to the same naming and shaming policy which was adopted towards the tail end of the urban implementation campaign. There are a number of reasons why this kind of approach was not necessary, and these will be discussed later in the chapter.

The lead up to national implementation culminated in the publication of State Council circular number 19 'State Council circular regarding the establishing of a national rural minimum livelihood guarantee system' on 11 July 2007 (hereafter the 2007 Circular) (State Council 2007). The 2007 Circular is strikingly similar to the 1997 Circular and 1999 Regulations which determined the form and function of the urban *dibao* programme. In particular, the vagueness of how the *dibao xian* was to be calculated persists as well as the devolution of decision making on the calculation and running of rural *dibao*. As will be discussed, this is an area which has caused a number of problems.

The 2007 Circular also differed in a number of key areas, namely: an explicit linking to a policy problem and explicit focus on poverty alleviation, a call for standardisation, different funding mechanisms, and different calculation mechanisms. In the first section of the 2007 Circular the importance of addressing the '*san nong*' is raised, and while success in alleviating poverty in rural areas is mentioned it is also noted that rural poverty persists with some people unable to afford the basics (*wenbao*). Rural *dibao* is presented as a programme to support those with the ability to work, ensuring their basic livelihoods, so that they can lift themselves out of poverty (*tuopin*). It is worth noting that the means to alleviate poverty is through work and not receipt of *dibao*. This is very different to the opening of both the urban *dibao* regulatory texts, suggesting that the justification for rural *dibao* was slightly different.

MCA officials did assert during interviews that the ministry had learned from the experience of implementing urban *dibao* (Interview 21). There are three areas where this is apparent in the 2007 Circular. First, it includes an explicit call for a standardised form of *dibao* when implemented. This was not something explicit in the 1997 Circular but it did become a consistent issue in discussion of the urban *dibao*. Second, funding mechanisms in the 2007 Circular are different, with an explicit commitment to central subsidies in section five, paragraph one. This is important because a large number of problems experienced by urban *dibao* revolved around the allocation of resources as shown in the previous two chapters. Third, and finally, the calculation of the *dibao xian* is based on annual household income rather than monthly household income. When questioned about learning from urban *dibao*, Interviewee 20 noted that the framework for running *dibao* was the main thing learned and adopted. While neither of the first two points noted above were raised, the issue of income calculation was – the explanation being that rural workers incomes are much more variable and dependent on seasonal changes so an annual income calculation would give a much clearer idea of what a household earned (Interview 21). It is worth adding, perhaps, that the experience of urban *dibao* also showed that calculating incomes for those households which applied was a problem precisely because of the informal nature of work and variable income for many people, so adopting an annual MLG line (*dibao xian*) makes sense.

As the discussion above has shown both the developmental timeline and also the regulatory framework for rural *dibao* shared similarities and differences with the urban programme. These similarities and differences in how the rural system was developed and implemented have led to both successes and challenges in terms of how the programme works on a day-to-day basis. Before explaining these outcomes, the next section will highlight a number of key areas where rural *dibao* can be said to have succeeded, and where challenges remain.

Successes and challenges of rural *Dibao*

As the previous section demonstrated, it is apparent that important lessons were learned when implementing rural *dibao* which arguably contributed to a number of successes; but there were also significant similarities and continuities which have, it will be argued, led to a number of difficulties when it comes to the day-to-day running of the system. Starting with the areas where rural *dibao* can be said to have been successful, there are two main points that are worth addressing. First, the comparative lack of difficulty when getting the rural programme implemented nationally; and, second, the scope and reach of rural *dibao*.

As noted in the discussion of rural *dibao's* timeline, there is a marked contrast in the way in which the MCA handled the national implementation of the programme compared to its urban counterpart. There was no newspaper campaign necessary to name and shame intransigent localities into implementing rural *dibao*. There were articles which exhorted implementation, highlighted practice in key provinces, and reported when different provinces achieved complete implementation, but there was no rural equivalent of the countdown boxes which appeared in 1999, discussed in Chapter 2. This lack of a problematic national push for implementation is interesting because one of the explanations put forward by Chinese scholars as to why the rural programme took so long to get implemented is the lack of interest and support from local government (Guan and Xu 2011). There is, therefore, a contrast between seemingly uninterested localities in the run-up to implementation and then a relatively smooth push to national implementation once that decision had been made. As will be discussed in the next section, there are a number of explanations for why this was the case.

The rural *dibao* system has also been successful in terms of the numbers it has covered. The scale of the programme is massive, dwarfing the urban programme and arguably most other social assistance programmes in other countries. At the end of 2015, rural *dibao* was paid to 49 million people per month, in 28 million households, costing RMB 87 billion (MCA 2016). While rural *dibao* might be criticised for the various gaps, exclusions and oversights which feature in its policy design and outcomes, it is an impressive achievement in terms of the number of people it reaches. Designing and implementing social policy on such a scale is profoundly challenging, not just in developing countries like China but also in developed countries like the UK, and it can be plagued by problems. The fact that something works at all is worth noting and appreciating.

Having noted the areas where rural *dibao* might be considered a success, the areas where it has faced challenges will now be discussed. There are two broad areas to consider here, first, the actual day-to-day running of rural *dibao* has faced a number of challenges; and, second, what rural *dibao* is actually for is arguably a significant challenge to the programme. There are three areas where the day-to-day running of rural *dibao* has been criticised. First, it has been noted that there is significant variation in the scope and coverage of rural *dibao* between different localities (Kuhn, Brosig and Zhang 2016). On the one hand this observation might be dismissed as pointing out the obvious given that one of the foundational ideas behind *dibao* was local variation, or that policy should be adjusted to suit local conditions. This local flexibility underpinned both urban and rural *dibao* and was in large part one of the reasons it has been so attractive to policy makers. However, as noted above the 2007 Circular also explicitly called for a standardised system in rural areas so the observation that there is a variation suggests a mismatch between policy design, intentions (or desires) and outcomes. Because of the policy design and general raison d'être of *dibao* such a criticism, while highlighting a significant issue, is not worth spending too much time considering. More significant are the other two challenges of the day-to-day running of *dibao*.

The second challenge is that rural incomes have proven extremely difficult for local officials to calculate (Interview 20). Although the *dibao xian* in rural areas is based on annual income, a change made in recognition of the variability of rural income, this has only addressed part of the problem. The issue in this case is that rural incomes are even more informal and difficult to measure than urban incomes. As noted by Cho (2013) the difficultly in calculating urban incomes has led to some problematic practices where a job or a particular role has an income assigned. This same problem is occurring in rural areas. Officials cannot, due to a lack of administrative capacity and necessary skills, gather the information required to accurately determine what a household's income might be. As a consequence, the allocation of *dibao* is determined by other means.

This contributes to the third day-to-day challenge, misallocation of *dibao* which leads to the twin problems of leakage and mistargeting when those who ought to get *dibao* do not, and those who should not, do. Interview data highlighted two problematic practices regarding the allocation of *dibao* which do not conform with what is set out in the 2007 Circular. What might be referred to as the arbitrary allocation of *dibao* was noted by one interviewee. This referred to the practice of quotas being used by local government when implementing rural *dibao* resulting in households receiving payments – so that successful implementation and meeting of quotas had been achieved (Interview 20). The second form of allocation described was the practice of using *dibao* as a means to make corrupt payments. This corrupt allocation reflects the problem of managing local administrative levels where the higher tiers of government and especially the central government are distant in terms of their oversight of local practices. There are two reasons for the corrupt use of *dibao*: first, personal ties with households facilitates payments; or, second, officials using payments as a means to get a household to cooperate with them – often as a means to facilitate local developments on property the household might occupy or work on (Interview 20; and Kuhn, Brosig and Zhang 2016; Li and Walker 2016).

A further challenge which still manifests today is that it is not particularly clear what rural *dibao* is supposed to be achieving as a policy programme. The introduction of rural *dibao* saw an additional form of social assistance to the traditional, and previously reformed, Five Guarantees system (*wubao*) being implemented in the countryside. How do rural *dibao* and the Five Guarantees systems work together? The Five Guarantees has been the main means for providing in-kind social assistance in China's countryside since the 1950s. In the reform era, regulations governing the Five Guarantees were first published in 1994 with a set of revisions set out in 2006. The policy explicitly provides for the three groups defined in the 2006 Regulations as: the elderly, those aged 16 or under, and those without the ability to work who are not provided for or who are unable to provide for themselves (State Council 2006). Applications are made to and subsequently handled by the village committee. If successful, an applicant is entitled to support for: basic foodstuffs and fuel; clothing and bedding; basic housing; medicines and support; arrangements for a funeral (Article 9, State Council 2006).

There is no explicit acknowledgement in the national programme regulations for either *dibao* or the Five Guarantees in terms of how one system relates to the other. It is therefore technically possible to envisage a Five Guarantees applicant being successfully considered for *dibao* if their income is deemed low enough. In practice this is not the case because as a rule those who receive the Five Guarantees do not and should not receive MLG payments (Interview 21). There are, however, exceptions to this practice and both Guizhou and Hubei local regulations allow both Five Guarantees and *dibao* recipients to enjoy the provisions of both programmes. For example, in Hubei if an individual receives MLG payments because they have no source of income, and therefore their income falls below the local *dibao xian*, they are also eligible to receive support through the Five Guarantees (Hubei Province 2016). Where both programmes operate in tandem they complement each other as one provides a basic minimum income while the other provides basic goods in-kind which are required to maintain a minimum standard of living. This highlights the challenge of what the purpose of rural *dibao* is, because they are both supposed to be providing the same thing – the means to a minimum standard of living in China. The extent to which there is overlap in recipients is not possible to state definitively as current statistics collected by the MCA do not address this issue.

It is possible to make a case for why the two programmes exist alongside each other in the countryside, but it requires thinking about the urban programme as well. This is because the urban and rural programmes developed in different sets of circumstances, which is not surprising given they were implemented a decade apart. A departure point is acknowledging that in rural areas the Five Guarantees survived the initial wave of reforms that radically altered the rest of social security, welfare and assistance in China. In urban areas, there was no equivalent to the Five Guarantees as the Three No's provided only cash payments, and the changes to social policy and the challenges facing the state-owned sector meant there was a widespread gap in basic provision. This meant that in urban areas, where provision had been rooted in the state-owned sector, a new set of policies had to be developed in order to provide a basic social assistance provision and this took place through the 1990s and early 2000s. In order to address the urgent issue of the new poverty the MLG was implemented first and subsequent gaps in provision were plugged under the umbrella of *dibao* in the early 2000s. In rural areas, in contrast, the Five Guarantees already existed and provided the basics which the expansion of social assistance in the cities had sought to provide. As with the urban situation, what was missing were adequate cash payments to support outside of the Five Guarantees; as the system remained based on categories and therefore excluded those who might be poor but did not qualify for the Three No's. The introduction of the rural MLG provided a missing element, the means to provide cash payments to those who fell outside of the Three No's and did not receive Five Guarantees; and in some areas it provided a combination of in-kind support (through the Five Guarantees) and cash payments (through *dibao*). Following this reasoning, the introduction of rural *dibao* followed a similar justification to the urban programme – the order was different and this reflected the established institutional structures as well as the political priority of leaders.

The countryside is also different to urban areas in terms of how poverty is viewed and has been treated in the past. In the urban context in which the MLG originally emerged, the concern of policy makers and academics was with the appearance (or the recognition) of relative poverty, whereas in rural areas the focus has been on absolute poverty within communities (Interview 20). This is an interesting distinction to highlight because it shows that the two areas were viewed as facing a different problem, but the promoted solution was the same: the *dibao* system. The implication of this is significant. Applying a policy system, which was developed and/or adapted to deal with a particular issue, to another different, albeit similar, problem will lead to incoherent policy and unintended outcomes.

Rural *dibao* is, as articulated in the opening paragraphs of the 2007 Circular, a policy which has poverty alleviation as one of its explicit goals. This marks it out as distinct from the urban system which, at a national level at least, never sought to specifically alleviate poverty – the focus of the urban system was always on maintaining social stability among particular groups that the CCP and state were concerned about (as discussed in Chapters 2 and 3). This difference between the urban and rural systems' policy objectives is important for two reasons. First, it explains why the rural MLG is seen, by some, as ineffective because realistically its aims are not going to be achieved by the policy in the first place. The 2007 Circular makes reference to both 'poverty alleviation' (*fupin*) and being 'lifted out of poverty' (*tuopin*). These terms suggest that the policy has proactive elements which will address poverty by radically altering the livelihoods and lived experience of those who receive MLG payments. The problem is that the MLG as it is designed and functions is not going to achieve these goals. The local *dibao* line is set as a means to ensure a minimum standard of living, not necessarily at a level which will lift a household out of poverty, as a cursory review of *dibao* levels demonstrates. In addition, receiving MLG payments does not provide additional support in order to pursue the traditional route out of poverty: employment. The danger with both forms of *dibao* is that those receiving it can get stuck due to a lack of support. Second, in seeking to explain why rural *dibao* was adopted at the time it was, it is worth acknowledging the values and institutional priorities at the time. The next section of this chapter will address this latter point in more detail as well as other explanations regarding the emergence and development of rural *dibao*.

How fragmentation facilitated and challenges rural *dibao*

As with the emergence, development and implementation of the urban *dibao* system the rural *dibao* system was shaped by the FA of the Chinese political system. And, as with the urban experience, the fragmentation of China's state both facilitated and impeded the development and implementation of the programme. In particular, the matching of particular values with the policy helped pave the way for the national implementation of rural *dibao*. The MCA also worked to ensure that some of the institutional experience implementing urban *dibao* was applied to the design of the rural system when it was rolled out nationally. However, there were also numerous challenges which have impeded the implementation and running of rural *dibao*. There are four key challenges highlighted in the following discussion and three of these are issues similar to those faced by the urban *dibao* system. The fourth, the overall incoherence of the rural *dibao* policy, can be considered an outcome of how China's fragmented state both facilitates and impedes policy developments.

The national implementation of rural *dibao* coincided with both the physical taking office of Hu Jintao and Wen Jiabao – as Party General Secretary/President and Premier respectively – and also a clear reorientation of China's policy away from coastal urban development at all costs towards a more comprehensive and inclusive developmental approach. As noted above, experiments with rural *dibao* systems had been taking place for as long as cities had been implementing urban systems. The foundation on which national implementation could be built had been in place from the 1990s, with encouragement of local implementation from 1996, but it was not until 2002 that implementing rural *dibao* became an explicit priority for the MCA when it was committed to in its work report for the year. From this commitment it then took five years to establish nationally, which neatly matches both the ideological and policy developments at the time. The implementation of rural *dibao* matched the values of the time and, as will be shown, with the support of the MCA this facilitated its elevation to national policy after a long period as an initiative specific to only a handful of localities.

Before discussing what values rural *dibao* reflected and how this facilitated its implementation it is necessary to set out what the values of the Hu regime were during this period. While it is tempting to see Hu as nothing more than a safe pair of hands who continued with Jiang's stability-first style of leadership there was a significant change in the broad ideological approach of the Party, policy objectives and the allocation of resources during his time in power. Specifically, there were two changes in values between 2002 and 2012: a focus on a more inclusive form of development across China, and a focus on a countryside which for many had been left behind during the reform era. The most widely publicised articulations of these value changes were Hu's canonical contribution of a harmonious society, and the more policy-oriented scientific development concept and the construction of a new socialist countryside. The development of a harmonious society was a more broad-brush effort to address growing social and economic inequalities which it was feared might begin to undo the progress made during the reform and opening period. Hu's effort built on specific aspects of Deng and Jiang's canon of CCP thought, emphasising the duty of care the Chinese state, and by extension the Party, had for its citizens. Arguably, the broadening out of urban social assistance during this period was a manifestation of this turn towards a more inclusive vision of China's development, and this is made clear in the frequent references to social security, welfare and assistance in decisions made by the Central Committee of the CCP (Xinhuanet 2006).

The focus on China's countryside was the outcome of years of growing concerns regarding the left-behind nature of the rural areas articulated through the *san nong* problem of China's agriculture, rural areas and farmers (*nongye, nongcun, nongmin*). While China's urban areas and coastal regions had benefited from reform and decades of subsequent growth, it was felt that the rural areas and inland regions were increasingly left behind and ultimately were the likely source of increasing social instability. Efforts to address the problem of the countryside were multifaceted and ranged from increased investment in infrastructure in rural areas, efforts to increase the productivity of agriculture, and the implementation of a number of social welfare programmes, and in particular the period saw the implementation of schemes providing rural pensions and medical care.

What connection does the implementation of rural *dibao* have with these developments? While social assistance in general reflected the shift in policy to more inclusive development, rural *dibao* reflected both more inclusive development and also the rural focus of the Hu–Wen years. The introduction of rural *dibao* systems across the country was a good policy fit with the dominant values of the time because it addressed various aspects that were relevant. This is supported by officials from the MCA (Interview 21) who made it clear that the change in priorities was key in getting the rural MLG implemented. First, it sought to address the inequality of reform in as much as urban areas had been viewed as having benefited from the largesse of the state to the detriment of rural areas. The provision of a rural MLG system would fit into a narrative of commitment to constructing both a harmonious socialist society and also a new socialist countryside. As with the urban programme before, implementing rural *dibao* would demonstrate that the state and the Party cared for the people who lived there and would provide for them. It also fits with the argument (of Wallace 2014) whereby the 2000s marked the point at which the Chinese state was assured of stability in its cities and could therefore consider distributing resources to the countryside in order to maintain stability there.

Second, the rural MLG also helps to addresses one of the *san nong* problems by providing a means to improve the income of a group which might not benefit from the more developmental elements of the new socialist countryside. While a significant amount of the policy instruments used during this period focused on the use of investment and construction to boost local development and generate jobs, not all of these would benefit those who might be eligible for rural *dibao*. Poverty in rural China is notorious both for being shaped by geography, with remote areas or those with poor environments getting stuck in spite of government efforts, and also for existing within administrative and geographic locations. For example, building a road might benefit those villages alongside it or at its final destination, but some areas will be excluded and, at the same time, some individuals or households will remain impoverished regardless of overall investment. The rural *dibao* would provide a means for incomes at the very bottom to be, at a minimum, levelled out and ideally brought up a notch in comparison to everyone else. As noted in Chapter 1, this appears to be what has happened even if the impact has been described as moderate (Li, Sato and Sicular 2013).

Third, the introduction of rural *dibao* allowed the Chinese state to pursue a goal of poverty alleviation which broke with a series of policies that had been patchy. In a similar fashion to the urban MLG in the early 2000s, which had enabled policy makers to escape the problems the established set of policies had created, the rural MLG provided policy makers interested in alleviating poverty with another set of tools that did not rely on the geographical investment of resources. As the urban MLG had been the policy which helped address the problem of the *xiagang* and the ineffectiveness of efforts based in SOEs, the implementation of the rural system allowed for a national effort to address rural poverty which bypassed the system of targeting poor counties. As Rogers (2014) notes, this system does not necessarily lead to resources going to those who need them most. Instead local government, due to tight fiscal constraints and a desire to see results, has a tendency to target villages with 'better existing conditions' (Rogers 2014: 198) such as good soil or infrastructure. This means that those villages most in need do not get the investment the system is supposed to provide and remain stuck in an impoverished state. The rural MLG provides a means to bypass this situation through the provision of both funds and a delivery mechanism which, in theory at least, will go to the households most in need.

The implementation of the rural MLG also provided an opportunity for the MCA to learn from the experience of implementing the urban system and apply changes that were deemed necessary. This reflects the fragmented and experimental nature of the policy process in China, which creates opportunities to learn and adapt policy before national implementation. As noted above officials in the MCA highlighted two areas where the state learned and changed policy when implementing the rural *dibao* (Interview 21), and both of these are borne out by the design of the system set out in the 2007 Circular. First, the rural *dibao* calculates income on an annual basis rather than monthly. This was implemented because rural income was viewed as more complex to determine than urban incomes, and urban incomes had proven a problem for both central and local Civil Affairs officials to determine since the introduction of the urban *dibao*. Rural incomes were expected to vary month to month even more than urban incomes because they would be affected by what agricultural products were being produced, the seasonal cycle, as well as informal work. In addition, rural residents would be exposed to the impact of natural disasters and a 'poorer service' in medical assistance which might have an impact on month-to-month incomes (Interview 21). Second, the 2007 Circular explicitly states that the central government will support rural *dibao* financially (section five, paragraph one, State Council 2007). In interviews, this was mentioned only in passing but it is a major difference with the urban system and negates one of the main problems which faced social assistance throughout the late 1990s and into the 2000s, that of the unfunded mandate. Taken together, this combination of experience with urban *dibao* and an understanding of the differences in how rural households earned income led to significant differences in how the rural *dibao* system was designed.

Despite the favourable context in terms of values for rural *dibao* the implementation and day-to-day running of the policy was also negatively affected by the fragmented nature of the Chinese state. This manifests in four areas which will now be discussed. The first challenge rural *dibao* faced was its implementation. As has already been noted, the rural programme had some early adopters dating from around the same time that the urban system first appeared and was subsequently picked up by some provinces with the blessing of the MCA, but in many areas rural *dibao* was not implemented until the choice was taken away from local government. Why did rural *dibao* experience similar development issues to the urban system?

The problem of uneven early implementation of the rural *dibao* is a manifestation of the same problems which affected the urban system early on; although in the case of the rural programme central government benefited from local government being able to pursue and choose its own agenda. While the MCA was encouraging implementation in the countryside it did not have the means to either ensure or coax implementation. As noted previously, in China's fragmented system access to and allocation of resources is key when it comes to getting policy implemented, and in the case of the rural MLG the MCA did not have either authority or access to resources to ensure implementation. Ultimately this meant that until an opportunity arose for the MCA to exploit, in the form of the policy window opened by Hu and Wen's focus on rural underdevelopment, rural *dibao* was an unfunded mandate promoted by a ministry without the authority to order or the resources to coax implementation. At the same time localities could use the encouragement of the MCA as justification for implementation of a rural *dibao* system if it suited their local agendas. Where the rural programme deviates from the urban experience is that by the time the decision to implement rural *dibao* had been made systems had already been implemented in over 80 per cent of counties (Zhang, Xu and Wang 2012). While the use of two of three key resources, the highest authority in the system and a guarantee of funds, saw the national implementation of the rural MLG achieved, it is notable that a lot of the groundwork had already been done due to local government pushing ahead with its own systems.

Once the rural MLG was implemented nationally, notably with much less need for dramatic posturing by the MCA, the system still faced day-to-day problems in terms of its operations, which are also a consequence of China's FA. Similar problems which beset the urban system have been noted in the rural programme. These include the scope of coverage and the need to channel intended recipients onto the policy. As noted previously, the terms *yingbao weibao* even made an appearance in discussions of the rural programme, highlighting the similarities in the issues faced by both the urban and rural *dibao* systems. The similar language reflects a common problem in day-to-day implementation which has dogged social assistance in China and reflects a wider challenge of implementing policy in China's fragmented system. An issue with mandates to implement policy is not just that they are frequently non- or underfunded but that they also fall on the most basic levels of state administration, which has the least capacity in terms of personnel, time, finance and training. This was also the case with rural *dibao*, and explains the problems faced in terms of its implementation not protecting those intended to benefit from the policy.

A further unintended consequence of limited administrative capacity and the limited reach of the centre has been the 'incorrect' implementation of rural *dibao* – as highlighted in the preceding discussion of the misallocation of *dibao* payments. These problems reflect both structural issues of the Chinese state as well as the mixed and conflicting agendas of local officials. These problems are not just an issue of the emperor being far away. While interviewees did suggest the corrupt use of *dibao* funds by some local officials either to pay those close to them or facilitate other outcomes, there is also a policy design issue. The same interviewees intimated that rural areas appear to have had a quota to fill when it comes to rural *dibao* (Interview 20). The need to implement rural *dibao* and to spend a set amount on the needy, regardless of the reality on the ground, would explain some cases of mistargeting and suggests that issues with those receiving rural *dibao* are not entirely down to corruption or wilful misinterpretation of the rules.

There is also a larger issue regarding rural *dibao* which is a consequence of how the programme emerged nationally in response to the opportunity provided by the turn to the countryside and the nature of the policy design itself – and that is the overall incoherence of the policy in rural areas. The question of what rural *dibao* is for is challenging because of the more complex social assistance and anti-poverty policy context of China's rural areas. In urban areas the introduction of *dibao* was a clear policy intervention to address the emergence and, more importantly, the recognition of urban poverty beyond the narrow confines of the Three No's categories. Urban *dibao* also provided the foundation upon which subsequent targeted provisions could be built, such as medical, housing, education and legal assistance which matched the more inclusive development goals of Hu and Wen.

Arguably, rural *dibao* does not fit as comfortably with the overall set of rural provisions and it also does not have a particularly coherent set of policy goals. It is notable that at the same time as rural *dibao* was being put into operation there were provisions being built up to provide basic pensions, the new collective rural medical system, the long-established in-kind provisions of the Five Guarantees, and more developmental efforts to address the problem of poverty that dated back decades. Rather than serving as the foundation upon which the overall social assistance/anti-poverty policy strategy might be built, as with the MLG in the cities, rural *dibao* was the latecomer. Furthermore, in order to appear relevant to the rural context rural *dibao* has slightly different policy goals to its urban predecessor. The explicit reference to alleviation of poverty through the term *tuopin* (lit. to pull oneself out of poverty) rather than reference to livelihood maintenance sets rural *dibao* apart from the urban system in terms of its objectives (State Council 2007). What did not change was the policy design which only provides for maintaining a minimum standard of living as determined by the locality and therefore creates the potential situation of households getting stuck on *dibao* with little hope of moving on, as occurred for some in the cities (Cho 2010, 2013; Solinger 2011). A recent study disputes this somewhat and suggests that the rural MLG may, in spite of its limitations, be contributing positively to households moving out of poverty. Zhao, Guo and Shao (2017) note that recipients of rural *dibao* payments increase their spending in crucial areas – primarily on housing, education and, most of all, health. The authors do note that this is somewhat at odds with the intentions of the policy and, furthermore, that the more educated a household is the more likely it is to invest additional funds from *dibao* than spend them on the basics the programme was designed to cover. It is clear that, with regards to *dibao*, individual household circumstances and make-up will have a significant impact on the extent to which payments can help them escape poverty. This is not something a programme should rely on.

This concern regarding what rural *dibao* was supposed to achieve, and whether it was effectively doing anything at all, was neatly illustrated before national implementation in a cartoon published in an April 2007 edition of *China Society News*. A sparse rural landscape is the setting for a pipeline emerging from beyond a mountain range supported by RMB (¥ drawn to look like supports). At the end of the pipeline a man in caricatured peasant garments (patched suit and towel cap) stands with a bowl to receive a single drop from the pipeline (accompanies Liu 2007b). The cartoon could be interpreted as illustrating the lengths to which the Chinese state has gone in order to provide social assistance to China's rural poor. A more critical interpretation would suggest rural *dibao* as a significant investment of resources – the pipeline literally is built on money – which does not provide very much for those it is intended to benefit; the peasant receives a meagre amount for the resources invested. It is notable that these concerns were articulated in *China Society News*, the official newspaper of the MCA, in April 2007. This suggests that critical concerns were being aired in the run-up to implementation.

When combined with the issues of problematic day-to-day implementation of rural *dibao* discussed above, a picture is painted of general policy incoherence – a consequence of both the context within which the programme was implemented, matching the values of the time, and the structural issues that affect policy implementation on a day-to-day basis. This is a significant issue because normally social assistance is criticised solely on the basis of implementation efficacy (Barrientos 2013), but in the case of rural *dibao* there is arguably an issue in the underlying reasoning for implementing the programme that is then exacerbated by implementation issues.

Conclusion

This chapter has addressed the emergence, development and implementation of the rural *dibao* system, highlighting a number of areas where China's FA has affected the policy. While rural *dibao* did share a number of similarities in terms of how it emerged and subsequently developed – most notably ministerial-level support which encouraged implementation but without supporting resources – there were also significant differences. The values of the Hu–Wen leadership regime, focusing on the under-development of China's countryside, were important in terms of creating the opportunity for rural *dibao* to be implemented nationally, which the MCA pursued. Rural *dibao* also incorporated some elements of learning from the experience of the urban system, crucially a modification to the calculation of incomes to reflect the waxes and wanes of the agricultural year and also a guarantee of central subsidies to ensure implementation. Despite these changes, rural *dibao* has faced a number of problems similar to those faced by the urban system. These included an elongated and sporadic initial implementation due to the lack of authority or resources behind the MCA's early encouragement of adoption, and issues in the allocation of *dibao* payments related to points of rule interpretation and administrative capacity.

In addition, rural *dibao* also faced a number of issues specific to the programme; although it should be noted that these were not unique to policy under FA. In particular, allocation issues regarding rural *dibao* were not purely due to a lack of administrative capacity but were also, as reported in some cases, due to an implicit quota forcing local officials to find households that could receive *dibao* payments. More significant was a general lack of coherence regarding rural *dibao* brought about by its existence in the already crowded policy sphere of rural social assistance and anti-poverty, and some of the goals of the policy conflicting with its design. This was a consequence of rural *dibao* being implemented on the back of the value shift to prioritise development in China's countryside, and has been reflected in critical discussions of rural *dibao* in the run-up to and after national implementation.

Since the implementation of rural *dibao*, social assistance in China has been subject to a number of overarching challenges and efforts to consolidate the system. The next chapter will discuss these challenges, and how the MLG system in both urban and rural areas has been institutionalised. Having seen how FA has shaped the emergence, development and implementation of *dibao* in the 1990s and 2000s, the next chapter will look at subsequent changes leading to the introduction of the Temporary Measures in 2014.

Chapter 5

Institutionalisation? Achieving Policy in a Fragmented State

Introduction

The previous three chapters addressed issues which affected the urban and rural *dibao* systems during the initial emergence, development and implementation of the programmes. This highlighted the significant impact that China's fragmented policy-making system had on *dibao*, shaping not just how it emerged but also how it subsequently developed, the context of national implementation, and subsequent adaptations and expansion. The chapters also demonstrated that the significance of the actors who had an interest in *dibao* and where they were in the state hierarchy was significant in determining outcomes, especially with regard to the utilisation of resources (authority, financial, personnel or information). The preceding discussion also highlighted the various challenges that the *dibao* system has experienced during its implementation, including local government resistance to implementation and exclusion of those entitled, for example. This chapter will address how these issues might ultimately be addressed by discussing the question of whether or not both the urban and rural *dibao* systems have been institutionalised since the mid-2000s, and the implications of the answer. Overall it will argue that *dibao* has not been institutionalised and that the process of institutionalising was cut short in the late 2000s. This is primarily due to the purpose of the policy and the changing nature of China's development, but it is also indicative of certain aspects of China's FA and the impact this has on the policy-making process. Looking to the future this has implications for the policy long term in that it leaves the current system in a precarious state, but it also allows the Chinese state to respond to the changing nature of China's socio-economic context as well as more global developmental trends.

To this end the chapter is structured as follows. First, the concept of institutionalisation will be set out and discussed. This section will be broadly based on Fewsmith's study on the sustainability of experiments and reforms to local accountability in China, and Leung and Xiao's argument that social assistance in China has been institutionalised (Fewsmith 2013; Leung and Xiao 2016). The definition of institutionalisation set up in this section will go on to inform the rest of the discussion in the chapter. Second, the chapter will directly address the question of whether *dibao* has been going through a process of institutionalisation or not. Through three examples – the aborted Social Relief Law, the issue of responsive adjustment to price changes, and the changing nature of *dibao* policy goals illustrated through recent announcements – it will be shown that rather than fixing the parameters within which the policy operates, therefore contributing to resolving issues in the day-to-day running of *dibao*, these developments suggest that *dibao* is a policy programme in a state of slow, ongoing flux. Third, the chapter will discuss whether or not *dibao*'s lack of institutionalisation can be explained by the FA framework established at the beginning of the book. It will be argued that in large part the fragmentation authoritarianism of China's policy-making system does explain the challenges *dibao* faces, but that this is not sufficient as there are issues inherent in the design of the policy that need to be addressed in order to institutionalise *dibao*. Fourth, it is argued that the challenges facing *dibao* might be fixed by institutionalisation, but it requires political will and interest in order to see them addressed. This leads to the fifth point, that the question of whether institutionalisation can address *dibao*'s problems is ultimately going to be determined by those in positions of authority deciding that it should be used as the means to address the programme – in short, should institutionalisation be used to address *dibao*'s flaws? In the sixth section the chapter looks at examples beyond China and highlights both the advantages and dangers of adopting some of the policy tools suggested. In particular, the use of indexation in social policy programmes – highlighted in work on US policy (Weaver 1988) – will be discussed to illustrate that far from being a golden bullet the introduction of fixed rules addressing issues like adjustment in benefit levels can have unintended consequences. Finally, the chapter concludes by drawing the various threads together and returns to the question of whether or not institutionalisation might be the best way forward for the *dibao* programme. In order to do this, first the term institutionalisation needs to be defined.

The importance of institutionalisation

From a personal perspective, the question of whether or not *dibao* was institutionalising or not has been a question that I have pondered since the policy first became the focus of my research. This was initially because, when my engagement with social assistance in China started in 2005, the story of *dibao*'s development had already included a number of significant twists and turns – most notably the *yingbao jinbao* campaign of the early 2000s. The question of how the programme might be sustained, whether it served a broader purpose beyond the political needs of the Chinese state, was always in the background and an answer, as the discussion of the Social Relief Law which follows will illustrate, was elusive. It is apparent that I am not the only researcher of Chinese social assistance who has asked this question, as Leung and Xiao's discussion shows (Leung and Xiao 2016). However, their conclusion that social assistance in China is institutionalised, based on a detailed discussion of policy developments in social assistance, is not convincing for two reasons. First, the definition of the term is never particularly clear; and, second, what Leung and Xiao appear to be arguing is that *dibao* and other social assistance systems are going through a period of consolidation, but even this is arguable.

Institutions and institutionalism are both terms which have a long history in the disciplines of politics and policy studies. Traditionally the terms were used to refer to the typically visible organisational elements of the state such as ministries or offices of state which structured and therefore shaped the policy process. The emergence of neo-institutionalism in the last decades of the twentieth century provided a more nuanced conception of the terms; in particular, the introduction of unseen rules of the game in the policy process were broadly accepted as another set of important institutions that helped determine outcomes in the policy process (see for example Considine 2005; DiMaggio and Powell 1991; Hall and Taylor 1996; Hammond 2011b). Institutionalisation can therefore be understood as the process of establishing and sustaining institutions as either visible or unseen structures, or rules which shape the policy process.

In his study of experiments in political reform in China, in particular local accountability, Fewsmith argues that China as a political system is very good at policy innovation but not at institutionalising these innovations. The reform process and changes in policy therefore run into significant issues of sustainability (Fewsmith 2013). The fact that China has a political system which encourages experimentation and innovation is a widely accepted observation best illustrated in the work of Heilmann (2008a, 2008b). The important point that Fewsmith raises is that there are serious questions of sustainability when it comes to China's policy experiments because of problems getting them institutionalised. In Fewsmith's view this is primarily because fixing the rules in place is difficult in China, which means that policy becomes tied to particular individuals, and as these individuals move around the bureaucracy (as the system requires they do) innovations can be ignored, rolled back or countered by the successor.

Although Fewsmith discusses institutionalisation and the implications for China's reform process at length, he is not particularly explicit about what is meant by institutionalisation. Fewsmith alludes to establishing a set of rules to govern a particular policy area which are fixed and sustainable. This is broad enough as a starting point, because the rules required to govern a policy area could require the establishment of government structures in the traditional sense or unseen rules of the game which structure the options and behaviour of policy actors. That the rules are fixed means it is difficult, but not impossible, to change them. Sustainability in the Chinese context means, in particular, an initiative being able to survive changes in the key personnel who supported the initial implementation. While Fewsmith's work focuses on local initiatives this applies just as much at national level where, as was shown in the preceding chapter's discussion, the support of a minister or top leader can provide the impetus to get a policy adopted.

Both aspects of institutionalisation, the set of rules and sustainability, are important for three reasons with regards to both urban and rural *dibao*. First, they are important in terms of ensuring that a policy lasts. This does introduce a value judgement regarding a policy, something which will be discussed later in the chapter, but if it is determined that a policy should be carried out for some particular benefit then it can be presumed that ensuring that the policy is sustained for the long term is a good thing. For example, if social assistance in China ensures that vulnerable citizens are not falling into poverty and a minimum quality of life is provided then only providing this support for the short term would be problematic. If the final safety net that is *dibao* failed or disappeared, what would happen? Second, institutionalisation is important because it ensures that a policy matters to those whose job it is to carry it out. At present *dibao* rests on an unsteady foundation both in terms of the regulatory framework and also the financial mismatch between the regulations and actual sources. In some localities, the behaviour of local officials implies that the policy is almost optional. Although introducing regulations for the urban *dibao* system in 1999 went some way to addressing this issue, some interviewees argued to make it impossible for officials to avoid implementation by enshrining *dibao* in law (Interview 9). A third and final point is that institutionalisation matters because it can ensure that a policy works. The ad hoc nature of *dibao's* regulatory framework and the funding base means that there are various issues in the programme, as previously discussed, which then impact on those *dibao* is supposed to help. Institutionalisation could be one mechanism, through the setting of hard rules, which would address problem areas.

Dibao's lack of institutionalisation

As might have been implied by the end of the preceding section, *dibao* is not institutionalising, and this leaves a number of issues unaddressed. Since the implementation of the rural *dibao* programme it could certainly be argued that *dibao* has consolidated or settled to a certain degree. Additional elements have not been added to it after the rush of additions under the *dibao* umbrella of the Hu–Wen years where the urban programme became the gateway to a range of additional assistance. From 2007 there are three cases where it is clear that *dibao* has not institutionalised in terms of the criteria set out by Fewsmith, and which also highlight some of the problems that have dogged the system since its emergence in the 1990s. Three cases will be discussed to highlight this assertion: the abandoned Social Relief Law, *dibao*'s responsiveness problem, and the reimagining of the poor and repurposing of *dibao*.

Case One: The Abandoned Social Relief Law

During early fieldwork visits to China to discuss *dibao* with officials and researchers the desirability of a law governing the social assistance system was periodically brought up. Three interviewees brought up the need specifically in order to resolve the problem of local government not implementing the programme properly, and also as the logical development for a policy which had already moved to having its own set of regulations (Interview 9). At the time this interview took place in 2006 the MCA had already been drawing up a draft Social Relief Law for a year, initially called the draft Social Assistance Law but subsequently changed, for the State Council to consider. The draft law was ultimately checked by the State Council in November 2010, despite being included in the Standing Committee of the 11th National People's Congress legislative plan, when it declared that the draft law was not mature (*bu chengshu*) and required additional research and discussion (Haidian District Government 2012). Interviews with MCA officials in the years after the announcement suggested that the drafting of the Social Relief Law had merely been an exercise to see what such a piece of legislation would look like (Interview 21).

The documentary evidence surrounding the process of drafting the law does not suggest that it was an experiment but that it was actually a genuine effort to institutionalise the *dibao* and wider social assistance system through statute. First, the process was made public in a number of ways. A version of the draft law was opened to consultation and comment in August 2008 (Haidian District Government 2012). The process was also public and repeatedly discussed in the *China Society News*. Nine months into the process of drafting the law an article reported on six problems – the sixth of these was the need to accelerate the construction of social relief's regulatory structure including a law on social security, social relief, and disaster relief. This was deemed necessary as the poor could access all these sources but needed legal protection as well as the need for a standardised approach to social security and social relief work (Li 2005). Echoing this line of thinking a major article, starting on the front page and continuing to cover most of page four, in November 2005 pointed out the need for a social relief law in order to ensure that social relief work would be both standardised and protected or secure (Gu 2005). In September 2006 *China Society News* ran a story on social relief legislation, taking up four pages of the newspaper. The story led with the same justification for why a Social Relief Law was needed but this time quoted an NPC representative, Han Deyun, stating that 'We already have stable, strong, efficient social relief mechanisms, we need a law to protect these people's basic rights, to help those without the ability to enjoy social insurance, and those who are sick and disabled.' The article also noted that the impetus for drafting a Social Relief Law came from the *lianghui* in 2005 when thirty NPC representatives led by Han Deyun called for the legislation (Zhou 2006: 5). A final example from the newspaper appeared in March 2007 when another NPC representative and Deputy Director for the Shanghai Department of Civil Affairs, Zhang Lin, was reported as calling for an acceleration in the development of a Social Relief Law – this would help to address issues such as the lack of funding and the level of provision being ineffective, and a lack of standardisation (Liu 2007a). The process did not take place in private or in a manner which did not make it clear what was intended.

Second, the writing of the draft Social Relief Law was organised at a high level within the MCA. Responsibility was not delegated to a department but was guided by a leadership small group formed in January 2005 and headed by then Vice-Minister Li Liguo, with Vice-Minister Fan Baojun as his second. It should be noted that both individuals held senior positions in the ministry at the time and that Li Liguo went on to become Minister for Civil Affairs from 2010 to 2016. Additional participants were drawn from the MCA legal and *dibao* departments. The small group was tasked with cleaning up the social assistance system of individual regulations, to spend time in China and abroad investigating social assistance legislation, conduct grass-roots investigations and work with experts in other ministries on issues related to finance and taxation. The *dibao* department in particular was cited as being especially important in working on the detail of the law (Wang 2007a).

Third, the justification for the draft Social Relief Law implies that the MCA felt that it was striking while the iron was hot. Internal documents explain that the draft Social Relief Law was the culmination of a long development and significant efforts on the part of actors in the MCA. Significantly, the idea of a Social Relief Law was incorporated into the five-year legislative plans by the Standing Committee of the 8th and 10th National People's Congresses, elected in 1993 and 2002 respectively. According to internal discussion of the draft it was only in 2005 that 'ten years of unremitting effort' and the legislative conditions becoming 'warmer' allowed for the draft to be completed and sent up for ministerial approval (Wang 2007a). It was also noted as something that the current Minister for Civil Affairs Li Xueju and his predecessor, Duoji Cairang, were committed to. The timing of the start of the drafting process built on the plethora of developments in the social assistance system since 1993. This suggests that the MCA felt that the successful development and implementation of multiple programmes, and the subsequent development of a satisfactory local-level regulatory regime, meant the time was right for the law to be drafted.

Fourth, and finally, the context and nature of the draft Social Relief Law's final rejection implies that it was not simply an experiment to see what might be possible – for two reasons. First, the strength of the rejection was strong. Publicly reported, although in a low-key manner, the State Council killed the draft law stating that it was not appropriate and lacked maturity (Haidian District Government 2012; Zhang 2013). Second, the rejection of the draft law came at a time of relative uncertainty – with the Hu–Wen leadership coming to an end and Xi Jinping and Li Keqiang coming to power – although this was not absolutely clear at the time. If the draft law was simply a remote possibility or an experiment then during this period it could have been kicked down the line in terms of decision making or simply referred to as an experiment that was being ended. This was not the case; the draft law was rejected as immature and, as will be shown, a different tack was taken by the leadership and the MCA in terms of regulating the policy.

If the draft Social Relief Law had been passed, would it have addressed the problems that *dibao* had been facing? In short, no. Considerable thought and justification went into the explanations surrounding the draft law but the actual content, arguably, left a lot of issues unaddressed or in fact would have institutionalised known problems. It was noted that the choice for the drafting committee was between a 'backbone law' (*zhugan fa*) and a 'basic law' (*jiben fa*). The committee chose to draft a backbone law providing only the 'national perspective on system design' and the 'main method to develop and standardise the basic content of social assistance'. Wang suggests that the drafting committee came to this decision based on two factors. First, the number and status of bureaucratic organisations already involved meant that providing the key details in the law was not necessary. Second, the various components of social assistance already have or are in the process of having detailed regulations set out for them on an individual basis. Wang concludes that the law provides the framework within which social assistance can sit as a single national system. Within this system the details of the programmes are already in place, so the law is simply providing a backbone to connect the various parts of the social assistance system. Within this framework the system will continue to operate as before with the State Council being the only body able to make significant systemic changes and local government able to make changes within the established framework (Wang 2007a).

The approach taken by the drafting committee means that the draft law states very clearly what social assistance is, outlines who is responsible within the state for social assistance, and for individual components of the system sets out some basic ground rules relating to what each programme should do. The introduction of the special assistance measures provides the only real significant innovation within the law. What the law leaves out, because it is not a detailed 'basic law', is of real concern. There are at least four areas which would have significant long-term impacts on the long-term function and efficacy of the MLG.

The first area that goes unaddressed is any comment regarding the increasing dependence of the MLG on central-level transfers for support. In addition, there is no comment on the increasingly interventionist actions of the central government in the level and funding of the MLG. Since the national implementation of the programme in 1997 there have been at least four recorded interventions in the programme by the central government. These were in 1999 when the MLG was increased along with unemployment, pension and *xiagang* basic livelihood guarantee payments in celebration of the PRC's fiftieth anniversary; between 2000 and 2002 when Zhu Rongji supported and funded a doubling in the number of MLG recipients; and in 2007 and 2008 to compensate for increasing food prices, particularly pork prices. The MLG is supposed to function as a local programme with no intervention from central government and although this has now become common practice the draft law did not seek to address the issue at all.

The second and third areas of concern are related. These are the failure to address the lack of a clear standardised mechanism for calculating the MLG line and also the lack of a standardised mechanism for the subsequent adjustment of the MLG line. Neither of these issues was addressed in the draft law. This can be put down to the decision to draft a backbone law, but it would certainly have been a missed opportunity. Both the 1997 Circular establishing a national MLG system and the 1999 MLG Regulations offer vague instructions regarding these two issues. Subsequently, the issue of standardising and improving both the calculation and the adjustment of the MLG have been significant issues discussed extensively by the MCA and also by researchers specialising in social protection – it was also a repeated concern in the newspaper articles discussed above. The draft law provided an opportunity to resolve this problem by either providing a model calculation and adjustment method or providing the minimum elements that every local government should include in its own local regulatory framework.

Finally, the introduction of the special assistance provisions for low-income households raise a number of concerns. First, what is meant by low-income households? This is a problem which has dogged the MLG and as pointed out above has not really been resolved with any kind of standardised definition of a low-income or poor household. Second, the draft law states provision of special assistance should be determined according to regional economic development. This statement essentially means that extra provisions in social assistance will be determined by the ability or willingness of local government to provide funding. Finally, the draft law provides an impressive list of provisions that should be made for each of the areas covered by the special assistance measures, but there is no clear outline of what the minimum requirement might be. For example in medical assistance, Article 17 mentions subsidies for insurance/cooperative medical schemes, 'appropriate medical expense assistance' and 'appropriate medical fee waivers or discounts'. It is not set out in any form at all what a subsidy should be nor is it stated what is meant by 'appropriate' (MCA 2007b).

The case of the draft Social Relief Law highlights two problems with regards to the institutionalisation of *dibao*. First, the process to try and institutionalise a set of rules governing the policy failed. The after-the-event assertion that the draft law was an experiment can probably be dismissed due to the documentary evidence and the efforts made to have the draft law considered by the State Council. As a serious attempt to take advantage of a favourable political context to get social assistance onto statute, the MCA failed; and this highlights, again, the need for support from top-level leaders when seeking to implement policy in China's system. Second, even if the draft law had been passed it is questionable if it would have helped in terms of addressing the challenges that *dibao* faces. Institutionalising the ambiguity and local decision making of the programme would have ensured that the problems in the system would have been more firmly ensconced. In this case, institutionalising as a process failed, and even if it had succeeded it would have been locking in poor practice.

Table 5.1 Consumer price index by category (urban)

Category	CPI 2007 (2006 = 100)
All	104.5
Food	111.7
Tobacco and liquor	101.8
Clothing	99.1
Health and cosmetics	101.7
Transport	98.4
Entertainment	99.3

Source: NBS (2008).

Case Two: Dibao's Responsiveness

As a precursor to what became the great financial crisis in 2007 a number of developing and developed countries were faced with increases in food prices. The long-term implications for this in some countries was profound, triggering cost of living rises in the US which contributed to the collapse in subprime mortgage payments, or leading to the uprisings which went on to constitute the Arab Spring. China did not escape these challenges, which saw various food prices increase at a rate which alarmed the leadership enough to go on a publicity offensive (Global Voices 2007). Increases in the cost of living, and particularly in basic foodstuffs, has a disproportionate impact on the poorest in society, reduces the effectiveness of *dibao*, and ultimately led to a central government intervention in the level of subsidy provided by the urban programme.

Were food prices particularly affected in 2007, and to what extent were inflationary pressures on food prices a problem? A cursory glance at the general consumer price index data for 2007 in Table 5.1 does show that overall prices had increased in comparison to the year before but not particularly dramatically. Food prices however had increased dramatically in comparison to 2006, as well as in comparison to other categories.

Breaking down further the category of food it is clear that, with the exception of fresh fruit, prices increased in all categories. It is worth noting that prices increased substantially for what might be considered basic foodstuffs (rather than luxuries) with rice, flour, bean products, oil, meat, eggs and vegetables all showing substantial increases in price, as shown in Table 5.2.

Basic foodstuffs like oil, meat and eggs saw the greatest increase in price and this is where pressure was exerted not only on poor families but on the general urban population in China as well. The implication for those receiving the MLG was worse because their household income, supported by or entirely dependent on *dibao* payments, would be spent disproportionately on basic foodstuffs and would, therefore, be affected disproportionately by increases in basic food prices.

The *dibao* system is supposed to respond appropriately to changes in local circumstances and this includes the prices for items that are considered part of

Table 5.2 Consumer price index for food (urban)

Category	CPI 2007 (2006 = 100)
Rice	105.3
Flour	107
Beans and bean products	107.6
Oil and fat	125.5
Meat and poultry	131.6
Eggs	122.2
Vegetables	107.3
Fresh fruit	99.8
Milk and dairy products	102.8
Tea	101.6

Source: NBS (2008).

a minimum livelihood, such as basic foodstuffs. It is apparent that the average *dibao* line and pay-outs provided to recipients did not change until September 2007 when the central government intervened. The lack of response was the cause of some consternation within the MCA and higher tiers of government. Newspaper articles in *China Society News* had highlighted concerns about prices and *dibao* since 2004, when an article argued that the *dibao* level should be adjusted in line with price increases (Liang 2004). Cartoons were also used to illustrate concerns, with one example, preceding action by the government, showing a packet of instant noodles (*fangbian mian*) on a carpet labelled raw materials (*yuanke zhangjia*) being dragged away by price rises (*tijia*); the onlookers are shocked, confused or crying (Zhang and Gao 2007). The MCA twice called for local government to respond to price increases in basic goods by increasing their MLG line, first on 1 June and then on 23 June (MCA 2007a). This was followed up on 31 August when the State Council, the MoF and the MCA jointly issued an order to increase the MLG line nationwide by 15 RMB, and was made public on 5 September (Wang 2007b) and subsequently reinforced in February of the following year in a joint circular from the MCA and MoF (MCA and MoF 2008). The order was made specifically in order to increase the MLG line so that it would compensate for increasing prices. It also underlined how ineffective local *dibao* governance had been in responding to fluctuations in food prices. The perception and concerns regarding price increases is borne out by quantitative studies, with Gao (2017: 29) arguing that urban *dibao* lines were increasing during the period in question but they were increasing at a slower rate than the urban consumer price index.

Regardless of whether *dibao* can be argued as responsive or not, the issue is that the central government perceived it as such. Inflation continued to be a concern for China's leaders after 2007, with another intervention in 2008 (MCA and MoF 2008). If *dibao* was perceived as being unresponsive then this would suggest a good case for the state to institutionalise the system by firming up the rules governing key processes such as adjustment. The draft Social Relief Law would not have addressed this problem but neither have subsequent measures introduced by the MCA. In 2011 the MCA produced a document with the title 'Guidance on the further regulation of the urban and rural resident MLG standard system and adjustment work' (MCA 2011). The document represents a first clear elaboration of how the central government saw the MLG working outside of references to the existing framework of the 1997 Circular, the 1999 Regulations and 2007 Circular. It is, therefore, of some significance and worth reviewing briefly here. The first point to note is that the work of local government in setting the MLG line according to scientific decision making and subsequently adjusting the MLG line has 'met with some success', but there is also recognition of problems. Calculations in some areas are simply a reference to national averages, and fail to reflect the needs of local residents. Another problem is that the MLG line is not adjusted in a timely manner to reflect local economic circumstances.

The guidance extorts local government to unify thinking and approaches to calculating the MLG to improve and perfect the system. The two most important elements of the guidance are: first, it provides for the first time explicit methods on how to calculate the MLG line; and, second, it provides guidance on the adjustment of the MLG line. In brief the three methods outlined are a shopping basket method (called the basic living expenses method), the Engels method and a consumption-expenditure ratio method. It is worth noting that these three approaches were used together by Beijing to calculate its MLG line in 2006 and that the shopping basket method appears to be the most common (as well as the simplest) approach chosen by local governments (Hammond 2010). The guidance on adjustment focuses on principles rather than explicit methods. These principles are organisation, to use scientific calculations for adjustment, to use a standard procedure and, finally, to strengthen guidance. The data which should be used to inform adjustment are set out and it is stated that this should be used in conjunction with one of the three calculation methods to assess the need for an adjustment. This was not as radical a development as the explicit identification of methods for the setting of the MLG line, but it did mark a significant shift in the direction of a formalised system of adjustment. For example, it is only implicit that adjustments should be made annually but, as 2007 demonstrated, inflation can have a significant impact on prices within this time frame (MCA 2011).

The developments outlined in the 2011 Guidance suggest that institutionalisation has been occurring, inasmuch as some of the rules governing the system have been consolidated, but it is incomplete. The rules which consolidated the MLG systems were only concerned with the initial setting of *dibao* lines and not the more troublesome issue of subsequent adjustments. The measures introduced to address adjustments were vague and did not fix the process in terms of how adjustments should be practised. In this respect, the 2011 Measures fell short of institutionalising a set of rules that governed the policy. It could be argued that the 2011 Guidance was addressing issues which had affected the setting up and running of the MLG on the ground rather than adjustment which is a slightly higher-level issue in terms of which parts of the state are involved. That the initial setting up and running of *dibao* was a concern in the early 2010s, over a decade and a half after the policy first appeared and a decade after the first regulations were announced, suggests that there were concerns regarding what was happening on the ground. A different example of this which concerns the day-to-day running of the system was a storyboard article published in *China Society News* which illustrated how *dibao* should be handled by local officials from the initial application through to the award and management of recipients (Anonymous 2010). The state's concern appears to have been with problems the MLG was facing as a consequence of how it had been set up initially and then expanded, with the main concern being to resolve these through confirmation of good practice, illustrating this further through a visual medium that would help avoid confusion – compared to the issues that vague texts can cause. However, even taking this explanation into account, the responsiveness of *dibao* has not been addressed as adjustment has not been properly addressed, and this leaves a significant portion of both the rules and their practice posing the same problems they have since the MLG first began to be widely adopted.

Case 3: Reimagining the Poor and Repurposing Dibao

The last case discusses the regulatory and policy developments concerning the *dibao* system which followed the inflation crisis of the 2000s and the 2011 Guidance. The first development to discuss is State Council document number 649, published on 1 May 2014, named the 'Social Relief Temporary Measures' (hereafter, Temporary Measures) (State Council 2014). The Temporary Measures are an important development for the institutionalisation of the social relief system as a whole but not for *dibao* as the document only addresses a few aspects of the system, although these have significant implications. There are four main areas worth highlighting regarding the document.[1] The first area to highlight is in the first section, where the Temporary Measures outline what is referred to as the 'social relief administration' which consists primarily of the bureaucratic organisations for Civil Affairs, health planning, education, housing and urban construction, and human resources and social security at central through to county level. In and of itself this is not a ground-breaking development and echoes previous documents which outlined relevant actors; however, it does break with previous documents by outlining these bodies as working within a single, specific social relief bureaucracy. Second, the Temporary Measures further consolidate principles of social relief, and by extension *dibao*. This is also set out in the general comments of articles one and two of section one. The measures are written in order to achieve 'strengthening social relief, protecting citizen's basic livelihood, promoting social equality, ensuring a harmonious society, and according to the constitution' (Article 1, State Council

2014). This is followed in article two by the principle to provide the lowest line of support, helps those in difficulties, be sustainable, converge with the social security system, and adapt to social and economic development levels (Article 2, State Council 2014). Taken together these two articles provide an updated justification of the social relief system which moves beyond the explicit concerns related to social stability and guaranteeing the reform project outlined earlier in Chapters 2 and 3, but also eschews the poverty alleviation goals of the rural programme noted in Chapter 4.

Third, in the section of the document specifically addressing the *dibao* system the Temporary Measures set out much the same system as that which had been articulated in the 1997 Circular, the 1999 Regulations and the draft Social Relief Law with one notable exception. The Temporary Measures introduced a requirement that not only should a household's income be calculated when determining its eligibility for payments, but also that the household is living together and that that property status of the household and any additional financial investments are taken into account. These changes make sense as they take into account changes in Chinese social and economic relations since the inception of the *dibao* system. The nature of work and family structures in China has become looser and more informal during the reform years and the requirement that a household be in one place takes this into account. The introduction of taking property status into account means that *dibao* has a more comprehensive understanding of the assets a family might have access to beyond just their income. This also means that *dibao* moves closer to the practices of more developed economies, with stringent assessment criteria which take into account not only income but also assets that need to be depleted before access to assistance is provided. From a more cynical perspective, taking into account the changes discussed below, the additional requirements also mean that there are more opportunities to remove households from the social relief provisions and mean that it will be harder to secure support in the future.

Fourth, and finally, the Temporary Measures focus on a prioritisation of the inspection process and the rooting out and punishing of malpractice by both recipients and officials managing the system. This takes up two whole sections and provides detail beyond what the policy-specific sections provide. The Temporary Measures place the same emphasis as previous regulatory documents on the household to promptly report changes in its circumstances – specifically changes in income, number of householders, or property status (Article 12, State Council 2014). The local levels of the state – county, township and street offices – are also required to conduct regular investigations into changes of *dibao* recipients' circumstances (Article 13, State Council 2014). Part 11 of the Temporary Measures details at length how the Civil Affairs offices at local levels of government should investigate applications, citing twelve distinct elements which might contribute to income, property status and residence status (Article 58). The cooperation of other actors, who will reply truthfully to all requests for information, is also required (Article 59); those who have access to citizens' private information should protect it (Article 61); local government is required to publicise regulations and policies through a range of media (Article 62); and also required is that those involved in decisions are subject to supervision (Article 63 and 64), and that decisions can be subject to administrative reconsideration or a lawsuit by households if they reject the decisions made (Article 65). Part 12 then sets out the punishments for seven types of malpractice which can be carried out by officials or recipients (Article 66). Malpractice includes: the rejection of eligible applications or the non-receipt of *dibao* payments; ineligible applications being accepted and payments provided; disclosure of private information; the loss of data regarding the numbers receiving and spending on *dibao*; and other instances of 'abuse of power', 'dereliction of duty', and 'favouritism'. Articles 67 and 68 then set out who can be held responsible and the nature of the fines that can be imposed (one to three times the total misappropriated). In comparison to previous documents addressing *dibao* the Temporary Measures provided a great deal of detail regarding the inspection regime and punishments for misuse in governing the system.

The 2014 Temporary Measures address a great deal regarding social relief[2] in China, but they do not address the problems that first emerged in the mid-2000s regarding responsiveness to prices. In terms of the specific operation of the *dibao* programme, the Temporary Measures continue the attention to processing applicants that the 2011 Guidance had set out – although the Temporary Measures build on the 2011 Guidance by providing explanation of and punishments for malpractice by officials and recipients. The 2014 Temporary Measures also set out the overall administrative structure for the social relief system as a whole and not just *dibao*. Institutionalisation in this respect is better understood as the process of bringing together the various aspects of the social relief system under one document. The draft Social Relief Law did this to a certain extent but, as pointed out by an MCA official, the Temporary Measures give the state time to see what works before concretely fixing arrangements as a law (Interview 21).

As has been highlighted in previous chapters, the *dibao* system has an ambiguous relationship with wider efforts to alleviate poverty in China. Often treated and criticised as a poverty alleviation measure, but operating separately and designed to maintain a minimum standard of living rather than lifting people out of poverty, the system does not sit easily with China's efforts to eradicate poverty. The introduction of rural *dibao* exacerbated this problem by introducing the system to an already crowded policy market place and, as argued in the previous chapter, it appeared to be a policy in search of problem to solve rather than a response to a clear need. The decisions made in the lead-up to the 2016 National People's Congress and the Thirteenth Five Year Plan mean that rural poverty is, once again, a high priority area for the government and this is going to change the role and function of rural *dibao* further.

Poverty alleviation is referred to as a 'big wind' (*da feng*) policy area in China – indicating that it periodically blows strongly and shakes things up before winding down to become of little consequence (Interview 21). The plans outlined in 2016 are to alleviate poverty for the remaining 70 million rural residents the state has determined still live in poverty. The means to do this is a four-pronged approach of which the final approach is of most interest to the discussion here. Approximately 30 million people will be helped through industrial development, 10 million through the transfer of employment, and 10 million through relocations (*China Daily* 2016, Qu 2017). It has been noted that this is a significant change in poverty alleviation policy with a shift from targeting geographic regions to targeting poor household, which should avoid some of the problems with mistreating and perverse incentives which plagued rural poverty alleviation in the decades before (Rogers 2016). The fourth prong will pull the remaining 20 million people out of poverty using rural *dibao*. These remaining poor were specifically identified as those who are 'fully or partly disabled' in one report (*China Daily* 2016; Qu 2017).

There are a number of problems this approach raises which are indicative of both a lack of institutionalisation and a sustained policy dissonance. First, the introduction of targeting of specific groups runs counter to the policy design of *dibao*. Those who are disabled and can demonstrate that their household income does fall below the locally set *dibao* line should be eligible. The introduction of such a category element will distort the allocation of *dibao* on the ground. The use of category criteria has already been recorded as an issue in the allocation of *dibao* status resulting in those who do not fit a category being told they cannot receive payments (Cho 2010, 2013). The great difficulty of getting disabilities recognised by the state noted by Kohrman further highlights the problem of using categories to determine access to state help (Kohrman 2005). Second, the quota of 20 million to be reached through this use of *dibao* is problematic. Again it runs counter to the design of the policy although, as noted in both Chapters 3 and 4, the targeting of particular groups and the desire to be seen to be doing something has led to the use of quotas in the past which has, at times, resulted in mistargeting and leakage. Third, there is a serious question about the extent to which this will be an effective poverty alleviation measure. *Dibao* payments are traditionally very low relative to the average wage or unemployment payments and, as discussed above, they can be slow to respond to changes in the cost of living. In addition, *dibao* does not include specific measures (bar local innovations) to move people on from the policy. In one interview it was noted that the intention with rural *dibao* was to force annual 10 per cent increases in the local *dibao* line to ensure pulling people out of poverty (Interview 20), but it is questionable as to whether this would be enough in some areas as rural *dibao* payments are very low (see Chapter 1). It is also problematic as it will increase *dibao's* dependence on subsidies, and again runs counter to concerns that *dibao* is too generous and acts as a disincentive to work (Interviews 17 and 21). A final issue with the use of *dibao* for poverty alleviation is the nature of the means test and the message sent out by its use for the disabled. For a low-income family just the other side of the *dibao* line no help will be forthcoming due to the way in which the system is set up, so some households inevitably will be left to struggle. In addition, the message these decisions send out is that the disabled are incapable of escaping poverty through engagement in the labour market. Taken together, these points suggest that the 2016 decisions on the use of *dibao* sustain the dissonance in policy design and intentions where targets have frequently been categories but the policy is supposed to capture households with a sufficiently low income – which might or might not happen to fall into the category. Despite the general tightening of the application and inspection regime in the 2014 Temporary Measures, the means tested element of *dibao* has remained consistent and clear (State Council 2014).

The longer-term issues facing *dibao*, in terms of institutionalisation, the setting of rules and establishing sustainability, have only partially been addressed. The process of the draft Social Relief Law illustrated the relative impotence of ministries when top leader support is lost and subsequently fails. The 2007–2008 food price crisis illustrated the relative dysfunction of *dibao* and the need for the central government to intervene to ensure the system worked as intended. These developments were then followed by a notable change in tack. The 2014 Temporary Measures did go some way to institutionalising the practice and function of *dibao* by establishing, or reiterating, some of the rules governing the policy. The Temporary Measures did, however, fall short in addressing crucial areas that affect the rules and sustainability of *dibao*, such as adjustment to price changes and the temporary nature of current regulations. The 2016 developments complicate the picture further for rural residents by introducing criteria for eligibility which, if previous experience is to be factored in, may lead to mistargeting and leakage according to the established rules. This also illustrates why institutionalisation matters because *dibao* was, once again, being adapted to fit a particular agenda. The answer to the question of whether *dibao* has been institutionalised would therefore be no, it has not. The system is still in flux, the rural programme in particular; key elements of the policy still do not have central government guidance to set the rules, such as adjustment; and the sustainability of the system can still be questioned despite the assertions of interviewees, as the latest administrative guidance is by its very name temporary and the 2016 developments suggest another change in direction at the whim of top leaders (Interviews 18 and 21). Ultimately, it is not clear what the Chinese state wants *dibao* to be for, especially in rural areas. The rules have not been fixed for all areas, and the changes introduced by the Temporary Measures suggest a tighter, stricter delivery of *dibao* at the same time as the programme is being treated as an expansive anti-poverty and poverty alleviation measure in the countryside.

A consequence of fragmentation?

Returning to the broader argument of the book, to what extent has the lack of institutionalisation been shaped by the fragmentation of the Chinese state and the policy process? Fragmentation has affected the process of institutionalisation in a number of ways, but there are also important arguments to make that even without institutionalisation *dibao* might have faced the same or similar challenges. The failure of the draft Social Relief Law and the subsequent efforts to address the specific problems of how the MLG line is calculated, rooting out malpractice and maladministration, and tweaking eligibility, all reflect challenges that can be summed up by three aspects of the FA framework set out at the beginning of this book. First, the fragmented nature of centre-local relations regarding policy implementation is the root of many problems that the central government has been seeking to fix, either through the draft law or subsequent regulatory documents. The perceived lack of response by local government to the price crisis and the incorrect administration and monitoring of *dibao* have both resulted in interventions, clarifications and additional rules being outlined by the central government. This reflects the persistent tension within the Chinese system between central and local government allowed by the space and multiple decision-making points noted by Lampton (2014).

The piecemeal process of institutionalisation also reflects the fragmented nature of the centre and the relative importance of access to resources, especially authority. The failure of the draft Social Relief Law demonstrated the relative lack of authority ministries have within the overall state structure. While the early years of both urban and rural *dibao* development illustrated the extent to which a ministry could exploit the fragmentation of local government to encourage innovation and adoption of policies, it also demonstrated the weakness of moving from encouragement to implementation without a top leader's support. The draft Social Relief Law further demonstrates the inability of the MCA to achieve specific aims as it does not have the authority. As an interviewee noted, 'it is not up to the MCA, it is up to the State Council' (Interview 21). The institutionalisation or lack thereof of *dibao* illustrates how changes in the priorities of top leaders, and therefore the allocation of the authority to implement, can dramatically change the prospects for a policy development to be adopted. In the case of rural *dibao* the MCA was able to take full advantage of a supportive environment but the draft Social Relief Law demonstrated clearly that this support had ebbed away as priorities changed and the leadership transition loomed.

Finally, the lack of progress institutionalising the MLG in urban and rural areas illustrates the extent to which politics trumps policy, as noted by Lieberthal (1992). In particular, the changing of the intended goals of *dibao*, regardless of the actual policy design elements in place, demonstrates the changing political agenda of central government taking priority. In particular, the 2014 Temporary Measures and the 2016 poverty alleviation targets were more about implementing measures which fitted with broader central government concerns – regarding perceived malpractice and maladministration in *dibao* and the need to continue to eliminate poverty in the countryside respectively – than being indicative of prioritising problems of responsiveness for example. While it could be argued that the Temporary Measures would address the mistargeting of *dibao* payments, the introduction of the 2016 poverty alleviation plans will reintroduce issues of targeting and using quotas as provinces seek to achieve targets set by the centre. Furthermore, the 2016 decisions confuse what *dibao* is supposed to be for and risk distorting the perception of the public (*dibao* is only for the disabled because they cannot work) and practice by local officials (you are not disabled and therefore cannot receive *dibao*).

There are, however, arguments which can be made to suggest that fragmentation is not the issue affecting *dibao*. First, while it should be acknowledged that there are problems which are tied to fragmentation which do explain ongoing issues, these are secondary to the problem of the policy design itself or at least how it is currently articulated; simply put, problems related to eligibility, level of payments and adjustments could be fixed through further guidance along the lines of that released in 2011. The policy itself could, therefore, be focused in order to address some of these issues, and this will be discussed further in the next section.

Second, one of the main criticisms of *dibao* is the variation in how it is implemented. While this is a consequence of both the policy design and also the fragmentation of the Chinese state, it also makes sense as a design choice for China. This is because China is still a developing society experiencing rapid (if slowing) economic growth, and policies like *dibao* need to remain adaptive in order to respond to the changing socio-economic environment in which they exist. They also need to reflect the fact that development in China has not been uniform and the minimum cost of living in Beijing is going to be substantially higher than in parts of Gansu or Qinghai. In addition, significant change is on the way, *hukou* reform will change a range of policies including *dibao* and the status quo in this area is not sustainable even if controlling population movements is favoured by the government.

This does not excuse the programme becoming a dumping ground for those who are perceived as being unable to keep up or adapt to the changing context though; and if it is to become a true poverty alleviation measure then it needs to actually provide more support than the vague measures alluded to in the 2014 Temporary Measures regarding re-employment, as well as addressing the fact that there are some in poverty who – for social reasons such as discrimination against the elderly, the unskilled and the disabled, and for reasons based on gender – cannot necessarily pull themselves out by finding work.

Can institutionalisation resolve fragmentation?

If it is accepted that the nature of the Chinese state, manifest in FA, contributes to the challenges that the *dibao* systems faces; is institutionalisation a potential remedy? If we recall the discussion at the start of this chapter institutionalisation was defined as consisting of a clear set of rules which were also sustainable. Without seeking to trivialise the challenges facing *dibao* a simplified understanding of the situation would highlight the vagueness of the rules which are currently in place, the ability of local government to implement at variance with these rules, and the fact that the resources required for effective implementation are not currently sustained. As one interviewee in China put it, the complexity in social policy, not just for social assistance, is that the 'local policy practice is usually different from the central [policy]' (Interview 20). If the challenges facing *dibao* can be reduced to these points, can institutionalisation address them?

An affirmative argument would be that an institutionalisation of the *dibao* system would address these challenges for two reasons. First, a process of institutionalisation could progress to fix the specifics of the various announcements that the government has provided over the years. This is not beyond the capability of the central government as it has been forthcoming on specifics when a particular agenda or problem is being addressed, for example in 1999 and 2007 increases in the *dibao* were sanctioned. Specifically, the adjustment of the *dibao* line and a clear set of rules on eligibility that fleshes out the definition of terms needs to be set out. Setting hard rules and definitions would leave less space for local government to interpret criteria and therefore reduce the possibility of poor households being excluded on the ground; for example, at the moment it is possible to interpret the eligibility criteria in multiple ways regarding the ability to work and how to calculate income. In this sense institutionalisation would be useful because it would establish clear rules that would address the policy nationally and ensure that a Chinese citizen in area X would be treated the same as a citizen in area Y. Second, fixing the rules would require fixing the funding arrangements which are at present still rather vague, with local government still primarily responsible in spite of central government transfers providing the bulk of the funding, with the exception of poorer rural areas. Addressing both of these points would fulfil the criteria set out by Fewsmith (2013) by providing a clear set of rules and also ensuring that *dibao* could be sustained to survive beyond the whims of a change in leadership or a larger systemic shock like a crisis in government funding.

It is also possible to take an opposing view and argue that simply making more specific or detailed rules, or guaranteeing funding, will not address the challenges affecting the MLG. First, fixing the rules will not stop intentional or unintentional misinterpretation during implementation by local government. The centre-local dynamic which shapes a great deal of how policy plays out in China will not be affected by stricter rules – the problem in this regard is administrative capacity, the incentives for implementation by local government, and the limitations of central government oversight in the regions. These are big issues in the Chinese state and go far beyond the *dibao* system. Addressing these issues will be part of a much longer-term process of reform, investment, training and change in work practices. Second, local variation is a fundamental part of what made the *dibao* attractive to the government in the first place. Any move to make the rules clearer lessens the space for local government to adapt the programme for local conditions, which is fundamental to how it is supposed to operate. Third, the introduction of fixed rules on a policy and formal funding commitments would require specifics in terms of policy announcements that would go beyond what the central government has been typically prepared to provide. There would need to be a change in behaviour and expectations regarding how the Chinese state governs. This is, in part, linked to what the current Chinese government desires when it comes to implementing certain policies.

Should institutionalisation resolve fragmentation?

The preceding discussion makes one fundamental assumption: that the current state of affairs regarding *dibao* and the fragmentation of the policy in the PRC ought to be resolved. There are two arguments which can be made to counter this assumption which should be factored into the ongoing debate regarding what happens to *dibao*. First, critics of the current situation need to think about what it is we think *dibao* should be achieving and how closely this matches what the Chinese government intends. This takes the discussion back to one of the observations made in the Introduction to this book: that much of the criticism of *dibao* focuses on its effectiveness at alleviating poverty when for long periods this has arguably not been the intention of the policy. *Dibao* has served as the means to catch and minimally support the poorest in urban areas but not to serve as a way out of poverty – the expectation has always been that work would provide the route out of poverty. In rural areas this now appears to be the case as well, with the 2016 plans to use rural *dibao* as a means to provide for those who it has been decided cannot work. Wallace argues, when discussing the broad spectrum of social stability and internal migration in China, that state policy is often better understood as seeking to be seen to be doing something rather than actually achieving a particular outcome (Wallace 2014). A similar argument could be made about *dibao*. To a large extent it serves the state not as an actual poverty alleviation measure, even when that is intended, but more as something the state can point to which shows that it cares and is providing a basic livelihood to those most in need. This is, after all, one of the justifications that Minister Duoji outlined when making the initial case for adoption of the urban *dibao* in the 1990s. An understanding of the intentions of the state regarding *dibao* is important if specific policy measures or approaches are being suggested because it will have an impact on outcomes. Suggesting that *dibao* would be better served through a process of institutionalisation would mean the current system being fixed in place. This would mean an acceptance of the current system – with the strengths and weaknesses that go with it. When thinking in terms of whether a policy should be institutionalised an important question to address first is whether the particular policy in question is the best for the problem it is supposed to be addressing. There are arguments that *dibao* is not the best policy at present for helping China's poor in the long run and therefore should not be institutionalised.

Second, following on from the point made above, institutionalising *dibao* might not be the best policy in the long term given the wider developmental context of the PRC. As has been noted above, since 1978 China has been going through a sustained period of significant social and economic transformation. Part of this process created the situation in which *dibao* emerged as a policy possibility and also provided the impetus for eventual national implementation. Since its emergence *dibao* has served the needs of the central and local government, partly due to its flexibility. Future developments may well create a situation where a policy like *dibao* is not particularly useful if it is too fixed. The developments in 2014 and 2016 support this as they indicate changes in the direction of *dibao* provision which would not have been easy to achieve if the system had been institutionalised through the passing of the draft Social Relief Law. There are two significant changes on the horizon which China's leaders will need to address, and a flexible *dibao* could be a useful tool. First, changes to China's economy are going to have some significant impacts in particular areas as the number employed in industries such as manufacturing is reduced in response to changes in global demand and the more general shift to a consumption-based economy. This has the potential, as with previous transitions in the Chinese economy, to lead to concentrated unemployment in certain areas where *dibao* could fulfil its established role as a social stability mechanism (Hammond 2010, 2011b, 2013, 2015). Second, at some point in the future China's leaders will need to properly address the *hukou* system and institute wide-ranging reform. When this happens, policies like *dibao*, which are based on residence, will need to be reconfigured either to become fully national in the sense that all citizens access one programme or to be replaced by new programmes that are better suited to the new circumstances. In either case, having a policy system which is fixed in place through a law or through highly detailed policy guidance would be a hindrance to such changes; even in a system like China – where top leaders can force through decisions quickly – process would still need to be followed, laws changed and guidelines reviewed.

Could China learn from other countries?

During early interviews, it was always intimated that China had observed and learned from other countries when developing *dibao*, but the specifics did not go beyond vague references to study tours and were disputed by other interviewees. What has been apparent through China's reform of its social protection system is a willingness to learn from both implementation of domestic policies and other countries' experiences. In the case of *dibao* there are numerous systems throughout the world which China could learn from, but to what extent might these address the challenges highlighted previously? What are the possible dangers or consequences of introducing certain changes? Finally, to what extent are current social assistance systems, in China and elsewhere, fit for purpose in the context of a globalising and increasingly automated economy?

First, there are many examples in other countries which China could draw on when considering future changes to the *dibao* system. It is notable, when reviewing comparative studies of social assistance systems, that the Chinese system is an outlier relative to the approach of other developing countries. For example, Barrientos reviews ten programmes, including *dibao*, and with the exception of one other system all of the others determine eligibility based on categories rather than a means test. Furthermore, seven of the ten programmes include a conditional element which, to varying degrees, requires that recipients modify their behaviour in some way in order to ensure continued support. This includes guaranteeing children's school attendance or engagement with particular health programmes (Barrientos 2013: 101–103). Studies have shown that both the use of target categories for payments and the conditions attached can have a significant impact on the recipient household's behaviour and build up social inclusion as well as alleviating poverty (Leisering and Barrientos 2013).

How appropriate or relevant to the Chinese case would the possibility of these alternatives be? Essentially this would boil down to rethinking the means tested element of *dibao* through the reintroduction of categories as well as the addition of conditions for eligibility. At this point it becomes apparent that the policy incoherence highlighted earlier in this chapter again becomes clear. The *dibao* system in the regulatory documentation sets out clearly that it uses a means test to determine eligibility but also, as far back as the 1997 Circular, cites specific targets – the traditional Three No's. The 2016 plans for rural China make this even more explicit by specifically targeting those with disabilities deemed unable to work. In addition, the use of conditionality in *dibao* would not be a new development. The Community Public Service Agencies in Dalian, Liaoning Province, is one example highlighting the introduction of conditionality to *dibao* receipt (Hammond 2011a). Other examples highlighted in interviews include eligibility being tied to a lack of particular material objects such as phones or a household pet (Interview 3). Arguably the 2014 Temporary Measures also introduced conditions by introducing limits on income and property status as well as, more significantly, requiring that a household be living together in order to be deemed eligible.

The introduction of piecemeal categorisation and conditionality to *dibao* does not help in terms of resolving institutionalisation as it is an indicator of fragmentation rather than a means to resolve it. Ultimately the introduction of these measures would require a rethink by the government as to what *dibao* is supposed to be achieving and an adjustment of the policy programme to fit this. Categorisation and conditionality will mean that at some point a line will be drawn and a household which might need support will not receive it simply because it does not match a category or fulfil the required conditions. A final point is that *dibao* was introduced because the category-based system previously practised was determined to be failing to capture those who were poor but fell outside of the Three No's categories. In this respect, reintroducing categories would require a rethink on what they should be and, more fundamentally, on what the policy is seeking to achieve.

Second, a feature of social protection systems in more developed countries, where *dibao*'s association of poverty simply with income rather than categories shares similarities (Barrientos 2013), is the indexing of changes in benefit levels. The advantage is that this removes individuals from the decision-making process when it comes to calculating and deciding on increases to benefit levels – the process becomes automatic and is depoliticised. An example of an indexing solution would be the triple lock guarantee in the British pension system, which ensures that annual increases are based on price inflation, earnings growth, or 2.5 per cent – whichever is highest. While the triple lock has been credited with guaranteeing substantial increases in state pension payments, following a period where increases made were as highly political decisions and often not in the interests of recipients, it can be criticised as introducing a budgetary burden which is difficult to sustain and unjustified during a period of austerity spending. At the same time, suggesting changes to the system is politically controversial as demonstrated by the 2017 UK general election campaign. In his study of indexing in the US, Weaver (1988) highlights similar concerns. While indexing might address one set of problems, especially the failure of programmes to keep up with periods of inflation, it introduces three potential problems. First, indexing limits the agenda for change and moves the venue for decisions to an area of limited accountability. Second, indexing tends to create or strengthen 'clienteles' or beneficiaries changing the balance of power between policy actors. Third, when spending comes under pressure indexing makes it hard to reduce budget deficits and can also create divisions between groups who receive indexed benefits and those who do not (Weaver 1988: 249–253).

To what extent would the introduction of indexing, as a means to address some problems with *dibao*, work in the Chinese context? And how relevant are the concerns that Weaver raised to the Chinese example? As noted in the discussion of the 2007 price crisis the lack of responsiveness of *dibao* was as much about perceptions as the reality of the situation. This was the last time that there was concern extending to the top leadership regarding the responsiveness of the programme, and it seems unlikely at present that indexation would find its way onto the agenda, much less implementation – not least because the degree of specificity required would mark a significant break from the norms of how social assistance policy has been conducted in China to date. Furthermore, Civil Affairs officials point out that indexing already exists in the current MLG system, although this seems to be a generous interpretation of what is still, ultimately, a political decision (Interview 21).

Weaver's concerns regarding indexation once it is in place do not seem as relevant to the Chinese context as they do for more democratic systems. Concerns about accountability can be dismissed as decision making and oversight are basically black boxes in China compared to, for example, the UK or the US. The creation of vested interests which would block, or make politically expensive, future changes is also less relevant in China due to the way in which the system prioritises selection and social stability. Similarly, the third concern regarding the complexity of dealing with budgetary stress and indexing would not create the same problems for China's leaders unless it became a social stability issue. Indexing could, therefore, be a viable option for the Chinese government to introduce which would formalise adjustment measures, while the political system mitigates or negates the main criticisms of such developments. Having said this the adoption of similar measures to the UK triple lock, for example, seems unlikely in the present context as the political will to commit to and implement such a measure appears lacking. *Dibao* suits China's leaders much better as a flexible tool which can be used to address particular problems as and when they emerge rather than a longer-term commitment to alleviating poverty or guaranteeing citizens' rights.

Third, and finally, the challenges facing social protection in many states, not just China, are changing rapidly and will require radical reconsideration as increasing automation changes the nature of work in a way that previous labour revolutions have not. Reforming or reconfiguring the current social assistance system to fit within current expectations regarding work as a means to long-term income might not make sense when the jobs these expectations are based on might not exist in the future. With some reports estimating that close to 50 per cent of jobs could be automated, the current conventions surrounding state payments to citizens will need to change (Frey and Osborne 2013). Increasingly, discussion on social security and social assistance is moving away from the conventional models of social insurance and residual welfare to more radical options like the basic income. For countries like China this is both a challenge and an opportunity. The challenge is managing a transition from the current work-based paradigm at a time when resources are still limited, during a significant demographic transition, and while the economy is still relatively dependent on manufacturing. The opportunity is that, compared to other states, China can manage this transition before other social and economic norms regarding the nature of social protection become so imbedded they are difficult if not impossible to change. Rather than institutionalising the current set of policy systems regarding social protection China could, and perhaps should, be looking to the future with a willingness to embrace radical solutions to what will be a radically different world.

Conclusion

This chapter began by setting out the importance and definitions of institutionalisation in relation to the *dibao* system. The main reason for asking the question, beyond academic interest in the consolidation of policy innovations, is that institutionalisation marks the fixing in place of a policy development which means that the rules of the game are clear and that the policy is sustainable. This definition broadly follows that set out by Fewsmith (2013) in his discussion of democratic reforms and reflects one of the concerns regarding the Chinese policy process – i.e. that innovation comes easy, but sustaining it is much harder. The other reason the term is worth discussing is because the literature on *dibao* has started to discuss its institutionalisation, and it is worth investigating this in a critical manner. While the preceding chapters have highlighted a number of areas where *dibao* would benefit from institutionalisation, this chapter also set out three additional cases which highlighted either the need to institutionalise or where the process had fallen down. In each of these cases – the aborted draft Social Relief Law, the food price crisis of 2007, and the developments in measures of 2014 and 2016 – *dibao* was shown to lack institutionalisation as the system was either operating in a manner that consolidated existing practices where clear rules and sustainability were not clear or was operating in contradiction with existing practice as new rules or agendas were introduced. Rather than institutionalising, *dibao* appears to be as incoherent as it was before as the regulations and policy goals continue to run counter to each other.

To what extent is the lack of institutionalisation of *dibao* a consequence of China's FA? This chapter argued that the same features of China's policy process which shaped *dibao* continued to do so in the period after 2005 when all three cases took place. In particular, the fragmented nature of both the central and centre-local government relationship played a significant role. In the case of the draft Social Relief Law the lack of support from a top leader meant that the MCAs efforts came to naught. This is not necessarily a bad thing as the draft law would have fixed in place the vagaries of the *dibao* system. The food price crisis and the central government's response highlighted the continued issue of local government implementation not matching central government expectations. Finally, the developments of 2014 and 2016 illustrate the extent to which politics, in this case a harsher interpretation of eligibility unless you fall into a particular category, can trump policy – which is also an expectation under fragmentation.

While the lack of institutionalisation appears problematic this chapter discussed both sides of the debate. Institutionalisation would be positive in terms of fixing the rules for policy, and if legislated would, to some degree, ensure sustainability. In contrast, institutionalisation could be viewed as problematic if policies like *dibao* are required to be flexible in order to suit the needs of the state. This brings us to the question of what *dibao* is really for. If it is regarded as a poverty alleviation measure then it requires further refinement as well as institutionalisation. If it is a social stability mechanism which can be adapted and deployed as the state sees fit then the vagaries of policy interpretation and implementation are well suited to such a requirement. The possibility of China learning from the example of other states was discussed, but it was shown that in most cases the alternatives are either versions of the systems that *dibao* replaced, in terms of categorisation, or included elements already adopted by *dibao*, in terms of conditionality. The use of indexing was also discussed, and although the concerns about the approach are not as problematic in China's political system the political inclination to adopt such an approach appears to be lacking.

In sum, *dibao* is not institutionalising and this is mainly due to such a process not suiting those at the very top of China's political system. Even when those lower down the hierarchy have sought to pursue this agenda it has been blocked, and rather than clarify existing practices China's leaders have introduced additional complications that suit their agenda at a given moment in time. This does not indicate that *dibao* and the challenges the system faces as a consequence of fragmentation are going to be resolved at any point in the near future but, as noted in this chapter, this might not be as serious an issue as some critics might suggest. The social and economic space in which *dibao* is operated is changing and this will have a profound effect on the nature of social assistance and state provision to its citizens. Specific to China is the future need to address the way in which residence determines access to social provision; at some point the *hukou* will need to be significantly reformed, if not abolished, and at this point *dibao* will need to change dramatically. A more global issue to address is the changing nature of work, as increased automation forces states and society to reconsider the relationship between labour, income and how the state supports subsistence. *Dibao* as a system of social assistance suited its purpose at the time it was implemented, but looking to the future a more radical approach to guaranteeing minimum standards of living will be required and a new set of policies can be built in its stead.

Notes

1. The Temporary Measures do address the full range of social assistance programmes, but this book focuses on the *dibao* system and so discussion will focus on this.
2. The Temporary Measures also discuss and encourage the role of 'social forces' in the provision of social relief and social relief services, but the regulatory elements determining this do not form part of the document; rather, readers are directed to the relevant laws and regulations – which are not stated (see part ten of the Temporary Measures).

Conclusion

Introduction

A point which has been stated and restated at different points during this book has been the remarkable transformation that China has experienced in the almost four decades since the twin policies of reform and opening were implemented. It is almost a cliché nowadays to touch on how much the economy has grown year on year, how villages have been transformed into metropolises, or how historically great cities like Shanghai have re-entered the limelight. The shift from a poor but comparatively equal society, at least in material terms, to one of moderate wealth but greater inequality is a common thread to the narrative of China's transformation. Less frequently told outside of China studies is the story of how China's state-owned sector almost drowned in debt and how the social assistance, social security and social welfare systems all creaked under the contradictions of market reforms and ongoing obligations inherited from the planned economy. The emergence, implementation and subsequent development of *dibao* is part of this story although it has frequently been passed over to discuss seemingly more pressing concerns, such as China's rapidly ageing population or the difficulties in reforming the delivery of healthcare; and all are dwarfed by the mammoth poverty alleviation projects imposed on the countryside in the last few decades. Fundamentally, the MLG system, in both rural and urban areas, matters as it might not involve the same fiscal resources, nor might it cover as many people, but it tells us a great deal about how the policy process in China works, and day-to-day it affects a similar number of people to those living in the UK.

Goals of the study

While the importance of the *dibao* programme is now reflected in a growing literature produced by both Chinese and international scholars, the origins and development of the MLG have been treated relatively superficially. This has meant, as noted in the Introduction, that a dominant narrative has emerged regarding *dibao* which suggests that the system was implemented as a consequence of rational decision making by an omnipotent and benevolent governing system. The documentary and interview evidence suggested very early on when researching this topic that this narrative did not hold up and the reality of the policy process was much messier than subsequently presented or described. A secondary issue is that by skirting the origins and development of a policy subsequent critical assessment can be based on a set of misplaced assumptions. In the case of the MLG this is where social assistance, political expediency and poverty alleviation meet. Both the rural and urban *dibao* have been criticised for failing or ineffectively contributing to poverty alleviation, but if the programme was never intended to do this such criticism is unfair.

The puzzle this study has addressed, therefore, is what is the explanation for the emergence and development of the MLG in the PRC? This is not an attempt to analyse poverty in China, how it is experienced, or how the *dibao* notionally impacts on poverty alleviation. These questions are all important and interesting but the focus here is on the origins, implementation and subsequent development of the *dibao* as a policy programme. By extension, because of its targets *dibao* is about poverty, but the argument made here is not specific to poverty alleviation, in part because the argument made suggests that poverty alleviation was secondary to a broader set of concerns.

In order to address the puzzle of *dibao's* emergence and subsequent implementation the book adopted the FA framework to analyse and explain the developments. As argued in the Introduction this is because it provides the most comprehensive and flexible approach to understanding and explaining policy developments in the PRC. While it might be getting on in years, as an idea the FA approach to understanding and explaining policy in China has maintained its appeal in the thirty years since Lieberthal and Oksenberg published *Policy Making in China*, because of its flexibility and also because it addresses the workings of the Chinese state (Lieberthal and Oksenberg 1988). Subsequent efforts to explain or describe the Chinese policy process all touch on an element or elements addressed by FA. With some modification to account for the role of both state and non-state actors in China the FA framework still explains the fundamental elements that influence and shape China's policy process. As noted in the Introduction there are three institutional elements – values, political structure, and decision making and implementation – and the role of actors, as bounded rational actors or PEs. The policy process in China is about how policy actors, either as rational participants or more entrepreneurial policy makers, ensure that they match the dominant shared values of the time, navigate the complex web of vertical and horizontal relationships between and within different levels of the state, and how resources are utilised to achieve decisions and implementation. While the complexity of the policy process might tend towards drawn out consensus building it also means that there is space in the system for innovation to occur and, when values and resources align, significant change can occur in short space of time.

Main findings

The analysis in the preceding chapters provides not only detail on the historical development of the MLG in China, as set out in Chapter 1, but also six main findings. Before addressing each of these in turn, a simple first point to make is that the FA framework does help to explain the development of *dibao*. This is significant in and of itself as a criticism levelled at FA has been that it only applies to resource-intensive policy sectors, where there is something for policy actors and interests to negotiate over. *Dibao*, while a substantial set of programmes in and of itself, does not involve the kind of fiscal and personnel resources that other parts of government might command. As the preceding analysis shows a fiscally poor ministry like the MCA can make use of other resources to try and negotiate or force policy implementation – either as a result of applying pressure through media resources as shown in Chapter 2 or by invoking the political authority of ministers or more senior leaders as shown in Chapters 2 and 3.

Moving on to the first point raised in the core chapters, the structure of the state facilitates innovation at the local level as well as constrains both central and local government when seeking to implement or adapt policy. The emergence of the MLG in Shanghai during the early 1990s is an example of the kind of space that exists within the Chinese state, as noted in Chapter 2. The city was able, through the combination of local actors including the mayor and Civil Affairs bureau, to devise and implement a system of social assistance that was a marked innovation on what preceded it. The relative looseness at the local level also meant that other cities and some rural areas adopted *dibao* systems in the years following Shanghai without support or pressure from the central government. If local government resists implementation then the same structure can help impede the spread of policy developments. As shown in Chapters 2 and 4 regarding urban and rural *dibao* respectively, as well as when considering efforts to institutionalise the system in the late 2000s, local interests or the lack of elite support can be the reasons behind limited expansion, or when institutionalisation and standardisation falters. The fragmentation of the Chinese state ensures that politics and not policy remains king in China.

Second, and building on the first point, the issue of where a policy actor is situated within the cross-hatch of vertical and horizontal relationships of the Chinese state has a significant impact on the chances that a policy might be adopted or can shape the implementation that does take place in a profound way. An entrepreneurial official can only work within the confines imposed on them by the structure of the state. This might allow for some space to promote and implement policy but it also means that at a certain point an official will face opposition that they are unable to overcome. The only policy actors who can break through intransigence or opposition are those who are in a position to either pull rank by invoking their political authority and/or order the deployment of the necessary fiscal or personnel resources. In Chapters 2 and 3 it was shown that while Duoji Cairang, as Minister of Civil Affairs, had the authority

CONCLUSION   135

to cajole and persuade local government to adopt MLG systems in the years leading up to 1997, he had none of the political, fiscal or personnel resources required to force local or central government to support the adoption of *dibao*. As a minister, Duoji occupied a space at the apex of one bureaucratic system that generates limited authority, but this was not enough to negotiate or overcome the complex mesh of relationships when local government decides they cannot afford to implement a programme. In contrast, Li Peng in Chapter 2 and Zhu Rongji in Chapter 3 demonstrated how more senior leaders in the system, at the very apex of the state, do have the political authority and the means to distribute resources to force significant change in policy. Li Peng's support was identified as critical for the eventual national implementation of *dibao* and Zhu Rongji used the MLG as a means to address the challenge of laid-off workers in the state-owned sector by directing the necessary fiscal and personnel resources in a short space of time. After around 2003 it becomes harder to identify particular leaders who play a critical role in shaping the MLG. The transition to a new leadership pairing of Hu–Wen in 2002/2003 was important for the adoption of the rural *dibao*, but as noted in Chapter 4 this process was already ongoing and to some extent reflected the entrepreneurial behaviour of the MCA rather than the significance of having supportive officials in key positions. Similarly, in recent years the relative lack of support at the very top has been apparent. As discussed in Chapter 5 the failure of the draft Social Relief Law and the tightening of regulations in 2014 suggest a different set of priorities in the Xi–Li leadership. This suggests that while politics is key when it comes to policy, and who you are matters a great deal, where you are in the system matters even more.

Third, successfully matching the values of a given moment is critical in ensuring a policy is taken up and interest is maintained. One of the arguments made in Chapter 2 about why Duoji Cairang was able to work successfully within the limitations of the MCA to push the implementation of the MLG was because of the way he matched the policy to the dominant values of the period. By making *dibao* about maintaining both the reform programme and social stability he ensured that the policy closely matched the shared values of officials both within the Civil Affairs bureaucracy and beyond. This meant that it became very hard to object to the MLG as to do so would be to reject the shared values and move outside the established speech space of the time. In Chapter 3 it was noted that once Zhu Rongji had decided that the MLG was a useful programme to fulfil his own objectives, the MCA was quick to exploit these circumstances to resolve its own problem. The *yingbao jinbao* campaign became a way to address the *yingbao weibao* problem, even though the two were not explicitly linked before Zhu's intervention. The development of rural *dibao* in Chapter 4 again suggests that an entrepreneurial ministry can exploit changes in values to facilitate changes in policy. The shift in focus to the countryside at the very top of the Chinese system presented the MCA with a means to promote the implementation of a rural *dibao* system in spite of this being, perhaps, an unnecessary development when the plethora of poverty alleviation and social assistance measures already in place are considered. This also helps explain the differences in the way in which the rural *dibao* was presented. Unlike the urban programme the rural MLG was explicitly presented as a poverty alleviation measure when it was rolled out nationally in 2007. The discussion of developments since 2007 suggests that when values and policy do not match this can lead to policy drift and in some instances a tightening of provisions. The shift in priorities in the lead-up to and under the leadership of Xi and Li has made it difficult for the MLG and its supporters to establish a clear space in which it operates. This has led to legislative measures stalling, to the tightening of provision, and in some instances to the system being subsumed in other policy measures, as with the rural *dibao* during the most recent poverty alleviation announcements.

Fourth, as the discussion above has shown ultimately political authority and access to resources determine the adoption and spread of a policy beyond a local context. A PE relying solely on persuasion and matching values can get a policy so far but if it is to break through onto the national stage in a concerted and coherent manner then this is not enough. It was repeatedly shown throughout the discussion of both the urban and rural *dibao* that when faced with bureaucratic intransigence, non-implementation or incorrect implementation the only definite way to address these issues was to be supported by a leader at the very top of the system. This was the case with Li Peng and Zhu Rongji in the early years of the MLG's development, and the lack of such support is apparent in the later years. The case could also be made that when considering local-level innovations – as discussed in Chapter 2 in the case of Shanghai and discussed elsewhere regarding Dalian (Hammond 2011a) – this finding replicates itself within the narrower confines of the local hierarchy. The support of a local mayor or Party Secretary is crucial for the popularising and adoption of policy innovations.

Fifth, while the urban and rural *dibao* have different developmental stories which are distinct from each other the influence of FA permeated both. This is apparent in two particular issues which defined and dogged both programmes. The first is that the transition from innovation and opt-in to national policy for both the urban and rural MLG systems presented challenges to those who supported the programmes. This was due to a combination of the factors discussed above. For example, the support of certain policy actors only extending so far, a lack of resources to overcome opposition or to support local government who could not afford the system, and implementation on local terms all meant that the shift from a policy being implemented in only one or two cities to it being adopted nationwide was a piecemeal, mushy process that often sowed the seeds for subsequent problems that central government sought to address. The second factor, which underpins a lot of these challenges, is local government and non-implementation or incorrect implementation. Many of the problems identified by officials and scholars regarding both urban and rural *dibao* are linked to the problem of getting local government to do what central government wants. In many of the interviews conducted, and also in the documents consulted for this book, an overriding theme was that local government would wilfully or unintentionally misinterpret what was intended by central government. This happens generally speaking for two reasons. First, the distance between central and local government in China, because of the size of the country, is both physically and symbolically enormous. As studies have shown, in other policy areas it is relatively easy for local government to resist or misinterpret policy due to a general lack of administrative capacity. A second critical issue, often overlooked in the case of the MLG, is that the way the policy has been designed and articulated to officials further down the system has encouraged this kind of behaviour. In order to get *dibao* implemented initially adapting to local circumstances was encouraged, the later policy design for national implementation explicitly acknowledged the significance of local conditions, and even the draft Social Relief Law was only to act as the backbone to local regulations. While it might be a source of frustration in central government, and for those assessing the policy in research institutes and universities, the local variation and space for misinterpretation have been baked into the MLG through design choices that reflect both the unique features of the programme but more importantly the general practices of the Chinese state.

Sixth, and finally, it was argued that *dibao* has not yet institutionalised according to a definition developed from Fewsmith's work on local accountability (Fewsmith 2013). As discussed in Chapter 5, while the fundamentals which define the programme have now been in place for two decades in the urban programme, and a decade in its rural counterpart, this does not mean that it has institutionalised because the rules governing *dibao* are not yet fixed and arguably they are not sustainable in the sense that they might survive a change in leadership priorities. The draft Social Relief Law presented an opportunity to provide a clear set of rules, albeit flawed, which would have been difficult to renege on subsequently. As noted, the draft law was rejected and subsequent developments mean that there are a number of areas regarding urban and rural *dibao* that will be subject to ongoing change and development. These will have a significant impact on how it operates, who it reaches, and to what extent it helps them. As was the case previously, what direction *dibao* takes will depend largely on the priorities of the elite leadership in China. This ultimately reflects the role of *dibao* in the Chinese system of social assistance. It was never really intended as a panacea to poverty in China's cities or countryside. Rather it was a means to achieve particular political ends, placating particular groups at particular times who might have challenged the status quo. In this regard the lack of institutionalisation suits China's leaders and, especially when the ongoing changes to the *hukou* are considered, this is likely to remain the case for years to come.

Contribution to China studies

There are four contributions this study makes to China studies beyond the specifics of *dibao* and the questions of how it evolved and developing our understanding of social policy making in China. The first of these is that it adds to the already well-established literature demonstrating the continued relevance of the FA framework as a means for analysing policy developments. While the foundations of FA are now almost three decades old, and China has gone through significant developmental, political and administrative change, the fundamentals of the state and its relationship to the CCP and its citizens remain broadly the same. The need for policy actors to navigate and negotiate the complex mesh of structures and relationships, to work with and exploit the dominant values of the time, and the ultimate need for resources to drive policy all remain critical to getting things done in China. For analysts of Chinese policy making the approach provides a degree of flexibility which other options either cannot accommodate or only reflect a part of. The study of *dibao* also contributes to the growing number of studies using FA which do not focus solely on the realm of economic or energy policy making where the approach first gained traction.

Second, the discussion reinforces the need to study policy such as the MLG from a number of different angles – not just national or local – and illustrates the significance of understanding what a policy is really for before assessing what it has achieved. While it has been a national policy since 1997 the MLG has been shaped by its local origins and transition before this happened; and by the subsequent struggles to achieve national implementation and adaption that followed. Furthermore, what the policy has been intended to achieve has changed over the years as the political priorities and the scope of what was possible has shifted at national level. Taking a snapshot of a policy, without its developmental context, can lead to misleading or unfair criticism regarding what it has achieved. While *dibao* has typically found itself subject to analysis as a poverty alleviation measure, or criticised due to local variation, these are arguably unfair points as the programme was never really intended to achieve such a goal; the origins and design of the programme reflect this.

Third, the case of social assistance and how it has been used and adjusted to cater to different groups contributes to the arguments made by Huang regarding how social insurance policies have been used to co-opt, capture and placate particular interests in Chinese society (Huang 2013, 2014, 2015). The argument that social protection emerges as a means to head off challenges from particular emerging or established interests is not new and is the foundation of at least one of Esping-Andersen's original welfare regimes (Esping-Andersen 1990). What Huang has shown, and arguably the case of *dibao* supports, is that the Chinese state and the CCP have consciously changed social protection policies throughout the last thirty years in order to ensure regime legitimacy and to maintain the Party's position in power.

This links to the fourth and final contribution. While not a primary aim of the study, the way *dibao* has been used, and continues to be used, as a means for the CCP to maintain regime legitimacy means that social assistance should be part of our explanation when seeking to address resilience and regime stability in the PRC. The focus in these studies has typically addressed reform to the economy, so-called performance legitimacy, and ideological flexibility in the light of the policy shift away from Marxist-Leninist dogma and the historical collapse of the Soviet Union (for example see Fewsmith 2008; Gilley and Holbig 2009; Holbig and Gilley 2010; Shambaugh 2009). Maintaining legitimacy goes far beyond these areas and social assistance is one part of the bigger picture. When seeking to explain why China avoided the colour revolutions or has not fallen foul of the same challenges of other non-democratic regimes, the way in which social assistance has been used needs to be considered.

Contribution beyond China studies

Beyond the study of China this study contributes in three ways. First, it takes a single case study and discusses it in a manner that does not to treat China in a silo. There is a tendency to think of the Chinese case as in some way unique. While the historical circumstances and the way particular institutions might work in China have particular characteristics that are unique, it is important to note those features that are common to all states. In particular, the interaction of institutions and actors, of structure and agency, is a feature of policy systems. One of the interesting, but often overlooked, features of the FA framework is that it bridged China studies and the larger disciplines of policy studies and political science. The features identified and abstracted in the FA framework are not unique to China but are common to all political systems – what is specific is the way in which these different elements interact in the Chinese context. A small contribution this study makes is to reinforce the notion that when it comes to policy studies, China is not an island.

A second point is that it is critical to maintain an awareness of the political in studies of social policy. While excellent research is conducted on programmes like *dibao*, when these studies analyse a policy in isolation from the broader political developments and priorities then findings and recommendations will lack critical insights. The most significant example of this is the way poverty alleviation and *dibao* are often conflated and the programme is criticised for not helping to pull individuals and households out of poverty or for trapping recipients in a cycle of dependence, or that the *dibao* varies across the country. These outcomes are problematic especially where recipients find themselves stuck on *dibao* in dire circumstances as scholars have shown (Cho 2010, 2013; Solinger 2011), or where the utility of *dibao* is dependent on other features of a household's composition such as education levels (Zhao, Guo and Shao 2017). It is important, however, to separate out intended outcomes, unintended outcomes, and those which are misattributed to the policy. It is impossible to do this without considering the politics which motivate new developments. Social assistance policy does not take place in a vacuum nor is it framed solely by good intentions. Rather it serves the interests of those in power and their objectives. In the case of *dibao*, policy served the regime not because it helped people out of poverty but because it ensured they had a minimum standard of living and would not protest.

The final area to which this study contributes is how China fits within our understanding of development and the role played by social assistance. The preceding discussion of *dibao* highlights that, at present, China presents as something of an outlier which does not easily fit into the narrative or work in other areas. There is no case to suggest that China is in some way constructing a new system of social assistance, but it has developed a model that works differently to the majority of other systems. As noted in Chapter 5, China has dealt with social assistance in a manner at variance with other major programmes that have been implemented (Barrientos 2013). The key difference in China is the lack of conditionality and the lack of clear objectives for recipients to achieve in the system once receiving payments. This difference reflects the origins and development of the programme, and the political motivations behind *dibao*. This meant that it was implemented primarily to maintain the CCP in power rather than to achieve more universal goals.

Reflection and future research

No study is without its limitations and this one is no different. The discussion throughout this book and the findings and contributions set out above are not intended nor should they be read as the final word on *dibao*. Rather this is a contribution to a growing body of literature in the English language which addresses social assistance and the MLG in China. There are a number of areas which are worth reflecting on before setting out areas for future research. A first point to consider is the challenges of working and researching in what can be a difficult field site. Access affects all scholars of China be they historians and archivists or social scientists seeking out interviews. This study was no different, and so the findings set out above must be understood as being based on the document base and interviewees accessible during fieldwork. Second, China is such a large unit of analysis that even taking into account local developments when considering national policy there will be oversights and areas that are not given the scope they deserve. Third, an iteration on the issue of access is that the black box of decision making at the very top, at provincial and at local levels, is still obscured. How power is exercised, who makes the ultimate decision, and what feeds into this, are all areas that are still opaque to scholars of China. This will remain the case until a more open climate permits interviews and critical questioning. Until then it remains for scholars to work collaboratively to piece together explanations for policy developments. Fourth, and more a lead-in to thinking about the future, there needs to be more on the day-to-day function of *dibao* and how it affects those who are on the programme. Experiences between cities and villages, and between households, vary enormously and this gets picked out by individual studies. This will be even more likely in light of recent developments. The more that is pieced together about local practice the more we learn about *dibao* and the policy process in China more generally.

Looking to the future, what is next for *dibao* and what should research on social assistance address? There are four critical areas which researchers on *dibao* could and should look to address. First, the current rural anti-poverty programme and its intended use of *dibao* is a fascinating development but is also a cause for concern, as noted in Chapter 5. Will rural areas see the re-emergence of categories as a means to determine access to the MLG? How will the MLG be managed so that it alleviates poverty? In the longer term it will be critical, when considering the well-being and dignity of those households who remain on *dibao*, to understand how it is anticipated that recipients of payments will be expected to escape poverty and eventually the programme itself.

Second, the extent to which the 2014 Temporary Measures have affected those on *dibao* is something that should considered. As intimated in Chapter 2 there has been a noticeable reduction in the number of individuals and households receiving both urban and rural *dibao* payments. It would be interesting to explore how the new requirements, especially regarding household eligibility and the more nuanced definition of income, are affecting both entry and exit from the programme. The Temporary Measures also made explicit the requirement that those on *dibao* receive support in order to find work. Given the relatively spotty history since the 1990s of government re-employment work in China, how this additional support has been operationalised and, given that this was articulated in 2014, how successful it has been is worth finding out.

Third, there are a number of reforms outside of social assistance which have the potential to dramatically change how it works. The reform of the *hukou* will have a profound impact on the way the *dibao* works. The shift from the classic rural-urban divide in services to a division based on place of residence has a range of implications, not least whether the current distinction between urban and rural *dibao* will be sustained in the longer term. As has been noted by Gao (2017) some regions have already abolished the distinction, and recent interviews in China highlighted changes in some cities which went as far as ensuring that benefits were accessibly to the partners of residents even if they themselves were registered elsewhere – for example a rural resident married to an urban resident can access *dibao* in some cases. At the same time, the emergence of professional social workers in China is changing how *dibao* payments are managed in some areas as the MCA experiments with paying social workers to work with recipients to ensure, according to interviewees, that they are better supported.

Finally, an issue which has implications that go beyond simply social assistance is the dramatic economic and social changes that technological development might have in China, as well as in the rest of the world. The extent to which *dibao* remains necessary or the best tool for the Chinese state to achieve its goals – assuming these are social stability and maintaining a minimum standard of living – is going to be challenged by changes occurring elsewhere in China's economy, society and administration. As China develops further and technology advances more generally the traditional paths out of poverty through work are going to be limited in their effectiveness. If developments in robotics and artificial intelligence – both industries in which China incidentally is investing heavily – continue as predicted then many jobs currently taken for granted will no longer be available. When work has been the primary means to alleviate poverty what happens when there are no longer the same employment opportunities? What happens when potentially many more require the final safety net of social assistance than it was designed to cope with? It may be that *dibao* is the answer or that the PRC will need to return once again to the question of social assistance and how it functions in the near future.

Appendix

Interview list

The list of interviewees is anonymised in line with ethical agreements and checklists secured before fieldwork was conducted. The number of the interview listed here corresponds with the number in the text, so (Interview 1) in text refers to the first interview on the list below. Interviews were conducted between 2006 and 2016.

1. CASS researcher, Beijing.
2. Official, Ministry of Science and Technology.
3. University researcher, Tianjin.
4. University researcher, Tianjin.
5. Official, People's Government, Anqing.
6. Official, Anqing Development Zone.
7. MLG recipient, Anqing.
8. Two university researchers, Beijing.
9. Three university researchers, Beijing.
10. NGO official, Beijing.
11. Official, Ministry of Civil Affairs.
12. Government researcher, Beijing.
13. NGO official, Beijing.
14. University researcher, HK SAR.
15. University researcher, HK SAR.
16. Government researcher, Beijing.
17. Official, Dalian.
18. Official, Ministry of Civil Affairs.
19. CASS researcher, Beijing.
20. Two CASS researchers, Beijing.
21. Two officials, Ministry of Civil Affairs.

Bibliography

ADB. 2004. Poverty Profile of the People's Republic of China. Asian Development Bank.

Anonymous. 1996. 'Regarding issues in overall plan for rural social security system (*Guanyu zhengti guihua juanli nongcun shehui baozhang tixi wenti*)'. *China Society News (Zhongguo Shehui Bao)*, 6 June 1996, 1–2.

Anonymous. 2000. 'Nationally over 1600 counties have started to develop rural "dibao" work (*Woguo 1600 yu xian kaizhan nongcun "dibao" gongzuo*)'. *Zhongguo Shehui Bao*, 20 July 2000, 1.

Anonymous. 2001. 'Rural dibao systems quietly flower (*Nongcun dibao zhihua jing qiaoqiao dikai*)'. *Zhongguo Shehui Bao*, 5 December 2001, 1.

Anonymous. 2003a. 'Jiangxi perfects rural social relief system (*Jiangxi wanshan nongcun shehui jiuzhu zhidu*)'. *Zhongguo Shehui Bao*, 26 August 2003, 1.

Anonymous 2003b. 'Ningxia decides to establish rural social relief system (*Ningxia jueding jinali nongcun shehui jiuzhu zhidu*)'. *Zhongguo Shehui Bao*, 4 November 2003, 1.

Anonymous. 2004. 'Liaoning comprehensively establishes standardised rural dibao system (*Liaoning quanmian jianli guifande nongcun dibao zhidu*)'. *Zhongguo Shehui Bao*, 3 December 2004, 6.

Anonymous. 2010. 'Flowchart for urban and rural dibao declaration, approval, and release process (*Chengxiang dibao shenbao, shenpi, fafang liucheng tu*)'. *Zhongguo Shehui Bao*, 1 November 2010, 2.

Anonymous. 2000. 'Urban MLG: Stepping up to a new journey (*Chengshi Dibao: Tashang Xin Zhengcheng*)'. *Zhongguo Minzheng* 2000 (1): 22–27.

Anonymous. 2001. 'Urban dibao: Increasing dynamics, increase protection (*Chengshi Dibao: Jiada Lidu Kuangda Baomian*)'. *Zhongguo Minzheng* 2001 (12): 38–40.

Barrientos, Armando. 2013. *Social Assistance in Developing Countries*. Cambridge: Cambridge University Press.

Baumgartner, F. and Bryan D. Jones. 1991. 'Agenda dynamics and policy subsystems'. *The Journal of Politics* 53 (4): 1044–1074.

Baumgartner, F. and B. Jones. 1993. *Agendas and Instability in American Politics*. Chicago: University of Chicago Press.

Beijing-Youthdaily. 2002. 'Whole country carries out "out to protect, fully protect" (*Quanguo shouci shixian "yingbaojinbao"*)'. *Beijing Qingnian Bao*, 29 July 2002.

Beland, Daniel and Ka Man Yu. 2004. 'A long financial march: Pension reform in China'. *Journal of Social Policy* 33 (2): 267–288.

Benkanpinglunyuan. 1998. 'Do not fear the laid-off (*Bu Pa Xiagang*)'. *Zhongguo Minzheng*, 7.

Cai, Yongshun. 2006. *State and Laid-off Workers in Reform China: The Silence and Collective Action of the Retrenched*. Edited by David S. Goodman, *Routledge Studies on China in Transition*. London: Routledge.

CCPCC. 1999. Central Committee of the CCP and State Council circular regarding the 'National Development Planning Commission regarding the current economic situation and main construction' (*Zhongfa (1999) 12 Hao: Zhonggong Zhongyang, Guowuyuan Guanyu Zhuanfa 'Guojia Fazhan Jihua Weiyuan Hui Guanyu Dangqian Jingji Xingshi he Duice Jianyi' de Tongzhi*). Beijing.

Chang, Yiyong and Xuejing Lü. 2005. *Contemporary Chinese Social Securty (Dangdai Zhongguo shehui baozhang)*. Beijing: China Labour and Social Security (*Zhongguo laodong shehui baozhang chubanshe*).

Chao, Xianhua. 1996. 'Jiaozhou: Formulates villager MLG line (*Jiaozhou: Zhiding cunmin zuidi shenghuo baozhang zhidu xian*)'. *China Society News (Zhongguo Shehui Bao)*, 25 April 1996, 2.

Chen, Honglin, Yu-Cheung Wong, Qun Zeng and Juha Hämäläinen. 2013. 'Trapped in poverty? A study of the dibao programme in Shanghai'. *China Journal of Social Work* 6 (3): 327–343.

Chen, Janet. 2012. *Guilty of Indigence: The Urban Poor in China, 1900–1953*. Princeton, NJ: Princeton University Press.

China Daily. 2016. 'Eight issues in spotlight at the two sessions'. Available at http://www.chinadaily.com.cn/china/2016twosession/2016-03/04/content_23735625.htm (accessed 14 April 2016).

Cho, Mun Young. 2010. 'On the edge between "the People" and "the Population": Ethnographic research on the minimum livelihood guarantee'. *The China Quarterly* 201: 20–37.

Cho, Mun Young. 2013. *The Spectre of 'The People': Urban Poverty in Northeast China*. London: Cornell University Press.

Commentary. 1994. "Five Guarantees provision for elders work enters a new stage (*Wubao gongyang gongzuo jinru xin jieduan*)'. *China Society News (Zhongguo Shehui Bao)*, 19 February 1994, 1.

Commentary. 1996. 'The basic livelihood of the poor masses are protected (*Pinkun qunzhong jiben shenguo you baozhang*)'. *China Society News (Zhongguo Shehui Bao)*, 13 February 1996, 1.

Considine, Mark. 2005. *Making Public Policy: Institutions, Actors, Strategies*. Cambridge: Polity Press.

Dai, Haijing. 2014. 'The discontents of reform: Boundary work and welfare stigma at mixed elder homes in China'. *Journal of Social Policy* 43 (3): 497–515.

Deng, Quheng and Bjorn Gustafsson. 2013. 'A new episode of increased urban income inequality in China'. In *Rising Inequality in China: Challenges to a Harmonious Society*, edited by Shi Li, Hiroshi Sato and Terry Sicular, 255–288. Cambridge: Cambridge University Press.

Dikötter, Frank 2016. 'The silent revolution: Decollectivization from below during the Cultural Revolution'. *The China Quarterly* 227: 796–811.

DiMaggio, Paul J. and Walter W. Powell (eds). 1991. *The New Institutionalism in Organizational Analysis*. Chicago: University of Chicago Press.

Dixon, J. 1981. *The Chinese Welfare System*. New York: Praeger.

Dixon, J. and D. Macarov (eds). 1992. *Social Welfare in Socialist Countries, Comparative Social Welfare*. London: Routledge.

Doak Barnett, A. 1974. *Uncertain Passage: China's Transition to the Post-Mao Era*. Washington, DC: The Brookings Institution.

Dong, Zewen. 1997. 'Establish a rural MLG system to protect the basic livelihood rights of the masses (*Jianli nongcun shehui baozhang zhidu, weihu qunzhong jiben shenghuo quanyi*)'. *China Society News (Zhongguo Shehui Bao)*, 4.

Dryburgh, Majorie. 2016. 'Living on the edge: Welfare and the urban poor in 1930s Beijing'. *Social History* 41 (1): 14–33.

Duckett, J. 2001. 'Political interests and the implementation of China's urban health insurance reform'. *Social Policy and Administration* 35 (3): 290–306.

Duckett, Jane. 2003. 'Bureaucratic interests and institutions in the making of China's social policy'. *Public Administration Quarterly* 27 (2): 210–237.

Duoji, Cairang. 1995a. 'Minister of Civil Affairs Duoji Cairang's work report to the 10th national civil affairs conference (*Minzhengbu Buzhang Duoji Cairang zai Di Shi Ci Quanguo Minzheng Huiyi shang de Gongzuo Baogao*)'. In *Minzheng Gongzuo Wenjian Xuanbian 1994 Nian*, edited by Minzhengbu Fazhi Bangongshi, 12–33. Beijing: Zhongguo Shehui Chubanshe.

Duoji, Cairang. 1995b. 'Positively push the urban minimum livelihood guarantee line system to effectively resolve residents livelihood difficulties, ensure social stability (*Jiji tuijin chengshi zuidi shenghuo baozhang xian zhidu qieshi jiejue jumin shenghuo kunnan, cuijin shehui wending*)'. *Jingji Ribao*, 15 June 1995.

Duoji, Cairang. 1995c. *New Era Chinese Social Security System Reform in Theory and Practice* (*Xinshiqi Zhongguo Shehui Baozhang Tizhi Gaige de Lilun yu Shijian*). Beijing: China Central Party Publishers.

Duoji, Cairang. 1998a. 'Minister Duoji Cairang speech at symposium of province, city and district civil affairs office heads regarding urban resident MLG line problems (*Duoji Cairang Buzhang zai Bufen Sheng, Shi, Qu Minzheng Ting(Ju) Zhang Yantanhui Shang Guanyu Chengshi Jumin Zuidi Shenghuo Baozhangxian Wenti de Jianghua 01/08/1995*)'. In *Chengshi Jumin Zuidi Shenghuo Baozhang Zhidu Wenjian Zike Huibian 1*, edited by Minzhengbu Jiuzai Jiujisi, 32–37. Beijing: Minzhengbu Jiuzai Jiujisi.

Duoji, Cairang. 1998b. 'Minister Duoji Cairang's instructions for urban resident Minimum Livelihood Guarantee line investigation work (*Duoji Cairang Buzhang dui Chengshi Zuidi Shenghuo Baozhang Xian Diaoyan Gongzuo de Zhishi 29/05/1995*)'. In *Chengshi Jumin Zuidi Shenghuo Baozhang Zhidu Wenjian Zike Huibian 1*, edited by Minzhengbu Jiuzai Jiujisi, 29–31. Beijing: Minzhengbu Jiuzai Jiujisi.

Duoji, Cairang. 1998c. 'Minister Duoji Cairang's speech at national meeting of civil affairs office/ bureaux heads (*Duoji Cairang Buzhang zai Quanguo Minzhengting(ju) Zhang Huiyi Shang de Jinaghua 22/12/1997*)'. In *Chengshi Jumin Zuidi Shenghuo Baozhang Zhidu Wenjian Zike Huibian 1*, edited by Minzhengbu Jiuzai Jiujisi, 26–28. Beijing: Minzhengbu Jiuzai Jiujisi.

Duoji, Cairang. 1998d. 'Minister Duoji Cairang's speech at the Eastern briefing on social secuirty (*Duoji Cairang Buzhang zai Shehui Baozhang Dongpian Gongzuo Huibaohui Shang de Jianghua 15-05-1997*)'. In *Chengshi Jumin Zuidi Shenghuo Baozhang Zhidu Wenjian Zike Huibian 1*, edited by Minzhengbu Jiuzai Jiujisi, 38–47. Beijing: Minzhengbu Jiuzai Jiujisi.

Duoji, Cairang. 1998e. 'Minister Duoji Cairang's speech to the Western area social secuirty work briefing (*Duoji Cairang Buzhang zai Minzheng Shehui Baozhang Xipian Gongzuo Huibaohui Shang de Jianghua 31/08/1997*)'. In *Chengshi Jumin Zuidi Shenghuo Baozhang Zhidu Wenjian Zike Huibian*, edited by Minzhengbu Jiuzai Jiujisi, 48–57. Beijing: Minzhengbu Jiuzai Jiujisi.

Duoji, Cairang. 1998f. 'Positively establish an urban Minimum Livelihood Guarantee system (*Jiji Jianli Chengxiang Zuidi Shenghuo Baozhang Zhidu 07/08/1997*)'. In *Chengshi Jumin Zuidi Shenghuo Baozhang Zhidu Wenjian Zike Huibian 1*, edited by Minzhengbu Jiuzai Jiujisi, 95–100. Beijing: Minzhengbu Jiuzai Jiujisi.

Duoji, Cairang. 2001a. *China's Minimum Livelihood Guarantee System Research and Practice (Zhongguo Zuidi Shenghuo Baozheng Zhidu Yanjiu Yu Shijian)*. Beijing: Renmin Chubanshe (People's Publishing).

Duoji, Cairang. 2001b. 'Minister Duoji Cairang speech to the national civil affairs department heads symposium (*Duoji Cairang Buzhang zai Quanguo Minzhengting(ju) zhang Zuotanhui Shangde Zongjie Jianghua Tigang (23/07/2000)*)'. In *Chengshi Jumin Zuidi Shenghuo Baozhang Zhidu Wenjian Zike Huibian 5*, 95. Beijing: Minzhengbu Jiuzai Jiujisi.

Duoji, Cairang. 2001c. 'Minister Duoji Cairang's opening speech to national meeting of civil affairs department heads (*Duoji Cairang Buzhang zai Quanguo Minzhengting(ju) Zhang Zuotanhui Kai Moushi Shangde Jianghua Tigang (20/07/2000)*)'. In *Chengshi Jumin Zuidi Shenghuo Baozhang Zhidu Wenjian Zike Huibian 5*, edited by Minzhengbu Jiuzai Jiujisi, 90–94. Beijing: Minzhengbu Jiuzai Jiujisi.

Duoji, Cairang. 2001d. 'Minister Duoji Cairang's speech to national civil affiars department meeting (*Duoji Cairang Buzhang zai Quanguo Minzhengting(ju) Huiyi Shangde Jianghua (08/01/2000)*)'. In *Chengshi Jumin Zuidi Shenghuo Baozhang Zhidu Wenjian Zike Huibian 5*, 82–89. Beijing: Minzhengbu Jiuzai Jiujisi.

Esping-Andersen, G. 1990. *The Three Worlds of Welfare Capitalism*. Cambridge: Polity Press.

Fan, Baojun. 1994. 'Explanation regarding the "Regulations for Rural 5 Guarantees provision for elders work" (*Guanyu "Nongcun Wubao Gongyang Gongzuo Tiaoli" de shouming*)'. *China Society News (Zhongguo Shehui Bao)*, 19 February 1994, 2.

Fan, Baojun. 1998a. 'Grasp well, deepen reform, push urban resident Minimum Livelihood Guarantee system speech (*Zhuahaojiyu, Shenrugaige, Tujin Chengshi Jumin Zuidi Shenghuo Baozhang Zhidu Jianshe 27/11/1997*)'. In *Chengshi Jumin Zuidi Shenghuo Baozhang Zhidu Wenjian Zike Huibian*, edited by Minzhengbu Jiuzai Jiujisi, 3–14. Beijing: Minzhengbu Jiuzai Jiujisi.

Fan, Baojun. 1998b. 'Vice-Minister Fan Baojun's speech at the urban MLG line work symposium held in Qingdao (*Fan Baojun Fubuzhang zai Qingdao Zhaokai de Chengshi Zuidi Shenghuo Baozhangxian Gongzuo Yantanhui Shang de Jianghua 05/1995*)'. In

Chengshi Jumin Zuidi Shenghuo Baozhang Zhidu Wenjian Zike Huibian 1, edited by Minzhengbu Jiuzai Jiujisi, 58–69. Beijing: Minzhengbu Jiuzai Jiujisi.

Fan, Baojun. 1999a. 'Vice-Minister Fan Baojun's speech in Shanghai on investigation into the Minimum Livelihood Guarantee system (*Fan Baojun Fubuzhang zai Shangahi Diaoyan Zuidi Shenghuo Baozhang Zhidu Shide Jianghua 26/04/1998*)'. In *Chengshi Jumin Zuidi Shenghuo Baozhang Zhidu Wenjian Zike Huibian 3*, edited by Minzhengbu Jiuzai Jiujisi, 31–38. Beijing: Minzhengbu Jiuzai Jiujisi.

Fan, Baojun. 1999b. 'Vice Minister Fan Baojun's speech at a conference on the reconstruction of disaster affected areas and the living arrangements of victims during winter (*Minzhengbu Fubuzhang Fan Baojun zai Quanguo Zaiqu Dao Fang Zhongjian Ji Zaimin Guo Dong Shenghuo Anpai Huiyi Shangde Jianghua 23/10/1998*)'. In *Chengshi Jumin Zuidi Shenghuo Baozhang Zhidu Wenjian Zike Huibian 3*, edited by Minzhengbu Jiuzai Jiujisi, 39–46. Beijing: Minzhengbu Jiuzai Jiujisi.

Fan, Baojun. 2000a. 'Fan Baojun: Perfect the urban resident MLG system system as the final security net (*Fan Baojun: Wanshan chengshi Jumin Zuidi Shenghuo Baozhang Zhidu Shehui Baozhang Tixide Zuihou Yidao Anquanwang (26/11/1999)*)'. In *Chengshi Jumin Zuidi Shenghuo Baozhang Zhidu Wenjian Zike Huibian 4*, edited by Minzhengbu Jiuzai Jiujisi, 1–12. Beijing: Minzhengbu Jiuzai Jiujisi.

Fan, Baojun. 2000b. 'MCA Vice-Minister Fan Baojun's speech to a symposium of 10 provinces on the urban resident MLG (*Fan Baojun Fubuzhang zai 10 Sheng Qu Chengshi Jumin Zuidi Shenghuo Baozhang Yantanhui Shangde Jianghua (29/06/1999)*)'. In *Chengshi Jumin Zuidi Shenghuo Baozhang Zhidu Wenjian Zike Huibian 3*, edited by Minzhengbu Jiuzai Jiujisi, 55–63. Beijing: Minzhengbu Jiuzai Jiujisi.

Fan, Baojun. 2000c. 'MCA Vice-Minsiter Fan Baojun's speech to a Five Province Sympsium on the urban resident MLG (*Minzhengbu Fubuzhang Fan Baojun zai Xi Nan 5 Sheng Qu Chengshi Jumin Zuidi Shenghuo Baozhang Yantanhui Shangde Jianghua (18/04/1999)*)'. In *Chengshi Jumin Zuidi Shenghuo Baozhang Zhidu Wenjian Zike Huibian 3*, edited by Minzhengbu Jiuzai Jiujisi, 47–54. Beijing: Minzhengbu Jiuzai Jiujisi.

Fan, Baojun. 2001a. 'Intensively carry out urban MLG work to establish a standardised and perfected social security system (*Fan Baojun: Shenru Xizhi Di Zuohao Chengshi Jumin Zuidi Shenghuo Baozhang Gongzuo Wei Jianli Guifan Wanshande Shehui Baozhang Tixi 20/07/2000*)'. In *Chengshi Jumin Zuidi Shenghuo Baozhang Zhidu Wenjian Zike Huibian 5*, 98–109. Beijing: Minzhengbu Jiuzai Jiujisi.

Fan, Baojun. 2001b. 'Vice-Minister Fan Baojun's speech at the provincial (city, district) work meeting on the urban resident MLG (*Fan Baojun Fubuzhang zai Bufen Sheng (shi, qu) Chengshi Jumin Zuidi Shenghuo Baozhang Gongzuo Diaoyanhui Shangde Jianghua (03/09/2000)*)'. In *Chengshi Jumin Zuidi Shenghuo Baozhang Zhidu Wenjian Zike Huibian 5*, edited by Minzhengbu Jiuzai Jiujisi, 110–115. Beijing: Minzhengbu Jiuzai Jiujisi.

Feng, Juan and Minh Cong Nguyen. 2014. 'Relative versus absolute poverty headcount ratios: The full breakdown'. Available online at https://blogs.worldbank.org/open-data/relative-versus-absolute-poverty-headcount-ratios-full-breakdown (accessed 1 August 2017).

Fewsmith, J. 2008. *China since Tiananmen: From Deng Xiaoping to Hu Jintao*. 2nd edition. Cambridge: Cambridge University Press.

Fewsmith, J. 2013. *The Logic and Limits of Political Reform in China*. Cambridge: Cambridge University Press.

Fitzgerald, John and Mei-fen Kuo. 2017. 'Diaspora charity and welfare sovereignty in the Chinese Republic: Shanghai charity innovator William Yinson Lee (Li Yuanxin, 1884–1965)'. *Twentieth-Century China* 42 (1): 72–96.

Frey, Carl Benedikt and Michael A. Osborne. 2013. The future of employment. *Oxford Martin School Working Paper*. Oxford: Univeristy of Oxford.

Gao, Qin. 2013. 'Public assistance and poverty reduction: The case of Shanghai'. *Global Social Policy* 13 (2): 193–215.

Gao, Qin. 2017. *Welfare, Work and Poverty: China's Social Sssistance 20 Years After*. Oxford: Oxford University Press.

Gilley, Bruce. 2001. 'Not China's Gorbachev'. *Far Eastern Economic Review* 164 (35): 36–37.

Gilley, Bruce and Heike Holbig. 2009. 'The debate on Party legitimacy in China: A mixed quantitative/ qualititative analysis'. *Journal of Contemporary China* 18 (59): 339–358.

Global Voices. 2007. 'China: Recently, can you afford meat?'. Available online at https://globalvoices.org/2007/11/24/china-recently-can-you-afford-meat/ (accessed 13 August 2017).

Gong, Guozheng. 2000. 'A number of misconceptions regarding "dibao" (*"Dibao" Zhongde Jizhong Cuowu Renshi*)'. *Zhongguo Minzheng* 2000 (4): 34.

Goodman, David S. (ed.). 1984. *Groups and Politics in the People's Republic of China*. Cardiff: University of Cardiff Press.

Gu, C. L. and H. Y. Liu. 2001. 'Social polarization and segregation in Beijing'. In *The New Chinese City: Globalization and Market Reform*, edited by J. R. Logan, 198–211. Oxford: Blackwell Publishers.

Gu, Zhibang. 2005. 'Further advance and perfect the social relief system (*Jinyibu tuijin he wanshan shehui jiuzhu tixi*)'. *Zhongguo Shehui Bao*, 19 November 2005, 1 and 4.

Guan, Xinping. 2000. 'China's social policy: Reform and development in the context of marketization and globalization'. *Social Policy and Administration* 34 (1): 115–130.

Guan, Xinping and Xu Bing. 2011. 'Central-local relations in social policy and the development of urban and rural social assistance programmes'. In *China's Changing Welfare Mix: Local Perspectives*, edited by Beatriz Carrillo and J. Duckett, 20–35. London: Routledge.

Guo, Sujian. 2013. *Chinese Politics and Government: Power, Ideology and Organization*. New York: Routledge.

Gustafsson, Bjorn and Deng Qiuheng. 2011. 'Di Bao receipt and its importance for combating poverty in urban China'. *Poverty and Public Policy* 3 (1): 1–32.

Gustafsson, Bjorn and Zhong Wei. 2000. 'How and why has poverty changed China? A study based on microdata for 1988 and 1995'. *The China Quarterly* (164): 983–1006.

Gustafsson, Bjorn, Shi Li and Terry Sicular. 2008. 'Inequality and public policy in China: Issues and trends'. In *Inequality and Public Policy in China*, edited by Bjorn Gustafsson, Shi Li and Terry Sicular, 1–34. Cambridge: Cambridge University Press.

Haidian District Government. 2012. 'Draft of the "Social Relief Law" has already been submitted to the State Council Office of Legal Affairs for studying (*"Shehui jiuzhu fa" cao'an yishang bao guowuyuan fazhiban zheng yanjiu'*)'. Available online at http://www.bjhd.gov.cn/ggfw/shbz/shjz/xgzx/dibao/201202/t20120209_392310.htm (accessed 18 June 2013).

Hall, P. A. and R. C. Taylor. 1996. 'Political science and the three institutionalisms'. *Political Studies* 44: 936–957.

Hammond, Daniel R. 2010. 'Explaining policy making in the People's Republic of China: The case of the urban resident Minimum Livelihood Guarantee system'. University of Glasgow, PhD.

Hammond, Daniel R. 2011a. 'Local variation in urban social assistance: Community public service agencies in Dalian City'. In *China's Changing Welfare Mix: Local Perspectives*, edited by Beatriz Carrillo and J. Duckett, 64–81. London and New York: Routledge.

Hammond, Daniel R. 2011b. 'Social assistance in China 1993–2002: Institutions, feedback and policy actors in the Chinese policy process'. *Asian Politics and Policy* 3 (1): 69–93.

Hammond, Daniel R. 2013. 'Policy entrepreneurship in China's response to urban poverty'. *Policy Studies Journal* 41 (1): 119–146.

Hammond, Daniel R. 2015. 'Enough to get by? A discussion of China's Minimum Livelihood Guarantee as social stability mechanism'. In *Non-Western Encounters with Democratization – Imagining Democracy after the Arab Spring*, edited by Christopher K. Lamont, Jan van der Harst and Frank Gaenssmantel, 163–179. London: Ashgate.

Hammond, Daniel R. 2017. 'Historical continuities in social assistance in China, 1911–2011'. In *Governance, Domestic Change, and Social Policy in China – 100 Years after the Xinhai Revolution*, edited by Jean-Marc F. Blanchard and Kun-Chin Lin, 21–66. London: Palgrave Macmillan.

Harding, Harry. 1981. *Organizing China*. Stanford, CA: Stanford University Press.

Harding, Harry. 1987. *China's Second Revolution: Reform After Mao*. Washington, DC: The Brookings Institution.

He, Ping and Yingfang Hua. 2005. *Urban Poor Groups: Social Security Policy and Measures Research (Chengshi pinkun qunti: Shehui baozhang zhengce yu cuoshi yanjiu)*. Beijing: Beijing Labour and Social Security Press (*Beijing laodong shehui baozhang chubanshe*).

Heilmann, Sebastian. 2008a. 'From local experiments to national policy: The origins of China's distinctive policy process'. *The China Journal* 59: 1–30.

Heilmann, Sebastian. 2008b. 'Policy experimentation in China's economic rise'. *Studies in Comparative International Development* 43: 1–26.

Holbig, Heike and Bruce Gilley. 2010. 'Reclaiming legitimacy in China'. *Politics and Policy* 38 (3): 395–422.

Hong, Dayong. 2004. *China's Social Assistance (Zhongguo Shehui Jiuzhu)*. Shengyang: Liaoning Education Press (*Liaoning Jiaoyu Chunbanshe*).

Huang, Xian. 2013. 'The politics of social welfare reform in urban China: Social welfare preferences and reform policies'. *Journal of Chinese Political Science* 18: 61–85.

Huang, Xian. 2014. 'Expansion of Chinese social health insurance: Who gets what, when and how?' *Journal of Contemporary China* 23 (89): 923–951.

Huang, Xian. 2015. 'Four worlds of welfare: Understanding subnational variation in Chinese social health insurance'. *The China Quarterly* 222: 449–474.

Hubei Province, Financial Service. 2016. 'Policy interpretation of Minimum Livelihood Guarantee, Rural Five Guarantees, and Medical Assistance'. Available online at http://www.ecz.gov.cn/wzlm/zdgd/lzjzdcjcgz/zcjd/74422.htm (accessed 31 January 2017).

Hurst, William. 2009. *The Chinese Worker after Socialism*. Cambridge: Cambridge University Press.

Hurst, William and K. J. O'Brien. 2002. 'China's contentious pensioners'. *The China Quarterly* 170: 345–360.

Hussain, A. 2003. 'Urban poverty in China: Measurement, patterns and policies'. In *InFocus Programme on Socio-Economic Security*. Geneva: International Labour Organization.

Jiang, Chengzhen. 1997. 'Shaanxi – Acclerate rural MLG system construction (*Shanxi – Jiakuai nongcun zuidi shenghuo baozhang zhidu jianshe*)'. *China Society News (Zhongguo Shehui Bao)*, 6 September 1997, 1.

Jiang, Zemin. 1998. 'General Secretary Jiang Zemin's report to the 15th National Party Congress (*Jiang Zemin Zongshuji zai Zhongguo Gongchandang Di Shiwu Ci Quangguo Daibiao Dahui Shang de Baogao 12/09/1997*)'. In *Chengshi Jumin Zuidi Shenghuo Baozhang Zhidu Wenjian Zike Huibian 1*, edited by Minzhengbu Jiuzai Jiujisi, 4. Beijing: Minzhengbu Jiuzai Jiujisi.

John, Peter. 1998. *Analysing Public Policy*. London: Continuum.

JRF. 2017. 'What is poverty?'. Available online at https://www.jrf.org.uk/our-work/what-is-poverty?utm (accessed 12 August 2017).

Ken, Guoying and Yongying Zhang. 2002. 'Investigating several problems in urban MLG work (*Chengshi Dibao Gongzuo Ryogan Wenti Tantao*)'. *Zhongguo Minzheng* 2002 (5): 16–18.

Khan, A. R. and C. Riskin. 2001. *Inequality and Poverty in China in the Age of Globalization*. Oxford: Oxford University Press.

Khan, A. R. and C. Riskin. 2005. 'China's household income and its distribution, 1995 and 2002'. *The China Quarterly* (182): 356–384.

Kingdon, J. 1984. *Agendas, Alternatives and Public Policies*. Boston: Little Brown.

Kohrman, Matthew. 2005. *Bodies of Difference*. Berkeley: University of California Press.

Kuhn, Lena, Stephan Brosig and Linxiu Zhang. 2016. 'The brink of poverty: Implementation of a social assistance programme in rural China'. *Journal of Current Chinese Affairs* 45 (1): 75–108.

Lai, Jiaceng. 1997. 'Xiamen establish rural MLG system (*Xiamen nongcun jianli zuidi shenghuo baozhang zhidu*)'. *China Society News (Zhongguo Shehui Bao)*, 11 September 1997, 1.

Lampton, D. M. 1987a. 'Chinese politics: The bargaining treadmill'. *Issues and Studies* 23 (3): 11–41.

Lampton, D. M. 1987b. 'The implementation problem in post-Mao China'. In *Policy Implementation in Post-Mao China*, edited by D. M. Lampton, 3–24. Berkeley: University of California Press.

Lampton, D. M. 1992. 'A plum for a peach: Bargaining, interest, and bureaucratic politics in China'. In *Bureaucracy, Politics, and Decision Making in Post-Mao China*, edited by G. Lieberthal and M. Lampton, 33–58. Berkeley: University of California Press.

Lampton, D. M. 2014. *Following the Leader: Ruling China from Deng Xiaoping to Xi Jinping*. Berkeley: University of California Press.

Leisering, Lutz and Armando Barrientos. 2013. 'Social citizenship for the global poor? The worldwide spread of social assistance'. *International Journal of Social Welfare* 22 (S1): S50–S67.

Leung, J. C. B. 2003. 'Social security reforms in China: Issues and prospects'. *International Journal of Social Welfare* 12: 73–85.

Leung, J. C. B. 2006. 'The emergence of social assistance in China'. *International Journal of Social Welfare* 15 (3): 188–198.

Leung, J. C. B. and R. C. Nann. 1995. *Authority and Benevolence: Social Welfare in China*. Hong Kong: Chinese University Press.

Leung, J. C. B. and Hilda S. W. Wong. 1999. 'The emergence of community-based social assistance programs in urban China'. *Social Policy and Administration* 33 (1): 39–54.

Leung, J. C. B. and Meng Xiao. 2016. 'The institutionalisation of social assistance'. In *China's Social Policy*, edited by Kinglun Ngok and Chak Kwan Chan, 33–50. Abingdon: Routledge.

Li, Bengong. 1998a. 'Do well next years natural disaster and social relief work (*Zuohao Mingnian de Jiuzai Jiuji Gongzuo 29/11/1997*)'. In *Chengshi Jumin Zuidi Shenghuo Baozhang Zhidu Wenjian Zike Huibian*, edited by Minzhengbu Jiuzai Jiujisi, 15–25. Beijing: Minzhengbu Jiuzai Jiujisi.

Li, Bengong. 2000a. 'Department Head Li Bengong's speech to the third training session on the national urban resident MLG (*Li Bengong Sizhang zai Quanguo Chengshi jumin Zuidi Shenghuo Baozhang Zhidu Di San Qi Peixunban Shangde Jianghua (08/1999)*)'. In *Chengshi Jumin Zuidi Shenghuo Baozhang Zhidu Wenjian Zike Huibian 3*, 64–70. Beijing: Minzhengbu Jiuzai Jiujisi.

Li, Bengong. 2000b. 'Li Bengong Sizhang zai Quanguo Chengshi Jumin Zuidi Shenghuo Baozhang Gongzuo Huiyi de Jianghua (28/11/1999)'. In *Chengshi Jumin Zuidi Shenghuo Baozhang Zhidu Wenjian Zike Huibian 4*, 13–17. Beijing: Minzhengbu Jiuzai Jiujisi.

Li, Bengong. 2001a. 'Department of Disaster and Social Relief head Li Bengong at the 2000 national meeting of civil affairs heads (*Li Bengong Jiuzai Jiuji Sizhang zai 2000 Nian Quanguo Minzhengting(ju) Zhang Huiyi Shangde Fayan (08/01/2000)*)'. In *Chengshi Jumin Zuidi Shenghuo Baozhang Zhidu Wenjian Zike Huibian 5*, edited by Minzhengbu Jiuzai Jiujisi, 124–127. Beijing: Minzhengbu Jiuzai Jiujisi.

Li, Bengong. 2001b. 'Director Li Bengong's Speech at Hainan MLG Training (*Li Bengong Sizhang zai Hainan Dibao Peixunban Shangde Jianghua (04/2000)*)'. In

Chengshi Jumin Zuidi Shenghuo Baozhang Zhidu Wenjian Zike Huibian, edited by Minzhengbu Jiuzai Jiujisi, 128–135. Beijing: Minzhengbu Jiuzai Jiujisi.

Li, Guixian. 1998b. 'State Concillor Li Guixian's speech at the national establishing of the urban resident MLG system teleconference (*Li Guixian Guowuyuan Weiyuan zai Quanguo Jianli Chengshi Jumin Zuidi Shenghuo Baozhang Zhidu Dianshedianhua Huiyi Shang de Jianghua 03/09/1997*)'. In *Chengshi Jumin Zuidi Shenghuo Baozhang Zhidu Wenjian Zike Huibian 1*, edited by Minzhengbu Jiuzai Jiujisi, 17–21. Beijing: Minzhengbu Jiuzai Jiujisi.

Li, Guixian. 1998c. 'State Concillor Li Guixian's speech at the national meeting of civil affairs office/bureaux heads (*Guowuyuan Weiyuan Li Guixian Tongzhi zai Quanguo Minzhengting(ju) Zhang Huiyi Shang de Jianghua 24/12/1997*)'. In *Chengshi Jumin Zuidi Shenghuo Baozhang Zhidu Wenjian Zike Huibian*, edited by Minzhengbu Jiuzai Jiujisi, 24–25. Beijing: Minzhengbu Jiuzai Jiujisi.

Li, Mingjin. 2005. 'Facing the difficulties of the "six lows" in China's social assistance (*Zhengshi woguo shehui jiuzhu zhongde "liu di" nanti*)'. *China Society News (Zhongguo Shehui Bao)*, 7 September 2005, 3.

Li, Minguan and Robert Walker. 2016. 'Targeting social assistance: Dibao and institutional alienation in China'. *Social Policy and Administration* Online Early: 1–19.

Li, Peng. 1995. 'Premier Li Peng's speech at the 10th National Civil Affairs Conference (*Li Peng Zongli zai Di Shi Ci Quanguo Minzheng Huiyi Daibiao Shang de Jianghua*)'. In *Minzheng Gongzuo Wenjian Xuanbian 1994 Nian*, edited by Zhengbufazhibangongshi, 2–8. Beijing: Zhongguo Shehui Chubanshe.

Li, Peng. 1998d. 'Premier Li Peng's important instructions regarding the second part of the State Council Office Secretary "Reflections" (*Li Peng Zongli zai Guowuyuan Bangongting Mishu Si Ju "Qingkuang Fanying" Di Er Qi Shang de Zhongyao Pishi 22/05/1997*)'. In *Chengshi Jumin Zuidi Shenghuo Baozhang Zhidu Wenjian Zike Huibian 1*, edited by Minzhengbu Jiuzai Jiujisi, 8. Beijing: Minzhengbu Jiuzai Jiujisi.

Li, Peng. 1998e. 'Premier Li Peng's report regarding the ninth national economic and social development five year plan and 2010 development goals (*Li Peng Zongli "Guanyu Guomin Jingji he Shehui Fazhan Jiuwu Jihua he 2010 Nian Yuanying Mubiao Gangyao de Baogao" 15/03/1996*)'. In *Chengshi Jumin Zuidi Shenghuo Baozhang Zhidu Wenjian Zike Huibian 1*, edited by Minzhengbu Jiuzai Jiujisi, 6. Beijing: Minzhengbu Jiuzai Jiujisi.

Li, Peng. 1998f. 'Premier Li Peng's speech at work meeting on enterprise worker's basic old age insurance system (*Li Peng Zongli zai Quanguo Tongyi Qiye Zhigong Jiben Yanglao Baoxian Zhidu Gongzuo Huiyi Shang de Jianghua 30/07/1997*)'. In *Chengshi Jumin Zuidi Shenghuo Baozhang Zhidu Wenjian Zike Huibian 1*, edited by Minzhengbu Jiuzai Jiujisi, 9–11. Beijing: Minzhengbu Jiuzai Jiujisi.

Li, Shi and Terry Sicular. 2014. 'The distribution of household income in China: Inequality, poverty and policies'. *The China Quarterly* 217: 1–41.

Li, Shi, Chuliang Luo and Terry Sicular. 2013. 'Overview: Income inequality and poverty in China, 2002–2007'. In *Rising Inequality in China: Challenges to a Harmonious Society*, edited by Shi Li, Hiroshi Sato and Terry Sicular, 44–84. Cambridge: Cambridge University Press.

Li, Shi, Hiroshi Sato and Terry Sicular. 2013. 'Rising inequality in China: Key issues and findings'. In *Rising Inequality in China: Challenges to a Harmonious Society*, edited by Shi Li, Hiroshi Sato and Terry Sicular, 1–43. Cambridge: Cambridge University Press.

Li, W. 2002a. 'Zhu Rongji: Strengthen civil affairs work, promote social progress (*Zhu Rongji: Jiaqiang minzheng gongzuo, cuijin shehui jinbu*)'. *Zhongguo Minzheng* 11: 35.

Li, Wanhua. 2001c. 'Ten long-standing misunderstandings regarding the MLG (*Zuidi Shenghuo Baozhang Shige Wuqu*)'. *Zhongguo Minzheng* 2001 (2): 18.

Li, Xueju. 2002b. *Trans-century China Civil Affairs Matters: Overall Status (Kuashijide Zhongguo Minzheng shiye: Zong juan)*. Beijing: China Society Publisher (*Zhongguo shehui chubanshe*).

Li, Xueju. 2008. *Thirty Years of Civil Affairs (Minzheng 30 nian)*. Beijing: Zhongguo Shehui Chubanshe.

Li, Yao. 2013. 'Fragmented authoritarianism and protest channels: A case study of resistance to privatizing a hospital'. *Journal of Current Chinese Affairs* 42 (2): 195–224.

Li, Youzhi and Qiansheng Zhu. 2000. 'The four principles of completing "dibao" (*Wanshang "Dibao" de Sige Yuanze*)'. *China Civil Affairs (Zhongguo Minzheng)* 2000 (11): 35.

Liang, Aimin. 2004. 'The dibao standard ought to follow adjustments in prices (*Dibao biaozhun ying sui wujia tiaozheng*)'. *China Society News (Zhongghuo Shehui Bao)*, 23 October 2004.

Lieberthal, K. G. 1992. 'Introduction: The "fragmented authoritarianism" model and its limitations'. In *Bureaucracy, Politics, and Decision Making in Post-Mao China*, edited by K. G. Lieberthal and D. M. Lampton, 1–30. Berkeley: University of California Press.

Lieberthal, K. G. 1995. *Governing China: From Revolution Through Reform*. New York: Norton.

Lieberthal, Kenneth and Michel Oksenberg. 1988. *Policy Making in China: Leaders, Structures, and Processes*. Princeton, NJ: Princeton University Press.

Lin, Alfred H. Y. 2004. 'Warlord, Social welfare and social philanthropy: The case of Guangzhou under Chen Jitang, 1929–36'. *Modern China* 30 (2): 151–198.

Lipkin, Zwia. 2005. 'Modern dilemmas: Dealing with Nanjing's beggars, 1927–1937'. *Journal of Urban History* 31 (5): 583–609.

Lipkin, Zwia. 2006. *Useless to the State: "Social Problems" and Social Engineering in Nationalist Nanjing, 1927–1937*. Cambridge, MA: Harvard University Asia Center and distributed by Harvard University Press.

Liu, Baocheng. 1997. 'The practice of establishing urban resident minimum livelihood guarantee system (*Jianli chengzhen jumin zuidi shenghuo baozhang zhidu de zuofa*)'. *China Civil Affairs (Zhongguo Minzheng)* 4: 15.

Liu, Pengcheng. 2007a. 'NPC Representative Zhang Lin: We ought to acclerate the development of a "Social Relief Law" (*Zhang Lin rendaibiao: ying jiakuai zhiding "shehui jiuzhu fa"*)'. *China Society News (Zhongguo Shehui Bao)*, 15 March 2007.

Liu, S. 2002. 'Zhu Rongji: Complete the social security system experiement, do well employment and re-employment work (*Zhu Rongji: Wanshan shebao tixi shidian, zuohao jiuye he zaijiuye gongzuo*)'. *People's Daily (Renmin Ribao)*, 25 July 2002, 1.

Liu, Yunyan. 2004. 'Fujian Province comprehensively establishes rural dibao system (*Fujian sheng quanmian jianli nongcun dibao zhidu*)'. *China Society News (Zhongguo Shehui Bao)*, 19 Februaury 2004, 1.

Liu, Yuting and Fulong Wu. 2006. 'The State, Institutional Transition and the Creation of New Urban Poverty in China'. *Social Policy and Administration* 40 (2): 121–137.

Liu, Zheng. 2007b. 'Rural Dibao: The major system arrangements for social relief (*Nongcun dibao: shehui jiuzhude zhongda zhidu anpai*)'. *China Civil Affairs (Zhongguo Minzheng)*, no date.

Lowndes, Vivien. 1996. 'Varieties of new institutionalism: A critical appraisal'. *Public Administration* 74: 181–197.

Lü, Yidian. 1998. 'Reflections on carrying out the Minimum Livelihood Guarantee (*Shishi Zuidi Shenghuo Baozhang Zhidu de Sikao*)'. *China Civil Affairs (Zhongguo Minzheng)* 1998 (4): 20.

Lü, Zhangping. 2003. 'Ought to establish and perfect dibao relief funds active examination mechanisms (*Ying Jianli Wanshang Dibao Jiuzhu Jin Dongtai Hecha Jizhi*)'. *China Civil Affairs (Zhongguo Minzheng)* 2003 (2): 45.

Luo, Yuanjie. 2003. 'Urban MLG work ought to carefully combine seven parts (*Chengshi Dibao Gongzuo Ying Zhuyi Qige Jiehe*)'. *China Civil Affairs (Zhongguo Minzheng)* 2003 (11): 44.

Ma, Jinhong. 1998. 'A few points on the carrying out of the urban Minimum Livelihood Guarantee system (*Shishi Chengshi Zuidi Shenghuo Baozhang Zhidu de Jidian Kanfa*)'. *China Civil Affairs (Zhongguo Minzheng)* 1998 (12): 27.

March, James and Johan Olsen. 1984. 'The new institutionalism: Organizational factors in political life'. *American Political Science Review* 78 (3): 734–749.

MCA. 1995. Ministry of Civil Affairs document number 14: Circular regarding implementing the spirit of the 10th National Civil Affairs Conference (*Minbanfa (1994) 14 Hao: Minzhengbu Guanyu Guanche Di Shi Ci Quanguo Minzheng Huiyi Jingshen de Tongzhi 16/05/1994*).

MCA. 1998. 'Developments in civil affairs matters from the ninth five year plan and 2010 development goals (*Minzheng Shiye Fazhan "Jiuwu" Jihua he 2010 Nian Yuanyin Mubiao Gangyao 1996*)'. In *Chengshi Jumin Zuidi Shenghuo Baozhang Zhidu Wenjian Zike Huibian 1*, edited by Minzhengbu Jiuzai Jiujisi, 12. Beijing: Minzhengbu Jiuzai Jiujisi.

MCA. 1999. 'MCA circular regarding accelerating the establishing and completion of the urban resident MLG system (*Minjiufa (1999) 4 Hao: Minzhengbu Guanyu Jiakuai Jianli yu Wanshan Chengshi Jumin Zuidi Shenghuo Baozhang Zhidude Tongzhi 28/01/1999*)'. Beijing: MCA.

MCA. 2000a. 'Civil affairs document (2000) no. 11: Circular regarding implementing the "Urban Resident MLG Regulations" to step-by-step standardise and perfect the urban resident MLG system (*Minfa (2000) 11 Hao: Guanyu Shenru Guanche 'Chengshi Jumin Zuidi Shenghuo Baozhang Tiaolie' Jin yi bu Guifan Wanshan Chengshi Jumin Zuidi Shenghuo Baozhang Zhidude Tongzhi (14/01/2000)*)'. Beijing: MCA.

MCA. 2000b. 'Office for the Department of Disaster and Social Relief (1999) document number 7: Circular from the Department of Disaster and Social Relief, Ministry of Civil Affairs, regarding establishing an information management system for the the urban resident minimum livelihood guarantee system (*Minjiuban (1999) 7 Hao: Minzhengbu Jiuzai Jiujisi Guanyu Jianli Chengshi Jumin Zuidi Shenghuo Baozhang Zhidu Xinxi Guanli Xitongde Tongzhi*)'. In *Chengshi Jumin Zuidi Shenghuo Baozhang Zhidu Wenjian Zike Huibian 3*, edited by Minzhengbu Jiuzai Jiujisi, 28–29. Beijing: Minzhengbu Jiuzai Jiujisi.

MCA. 2001a. 'MCA circular regarding developing urban resident MLG inspetion and supervisory work (*Minfa (2001) 192 Hao: Minzhengbu Guanyu Gan Kaizhan Chengshi Jumin Zuidi Shenghuo Baozhang Gongzuo Jianzu Diaocha Huodongde Tongzhi (25/07/2001)*)'. In *Chengshi Jumin Zuidi Shenghuo Baozhang Zhidu Wenjian Zike Huibian*, edited by Minzhengbu Jiuzai Jiujisi, 84–85. Beijing: Minzhengbu Jiuzai Jiujisi.

MCA. 2001b. 'MCA circular regarding step-by-step carrying out well 2001 work (*Minfa (2001) 16 Hao: Minzhengbu Guanyu Jinyibu Zuohao 2001 Nian Chengshi Jumin Zuidi Shenghuo Baozhang Gongzuode Tongzhi (22/01/2001)*)'. In *Chengshi Jumin Zuidi Shenghuo Baozhang Zhidu Wenjian Zike Huibian 5*, 80–83. Beijing: Minzhengbu Jiuzai Jiujisi.

MCA. 2001c. 'Minbanfa (2001) 87 Hao: Guowuyuan Bangongting Guanyu Jinyibu Jiaqiang Chengshi Jumin Shenghuo Baozhang Gongzuode Tonggzhi (12/11/2001)'. Beijing: MCA.

MCA. 2001d. 'Office of the MCA circular regarding accelerating the establishing of the urban resident MLG information management system (*Minbanhan (2000) 98 Hao: Minzhengbu Bangongting Guanyu Jiakuai Jianli Chengshi Jumin Zuidi Shenghuo Baozhang Xinxi Guanli Xitongde Tongzhi (14/06/2000)*)'. Beijing: MCA.

MCA. 2001e. 'Office of the MCA circular regarding carrying out well next years budget plan and establishing MLG target household record system (*Minzhengbu Bangongting Guanyu Zuohao Mingnian Chengshi Dibao Zijin Yongkuan Jihua he Jianli Chengshi Dibao Duixiang Jiating Bei'an Zhidude Tongzhi (19/12/2001)*)'. In *Chengshi Jumin Zuidi Shenghuo Baozhang Zhidu Wenjian Zike Huibian*, edited by Minzhengbu Jiuzai Jiujisi, 390–392. Beijing: Minzhengbu Jiuzai Jiujisi.

MCA. 2001f. 'Office of the MCA circular regarding the report on all levels of government MLG work situation (*Minbanhan (2001) 126 Hao: Minzhengbu Bangongting Guanyu Tongbao Gedi Chengshi Jumin Zuidi Shenghuo Baozhang Gongzuo Jinzhan Qingkuangde Tongzhi*)'. In *Chengshi Jumin Zuidi Shenghuo Baozhang Zhidu Wenjian Zike Huibian 5*, 86–87. Beijing: Minzhengbu Jiuzai Jiujisi.

MCA. 2002a. 'MCA circular regarding step-by-step strengthening the construction of the urban resident MLG information system (*Minfa (2002) 36 Hao: Minzhengbu Guanyu Jinyibu Jiaqiang Chengshi Jumin Shenghuo Baozhang Xinxi Xitong Jianshede Tongzhi (06/03/2002)*)'. Beijing: MCA. Available online at www.mca.gov.cn (last modified 16 March 2007, accessed 16 March 2007).

MCA. 2002b. 'Shehui Jiuzhu he Shehui Fuli: Chengshi Jumin Shenghuo Baozhang Zhidu'. In *Zhongguo Minzheng 2002 Nianjian*, 171–178. Beijing: MCA.

MCA. 2003a. '2003 Nian Chengshi Jumin Zuidi Shenghuo Baozhang Zhidu Jiben Gongzuode Qingkuang'. In *Zhongguo Minzheng 2003 Nianjian*, 236–239. Beijing: Zhongguo Shehui Chubanshe.

MCA. 2003b. 'Circular regarding implementing relief for 2003 ordinary high school graduates facing difficulties (*Minbanhan (2003) 116 Hao: Guanyu dui 2003 Nian Putong Gaodeng Xuexiao Kunnan Biye Shishi Lingshi Jiuzhude Tongzhi (17/07/2003)*)'. Available online at http://www.moe.gov.cn/s78/A15/xss_left/moe_780/s3265/201001/t20100128_80094.html (accessed 16 March 2007).

MCA. 2003c. 'MCA circular regarding matters related to establishing an urban medical relief system (*Minbanhan (2003) 105 Hao: Minzhengbu Bangongting Guanyu Jianli Chengshi Yiliao Jiuzhu Zhidu youguan Shixiangde Tongzhi (09/07/2003)*)'. In *Zhongguo Minzheng 2003 Nianjian*, edited by MCA, 403. Beijing: MCA.

MCA. 2003d. 'MCA circular regarding regulations in accordance with State Council demands to strengthen and perfect the MLG system (*Minhan (2003) 58 Hao: Minzhengbu Guanyu Anzhao Guowuyuan Yaoqiu Jinyibu Jianquan Chengshi Dibao Zhidude Tongzhi (25/03/2003)*)'. Beijing: MCA.

MCA. 2007a. 'MCA publishes circular demanding MLG recipients living situation be investigated'. Available online at www.mca.gov.cn/news/content/recent/200795154324.htm (accessed 5 September 2007).

MCA. 2007b. Social Relief Law, Draft (*Shehui jiuzhu fa, cao'an*), edited by Legal Office of the Ministry of Civil Affairs. Beijing: MCA.

MCA. 2011. 'Guidance on the further regulation of the urban and rural resident MLG standard system and adjustment work (*Guanyu jin yi bu chengxiang jumin zuidi shenghuo baozhang biaozhun zhidu he tiaozheng gongzuo de zhidao yijian*)'. Beijing: MCA. Available online at www.mca.gov.cn (accessed 19 May 2011).

MCA. 2016. 'MLG data (Dibao shuju)'. Beijing: MCA. Available online at http://www.mca.gov.cn/article/sj/tjjb/dbsj/ (accessed 1 January 2017).

MCA and MOF. 2008. 'MCA, MoF circular regarding the proper arrangement for the further increase of urban and rural MLG subsidies level for the poor masses in basic living difficulties (*Minzhengbu Caizheng bu guanyu jinyibu tigao cheng dibao buzhu shuiping tuoshan anpai dangqian kunnan qunzhong jiben shenghuo de tongzhi*)'. Beijing: MCA. Available online at http://dbs.mca.gov.cn (accessed 9 August 2010).

Mertha, Andrew. 2009. '"Fragmented authoritarianism 2.0": Political pluralization in the Chinese policy process'. *The China Quarterly* 200: 995–1012.

MoF. 2000a. 'Fiscal and Social Document (1999) No. 131: MoF, MoLSS, MCA circular regarding strengthening state owned enterprise laid-off worker basic livelihood guarantee, urban resident MLG funds and retired workers basic pension funds use (*Caishezi (1999) 131 Hao: Caizhengbu, Laodong he Shehui Baozhangbu, Minzhengbu Guanyu Jiaqiang Guoyou Qiye Xiagang Zhigong Jiben Shenghuo Baozhang Chengzheng Jumin Zuidi Shenghuo Baozhang Zijin he Qiye Tuixi Renyuan Jiben Yanlao Zijin Shiyong Guanli*)'. In *Chengshi Jumin Zuidi Shenghuo Baozhang Zhidu Wenjian Zike Huibian 3*, edited by Minzhengbu Jiuzai Jiujisi, 20–23. Beijing: Minzhengbu Jiuji Jiuzaisi.

MoF. 2000b. Tiaozheng Shouru Fenpei Zhengce de Juti Cuoshi (15/07/1999). Beijing.

MoF. 2005. *Ministry of Finance Statistical Yearbook (Caizheng tongji nianjian)*. Beijing: China MoF Press (*Zhongguo Caizhengbu Chubanshe*).

MoF. 2007. *Ministry of Finance Statistical Yearbook (Caizheng tongji niajian)*. Beijing: Caizhengbu Chubanshe.

MoLSS. 2000. 'Laoshebufa (1999) 13 Hao: Laodong he Shehui Baozhang, Minzhengbu, Caozhengbu Guanyu Zuohao Guoyou Qiye Xiagang Zhigong Jiben Shenghuo Baozhang Qiye Baoxian he Chengshi Jumin Shenghuo Baozhang Zhi du~ Jie Gongzuode Tongzhi (no date)'. In *Chengshi Jumin Zuidi Shenghuo Baozhang Zhidu Wenjian Zike Huibian 3*, edited by Minzhengbu Jiuzai Jiujisi, 9–12. Beijing: Minzhengbu Jiuzai Jiujisi.

Nathan, Andrew J. 1973. 'A factionalism model for CCP politics'. *The China Quarterly* (53): 34–66.

Nathan, Andrew J. 1976. 'Reply'. *The China Quarterly* (65): 114–117.

Naughton, B. 2002. 'Zhu Rongji: The twilight of a brilliant career'. *China Leadership Monitor* 1.

NBS. 2008. 'China Statisitical Yearbook 2008'. Available online at www.stats.gov.cn/ tjsj/ndsj/2008/indeexh.htm (accessed 11 August 2016).

NBS. 2016. 'National Data (Guojia shuju)'. National Bureau of Statistics of China. Available online at data.stats.gov.cn (accessed 31 May 2016).

Ngok, Kinglun. 2016. 'Social policy making in China'. In *China's Social Policy: Transformation and challenges*, edited by Kinglun Ngok and Chak Kwan Chan, 14–30. London: Routledge.

NPC. 1998. 'The Tenth National People's Congress approval for the People's Republic of China ninth five year plan of national economic and social development and the 2010 development goals (*Quanguo Renda Di Si Ci Huiyi Pizhun de "Zhonghua Renmin Gongheguo Guomin Jingji he Shehui Fazhan Jiuwu Jihua he 2010 Nian Yuanyin Mubiao Gangyao 17/03/1996*)'. In *Chengshi Jumin Zuidi Shenghuo Baozhang Zhidu Wenjian Zike Huibian 1*, edited by Minzhengbu Jiuzai Jiujisi, 3. Beijing: Minzhengbu Jiuzai Jiujisi.

NPC. 1999. *Constitution of the People's Republic of China (Zhonghua Renmin Gongheguo xianfa)*. Beijing: Foreign Language Press (*Waiwen Chubanshe*).

Oksenberg, Michel. 2002. 'China's political system: Challenges of the twenty-first century'. In *The Nature of Chinese Politics: From Mao to Jiang*, edited by J. Unger, 193–208. Armonk, NY: M. E. Sharpe.

Paine, L. 1992. 'The educational policy process: A case study of bureaucratic action in China'. In *Bureaucracy, Politics, and Decision Making in Post-Mao China*, edited by K. G. Liebertha and D. M. Lampton, 181–215. Berkeley: University of California Press.

Peters, B. Guy. 2005. *Institutional Theory in Political Science: The 'New' Institutionalism*. 2nd edition. London: Continuum.

Pye, Lucien W. 2002. 'Jiang Zemin's style of rule: Go for stability, monopolize power and settle for limited effectiveness'. In *The Nature of Chinese Politics: From Mao to Jiang*, edited by J. Unger, 209–216. London: M. E. Sharpe.

Qi, Jinming. 1999. 'Jilin Province establishes in general a rural MLG system (*Jilin Sheng – Nongcun zuidi shenghuo baozhang zhidu pubian jianli*)'. *China Society News (Zhongguo Shehui Bao)*, 17 March 1999, 2.

Qian, Zhihong and Tai-Chee Wong. 2000. 'The rising urban poverty: A dilemma of market reforms in China'. *Journal of Contemporary China* 9 (23): 113–125.

Qiao, Xianhua. 2003. 'MLG procedures ought to be equal (*Dibao Caozuo Chenxu Ying Hefa*)'. *China Civil Affairs (Zhongguo Minzheng)* 2003 (2): 37.

Qu, Tianjun. 2017. 'Poverty alleviation in China – plan and action'. *China Journal of Social Work* 10 (1): 79–85.

Ravallion, Martin and Shaohua Chen. 2015. 'Benefit incidence with incentive effects, measurement errors and latent heterogenity: A case study of China'. *Journal of Public Economics* 128: 124–132.

Rogers, Sarah. 2014. 'Betting on the strong: Local government resource allocation in China's poverty counties'. *Journal of Rural Studies* 36: 197–206.

Rogers, Sarah. 2016. 'The end of poverty in China?' *Research Brief.* Melbourne: Centre for Contemporary Chinese Studies.

Rowe, W. T. 1990. 'Modern Chinese social history in comparative perspective'. In *Heritage of China: Contemporary Perspectives on Chinese Civilization*, edited by P. S. Ropp, 242–262. Berkeley: University of California Press.

Sabatier, Paul A. 1991. 'Towards better theories of the policy process'. *Political Science and Politics* 24 (2): 147–156.

Sabatier, Paul A. (ed.). 1999. *Theories of the Policy Process.* Oxford: Westview Press.

Sabatier, P. and H. C. Jenkins-Smith. 1993. *Policy Change and Learning.* Boulder, CO: Westview Press.

Sabatier, P. and H. C. Jenkins-Smith. 1994. 'Evaluating the Advocacy Coalition Framework'. *Journal of Public Policy* 14 (2): 175–203.

Saich, A. 2008. *Providing Public Goods in Transitional China.* London: Palgrave Macmillan.

Saich, T. 2004. *Governance and Politics in China.* Basingstoke: Palgrave Macmillan.

Saich, T. 2011. *Governance and Politics in China.* 3rd edition. Basingstoke: Palgrave Macmillan.

Saunders, Peter and Xiaoyuan Shang. 2001. 'Social security reform in China's transition to a market economy'. *Social Policy and Administration* 35 (3): 274–289.

Saunders, Peter and Lujun Sun. 2006. 'Poverty and hardship among the aged in urban China'. *Social Policy and Administration* 40 (2): 138–157.

Shambaugh, D. 2009. *China's Communist Party: Atrophy and Adaptation.* Washington, DC: Woodrow Wilson Center Press.

Shanghai-BCA. 1997. 'Establishing a complete social assistance work system and guarantee urban residents basic livelihood (*Jianli jianquan shehui jiuzhu gongzuo tixi, baozhang chengzhen jumin jiben shenghuo*)'. In *Urban Resident Minimum Livelihood Gurantee System Document Collection (Chengshi jumin zuidi shenghuo baozhang zhidu wenjian zike huibian)*, edited by Minzhengbu Jiuzai Jiujisi, 85–91. Beijing: Minzhengbu Jiuzai Jiujisi.

Shanghai-RenminZhengfu. 1996. 'Shanghai social assistance methods (*Shanghai shi shehui jiuzhu banfa*)'. In *Urban Resident Minimum Livelihood Gurantee System Document Collection (Chengshi jumin zuidi shenghuo baozhang zhidu wenjian zike huibian)*, edited by Minzhengbu Jiuzai Jiujisi, 197–203. Beijing: Minzhengbu Jiuzai Jiujisi.

Shi, Derong. 2002. *Trans-Century China Civil Affairs Matters: Shanghai Status (Kuashijide Zhongguo Minzheng shiye: Shanghai juan).* Beijing: China Society Publisher (*Zhongguo shehui chubanshe*).

Shu, Shunlin. 2002. 'National urban MLG fundamental reality of "Ought to protect, fully protect" (*Quanguo Chengshi Dibao Chubu Shixian Yingbao Jinbao*)'. *China Civil Affairs (Zhongguo Minzheng)* 2002 (8): 38–39.

Social Relief Department, Ministry of Civil Affairs. 2013. 'Rural minimum livelihood guarantee system development report (*Nongcun zuidi shenghuo baozhang zhidu fazhan baogao*)'. In *China Social Relief Development Report 2013*, edited by Wang Zhikun, 38–46. Beijing: Zhongguo Shehui Chunbanshe.

Solinger, Dorothy J. 2001. 'Why we cannot count the "unemployed"'. *The China Quarterly* 167: 671–688.

Solinger, Dorothy J. 2005. 'Path dependency reexamined: Chinese welfare policy in the transition to unemployment'. *Comparative Politics* 38 (1): 83–101.

Solinger, Dorothy J. 2008. 'The *dibao* recipients: Mollified anti-emblem of urban modernisation'. *China Perspectives* 4: 36–46.

Solinger, Dorothy J. 2011. '*Dibaohu* in distress: The meagre Minimum Livelihood Guarantee system in Wuhan'. In *China's Changing Welfare Mix: Local Perspectives*, edited by Beatriz Carrillo and Jane Duckett, 36–63. London: Routledge.

Solinger, Dorothy J. 2013. 'Streets as suspect: State skepticism and the current losers in urban China'. *Critical Asian Studies* 45 (1): 3–26.

Solinger, Dorothy J. 2015. 'Three welfare models and current Chinese social assistance: Confucian justificaitons, variable applications'. *The Journal of Asian Studies* 74 (4): 977–999.

Solinger, Dorothy J. 2017. 'Manipulating China's "Minimum Livelihood Guarantee" – Political shifts in a program for the poor in the period of Xi Jinping'. *China Perspectives* 2: 47–57.

Solinger, Dorothy J. and Yiyang Hu. 2012. 'Welfare, wealth and poverty in urban China: The *dibao* and its differential disbursement'. *The China Quarterly* 211: 741–764.

Song, Zhiqiang. 2001. 'Assistant Director Song Zhiqiang: Course outline for national urban resident MLG work (*Minzhengbu Jiuzai Jiujisi Fusizhang Song Zhiqiang: quanguo chengshi jumin zuidi shenghuo baozhang gongzuo ban jingke tigang (19/03/2001)*)'. In *Chengshi Jumin Zuidi Shenghuo Baozhang Zhidu Wenjian Zike Huibian 5*, 136–143. Beijing: Minzhengbu Jiuzai Jiujisi.

Stapleton, Kristin. 2000. *Civilzing Chengdu: Chinese Urban Reform, 1895–1937*. London: Harvard University Press.

State Council. 1997. 'State Council publication number 29 (1997): State Council circular regarding the establishing of a national urban resident Minimum Livelihood Guarantee system (*Guofa (1997) 29 Hao: Guowuyuan Guanyu Quanguo Jianli Chengshi Jumin Zuidi Shenghuo Baozhang Zhidu de Tongzhi*)'. Beijing: MCA.

State Council. 1999. 'Urban resident Minimum Livelihood Guarantee regulations (*Chengshi Jumin Zuidi Shenghuo Baozhang Zhidu Tiaolie (28/09/1999)*)'. Beijing: MCA.

State Council. 2006. 'Regulations for the rural Five Guarantees (*Nongcun wubao gongyang gongzuo tiaoli*)'. Available online at http://www.gov.cn/zwgk/2006-01/26/content_172438.htm (accessed 31 January 2017).

State Council. 2007. 'State Council circular regarding the establishing of a rural minimum livelihood guarantee system'. Xinhuanet. Available online at http://news.xinhuanet. com/newscenter/2007-08/13/content_6524280.htm (accessed 14 April 2016).

State Council. 2014. 'Social relief Temporary Measures (*Shehui jiuzhu zanxing banfa*)'. State Council. Available online at http://www.gov.cn/zwgk/2014-02/27/ content_2622770.htm (accessed 31 January 2017).

Tang, Jun. 1998. 'China's urban resident minimum livelihood guarantee system research report (*Zhongguo chengshi jumin zuidi shenghuo baozhang zhidu yanjiu baogao*)'. In *Shehui fuli huangpishu: Zhongguo shehui fuli yu shehui shehui jinbu baogao 1998*, edited by Zhengxin Shi, 94–118. Beijing: Social Science Studies Publishers (*Shehui kexue xuewen xian chubanshe*).

Tang, Jun. 2001a. 'China urban social relief system report (*Zhongguo chengzhen shehui jiuzhu zhidu baogao*)'. In *China Social Security Development Report 1997–2001 (Zhongguo shehui baozhang fazhan baogao 1997-2001)*, edited by Chen Jiagui. Beijing: Social Science Studies (*Shehui kexue xuewenxian chubanshe*).

Tang, Jun. 2001b. 'The problem of urban poverty and the social assistance system'. *Social Security System* (7): 30–34.

Tang, Jun. 2003. *Report on Poverty and Anti-Poverty in Urban China (Zhongguo Chengshi Pinkun yu Fupinkun Baogao)*. Beijing: Huaxia Publishers.

Tang, Jun. 2004. 'Completing the social relief system thoughts and measures (*Wanshang shehui jiuzhu zhidude yikua yu duice*)'. In *Green Book of Chinese Social Security: Chinese Social Security System Development Report (Shehui baozhang lupishu: Zhongguo shehui baozhang fazhan baogao)*, edited by Jiagui Chen and Zhengzhong Wang. Beijing: Social Science Studies (*Shehui kexue xuewenxian chubanshe*).

Tang, Jun. 2005. *Urban MLG System, History, Current Situation and Future (Chengxiang dibao zhidu, lishi, xianzhuang yu qianzhan)*. Bejing: CASS.

Teets, Jessica C. 2015. 'The politics of innovation in China: Local officials as policy entrepreneurs'. *Issues and Studies* 51 (2): 79–109.

Tong, Weizhong, Bao Shouqing, Wu Zhengshan and Yu Jing. 1998. 'Comprehensively carry out the rural MLG system (*Quanmian shishi nongcun zuidi shenghuo baozhang zhidu*)'. *China Society News (Zhongguo Shehui Bao)*, 19 February 1998, 3.

Tsou, Tang. 1976. 'Prolegomenon to the study of informal groups in CCP politics'. *The China Quarterly* (65): 98–114.

Unger, Jonathan. 1985–1986. 'The decollectivization of the Chinese countryside: A survey of twenty-eight villages'. *Pacific Affairs* 58 (4): 585–606.

Wallace, Jeremy L. 2014. *Cities and Stability: Urbanization, Redistribution, and Regime Survival in China*. Oxford: Oxford University Press.

Wang, Bangwu. 2003. 'A few points regarding the construction of standardised MLG administration (*Dui Dibao Guifanhua Guanlide Jidian Jianli*)'. *China Civil Affairs (Zhongguo Minzheng)* 2003 (4): 39.

Wang, Laizhu. 2007a. Speech regarding 'Social Relief Law (draft)', edited by Legal Office of the Ministry of Civil Affairs. Beijing: MCA.

Wang, Ming. 2007b. 'Price subsidies show the government understands people's livelihood difficulties (*Wujia butie jinxian zhengfu liaojie minsheng zhijide guiji*)'. *China Society News (Zhongguo Shehui Bao)*, 17 September 2007, 1.

Wang, Pingping, Xin Xu and Yanhong Hao. 2015. 'Issues in Chinese rural poverty standards research (*Zhongguo nongcun pinkun biaozhun wenti yanjiu*)'. National Bureau of
Statistics. Available online at http://www.stats.gov.cn/tjzs/tjsj/tjcb/dysj/201509/
t20150902_1239121.html (accessed 1 August 2017).

Wang, Weiping. 2006. *Social Relief Studies (Shehui jiuzhu xue)*. Beijing: Qunxin Press
(*Qunxin chubanshe*).

Wang, Yaping and Alan Murie. 2011. 'The new affordable and social housing provision
system in China: Implicatins for comparative housing studies'. *International Journal of
Housing Policy* 11 (3): 237–254.

Wang, Zhaoli, Cui Jichao, Chen Liang, Qie Jianjun and Wei Anmin. 1994. 'Implement
the Five Guanrantee Regulations, carry out the Five Guarantee Policy (*Guanche
Wubao Tiaoli, Luoshi Wubao Zhengce*)'. *China Society News (Zhongguo Shehui Bao)*,
25 May 1994, 2.

Wang, Zhenyao and Wang Hui. 1998. 'Five relationships to deal with when carrying
out the urban resident Minimum Livelihood Guarantee funds (*Luoshi Chengshi Jumin
Zuidi Shenghuo Baozhang Zijin Ying Chuli Hao Wuge Guanxi*)'. *China Civil Affairs
(Zhongguo Minzheng)* 1998 (3): 18–19.

Wang, Zhikun. 1999. 'The urban resident Minimum Livelihood Guarantee enters a legal
systemisation administrative track (*Chengshi Jumin Zuidi Shenghuo Baozhang Buru
Fazhihua Guanli Guidao*)'. *China Civil Affairs (Zhongguo Minzheng)* 1999 (11): 18–19.

Weaver, R. Kent. 1988. *Automatic Government: The Politics of Indexation*. Washington,
DC: The Brookings Institution.

Weiyuanhui, Shanghai Tongzhi. 2005. *9th Shanghai Annual (Shanghai Tongzhi 9)*.
Shanghai: Shanghai Social Science Academy (*Shanghai shehui kexueyuan chubanshe*).

Wong, Linda. 1998. *Marginalisation in Social Welfare in China*. London: Routledge.

Wong, Linda. 2001. 'Welfare policy reform'. In *The Market in Chinese Social Policy*,
edited by Linda Wong and Norman Flynn, 38–62. New York: Palgrave.

Wong, Linda and Kinglun Ngok. 2006. 'Social policy between plan and market: Xiagang
(off-duty employment) and the policy of the re-employment service centres in China'.
Social Policy and Administration 40 (2): 158–173.

Wong, R. Bin. 1982. 'Food riots in the Qing dynasty'. *The Journal of Asian Studies* 41
(4): 767–788.

Wong, Yu-Cheung, Chen Honglin and Zeng Qun. 2014. 'Social assistance in Shanghai:
Dynamics between social protection and informal employment'. *International Journal
of Social Welfare* 23 (3): 333–341.

World Bank. 2015. 'FAQs: global poverty line update'. Available online at http://www.
worldbank.org/en/topic/poverty/brief/global-poverty-line-faq (accessed 1 August
2017).

World Bank. 2017. 'World Bank data'. World Bank Group. Available online at http://
data.worldbank.org/ (accessed 31 January 2017).

Wu, Alfred M. and M. Ramesh. 2014. 'Poverty reduction in urban China: The impact of
cash transfers'. *Social Policy and Society* 13 (2): 285–299.

Wu, Chunguo. 2001. 'The three issues currently affecting rural dibao work (*Nongcun
dibao gongzuo zhong cunzaide san ge wenti*)'. *China Society News (Zhongguo Shehui Bao)*.

Wu, Guimin. 1998. 'Energetically push, grasp well detailed practice – Vice Minister Fan Baojun talks on social assitance for impoverished urban residents (*Jiji Tuijin Zhuahao Zuoxi - Fan Baojun Fubuzhang Tan Chengzheng Pinkun Jumin Shehui Jiuji*)'. *Zhongguo Minzheng* 1998 (7): 6–7.

Xi, Ruixin. 1998. 'Vice Minister Xi Ruixin's speech at national meeting of civil affairs department and bureaux heads regarding establishing and implementing the urban resident Minimum Livelihood Guarantee line system (*Xi Ruixin Fubuzhang zai Quanguo Minzhengting(ju) Zhang Huiyi Shang guanyu Jianli he Shishi Chengshi Zuidi Shenghuo Baozhangxian Zhidu de Jianghua 01/1996*)'. In *Chengshi Jumin Zuidi Shenghuo Baozhang Zhidu Wenjian Zike Huibian 1*, edited by Minzhengbu Jiuzai Jiujisi, 82–94. Beijing: Minzhengbu Jiuzai Jiujisi.

Xinhuanet. 2006. 'The Central Committee of the CCP decision on several issues regarding the construction of a harmonious socialist society (*Zhonggong zhongyang guanyu goujian shehui zhuyi shehui ruogan zhangda wenti de jueding*)'. Available online at http://news.xinhuanet.com/politics/2006-10/18/content_5218639.htm (accessed 5 August 2016).

Yan, Jiaqi. 1995. 'The nature of Chinese authoritarianism'. In *Decision-making in Deng's China: Perspectives from Insiders*, edited by Carol Lee Hamrin and Shuisheng Zhao, 3–14. Armonk, NY: M. E. Sharpe.

Yan, Kun. 2016. *Poverty Alleviation in China: A Theoretical and Empirical Study*, Research Series on the Chinese Dream and China's Development Path. Berlin: Springer.

Yang, Tuan. 2003. *From without Position to Leadership – The Reality of Ten Years of China's Social Relief (Cong Wuwei dao lingpao – Zhongguo shehui jiuzhu shi nian jishi)*. Beijing: Chinese Academy of Social Sciences.

Yang, Yanyin. 2002a. 'Minzhengbu Fubuzhang Yang Yanyin zai Quanguo Chengshi Dibao ji Jiuzai Gongzuo Huiyi Shangde Jianghua (21/02/2002)'. In *China Civil Affairs 2002 Yearbook (Zhongguo Minzheng 2002 Nianjian)*, edited by MCA, 62–70. Beijing: MCA.

Yang, Yanyin. 2002b. 'Vice-Minister Yang Yanyin's speech at the national urban resident MLG work meeting (*Minzhengbu Fubuzhang Yang Yanyin zai Quanguo Chengshi Jumin Zuidi Shenghuo Baozhang Gongzuo Huiyi Shangde Jianghua (22/10/2002)*)'. In *Zhongguo Minzheng 2002 Nianjian*, edited by MCA, 70–77. Beijing: MCA.

Zhang, Haomiao. 2015. 'The social assistance in urban China: A critcial review'. *International Journal of Sociology and Social Policy* 35 (5/6): 403–418.

Zhang, Haomiao. 2016a. 'Frustration, shame, and gratitude: The meaning of social assistance for women recipients in China'. *Asian Women* 32 (1): 53–75.

Zhang, Haomiao. 2016b. 'Social assistance for poor children in urban China: A qualitative study from the recipients' perspective'. *Children and Youth Services Review* 64: 122–127.

Zhang, Shoujia. 2002a. 'Obligatory accelerate the complete establishing of temporary relief measures system (*Yingjinkuai Jianli Jianquan Linshi Jiuji Zhidu*)'. *China Civil Affairs (Zhongguo Minzheng)* 2002 (1): 51.

Zhang, Wenjie. 2016c. 'The evolution of China's pay inequality from 1987 to 2012'. *Journal of Current Chinese Affairs* 45 (2): 183–217.

Zhang, Xiulan, Xu Yuebin and Wang Xiaobo. 2012. 'The MLG system and rural anti-poverty (*Zuidi shenghuo baozhang zhidu and nongcun fanpinkun*)'. In *China Social Security Development Report No. 5: 2012 (Zhongguo Shehui Boazhang Fazhan Baogao No. 5: 2012)*, edited by Yanzhong Wang, 152–175. Beijing: Social Science Academic Press (*Shehui Kexue Wenxian Chubanshe*).

Zhang, Xixi (Cartoonist) and Yicun (Reporter) Gao. 2007. 'Price rises demand for a perfected temporary relief system (*Wujia shangzhang huhuan wanshan linshi jiuzhu zhidu*)'. *Zhongguo Shehui Bao*, 8 August 2007, 3.

Zhang, Y. 2002b. *Trans-Century China Civil Affairs Matters: Liaoning Volume (Kuashijide Zhongguo Minzheng shiye: Liaoning juan)*. Beijing: China Social Press.

Zhang, Yabo. 2013. 'Draft social relief law is not mature and "vetoed" by top level (*Shehui jiuzhu cao'an yin buchengshu zhongyang gaoceng "foujue")*'. Available online at http://news.cn.yahoo.com/ypen/20101124/98171.html (accessed 18 June 2013).

Zhao, Guochao. 1997. 'Minister Duoji Cairang points out during work inspection in Henan (*Duoji Cairang buzhang zai Henan kaocha gongzuo shi zhichu*)'. *China Society News (Zhongguo Shehui Bao)*, 6 May 1997, 1.

Zhao, Hongwen. 2002. 'Urban dibao: Accelerating the reality of "Ought to protect, fully protect" (*Chengshi Dibao: Jiankuai Shixian Yingbao Jinbao*)'. *China Civil Affairs (Zhongguo Minzheng)* 2002 (3): 19–22.

Zhao, Liqiu, Yu Guo and Ting Shao. 2017. 'Can the minimum income living standard guarantee scheme enable the poor to escape the poverty trap in rural China?' *International Journal of Social Welfare* Online Early: 1–15.

Zhong, Min. 2002. 'Dauntless and persistent: Winning initial success in the "Ought to protect, fully protect" campaign by overcoming all obstacles (*Zaiji Zaili: Dawang Yingbao Jinbao Gongjianzhan*)'. *China Civil Affairs (Zhongguo Minzheng)* 2002 (5): 10–12.

Zhong, Renyao. 2005. *Social Relief and Social Welfare (Shehui jiuzhu yu shehui fuli)*. Shanghai: Shanghai University of Finance Press (*Shanghai caijing daxue chubanshe*).

Zhou, Li. 2006. 'Social relief legislation (*Shehui jiuzhu lifa*)'. *China Society News (Zhongguo Shehui Bao)*, 6 September 2006, 5–8.

Zhu, Weiwei. 2003. 'Constructing an urban povery alleviation system with Chinese characteristics (*Gouzhu Zhongguo Tesede Chengshi Fupinkun Tixi*)'. *China Civil Affairs (Zhongguo Minzheng)* 2003 (1): 25–28.

Zhu, Xufeng. 2008. 'Strategy of Chinese policy entrepreneurs in the third sector: Challenges of "technical infeasibility"'. *Policy Sciences* 41: 315–334.

Zhu, Xufeng. 2016. 'In the name of "citizens": Civic activism and policy entrepreneurship of Chinese public intellectuals in the Hu-Wen era'. *Journal of Contemporary China* Online Early: 1–15.

Zhu, Yapeng. 2013. 'Policy entrepreneurship, institutional constraints, and local policy innovation in China'. *China Review* 13 (2): 97–122.

Zhu, Yapeng and Diwen Xiao. 2015. 'Policy entrepreneur and social policy innovation in China'. *The Journal of Chinese Sociology* 2 (10): 1–17.

Zhu, Yong and Sun Yuqin. 2002. 'Important work points for Dibao: To comprehensively push for standard administration (*Dibao Gongzuo Zhongdian: You Quanmian Tuijin Zhuanxiang Guifan Guanli*)'. *China Civil Affairs (Zhongguo Minzheng)* 2002 (11): 5.

Zhu, Yong, Ren Zhenxing and Zhao Hongwen. 2002. 'Shanghai: Establishing a modern social relief system (*Shanghai: Goujian xiandai shehui jiuzhu tixi*)'. *China Civil Affairs (Zhongguo Minzheng)* 2002 (9): 17–27.

Zou, Jiahua. 1998. 'Vice-Premier Zou Jianhua's speech at the establishing of the national urban resident MLG teleconference (*Zou Jiahua Fuzongli zai Quanguo Jianli Chengshi Jumin Zuidi Shenghuo Baozhang Zhidu Dianshedianhua Huiyi Shang de Jianghua 03/09/1997*)'. In *Chengshi Jumin Zuidi Shenghuo Baozhang Zhidu Wenjian Zike Huibian 1*, edited by Minzhengbu Jiuzai Jiujisi, 22–23. Beijing: Minzhengbu Jiuzai Jiujisi.

Index

administration
    limited administrative capacity for the
        rural *dibao*, 102
    malpractice by *dibao* administrators,
        119
    of the MLG by the Department of
        Disaster Relief and Social Assistance,
        82–3
    ranks of administrative agencies, 60
    uneven administration of the urban
        dibao, 68–70, 72

Barrientos, Armando, 127
Benxi Model, 68

care for the elderly, 43
central government
    dibao's increased dependence on
        support from, 112
    funding of the rural *dibao*, 101
    intervention in MLG policy (1999),
        74–6
    intervention in MLG policy (post-
        1997), 69
    perceptions of the responsiveness of
        dibao, 115–16
    state interventions for poverty
        alleviation, 42, 119–20
    subsidy of the urban MLG, 64
Chen, Janet, 22
Chen et al. (2013), 7
Chen Honglin, 3, 7
China Civil Affairs (ZGMZ), 69, 91

China Society News
    campaign on the urban MLG
        implementation (1997–9), 62–4
    countdown boxes for the urban *dibao*,
        63–4, 94
    coverage of food prices and *dibao*, 115
    coverage of the draft Social Relief Law,
        110
    coverage of the establishment of rural
        dibao, 90–2, 103
    storyboard article on how local officials
        should handle *dibao*, 117
Chinese Communist Party (CCP)
    ideological values of, 9, 12, 13–14, 40, 99
    the MLG and the state's overall policy
        aims, 54–5
    policy decisions and regime legitimacy,
        138–9, 140
    reforms of, 1, 4
    see also central government
Cho Mun Young, 3, 42
Chongqing Model, 68
classification guarantee measures (*fenlei
        baozhang cuoshi*)
    concept behind for recipient
        classification, 84–5
    development of, 33, 82
    Ministry of Civil Affairs (MCA)
        support for, 83
Confucian models, 43

Dalian Model, 28, 55, 56, 68, 70, 71
data collection on the *dibao*, 85

Deng Xiaoping, 40
Department for the Urban Resident MLG, 80
Department of Disaster Relief and Social Assistance (JZJJ)
  administration of the MLG, 82–3
  and the 'Ought to protect, fully protect' campaign, 80, 82, 83
dibao see Minimum Livelihood Guarantee (MLG); rural dibao; urban dibao
disabled, the
  within the classification guarantees for dibao, 84
  as one of the 'Three No's' categories, 24
  poverty alleviation for, 120–1, 123
  and the Social Relief Law, 110
  state support for in the Constitution, 25
Duoji Cairang
  commitment to the Social Relief Law, 111
  impact on support for MLG, 56–7
  limited political authority of, 134–5
  People's Daily editorial, 29
  personal intervention in Beijing's MLG implementation, 56
  personal intervention in Liaoning's MLG implementation, 56
  as policy entrepreneur, 53–4
  promotion of dibao adoption, 53–4, 65, 70
  promotion of rural dibao, 91
  speeches endorsing dibao, 7, 27–8, 51
  tactics for tackling challenges to MLG implementation, 54–6

education subsidies, 33
Eighth Five Year Plan, 47, 51
elite leaders
  generalist/specialist distinction, 80
  policy development by in pre-reform China, 8
  see also Duoji Cairang; Li Peng; Zhu Rongji

emergence of dibao
  official discourse of, 4–5, 7, 26, 132–3
  research on, 4, 7–8
  in Shanghai, 26–7, 47–51
  urban dibao, 97–9

Fewsmith, J., 108, 124, 129
Five Guarantees rural social assistance programme (wubao), 1, 24, 90, 91, 95–7
food prices
  consumer price index by category (urban), 114
  consumer price index for food (urban), 115
  dibao's responsiveness to via the MLG line, 114–16
  increases in (2007-8), 33–4, 114
  prices of basic foodstuffs, 114, 115
Fragmented Authoritarianism model (FA)
  applied to both urban and rural dibao, 136
  applied to policy development, 8–9, 133, 138
  criticism of, 11–12
  decision making and implementation, 10, 15–16
  as a flexible framework, 12, 133
  impact on institutionalisation of dibao, 121–6, 130–1, 137
  impact on the day-to-day running of the rural dibao, 101–2
  institutional elements of, 9
  and local innovation in Chinese policy, 47
  policy actor behaviour, 10–11, 82, 133
  political structure, impacts of, 9–10, 14–15, 64–5, 67
  and the unintended and unwanted outcomes of dibao, 68–73
  values and, 9, 13–14
funding of dibao
  consistency in and benefits of institutionalisation, 124

funding of *dibao* (*cont.*)
Dalian Model, 28, 55, 56, 68, 70, 71
during different iterations of the MLG, 5–6, **6**
as guaranteed by Zhu Rongji, 79, 80, 81–2
impact of weak local finances, 60–1, 72–3
increase to following SOE reforms, 78
increased spending on (1999–2003), 30, *31*, 73
increases from the Ministry of Finance, 29, 34, 74, 75, 80, 85
lack of resources for the implementation of, 72
regional variations in fiscal power, 68–71
for rural *dibao*, 93, 101
Shanghai model, 50, 68, 70
in urban areas (1997–9), 60
in urban areas (post-2000), 30, *32*
variations in urban *dibao* funding models, 68
Fuzhou Model, 68

Gao Qin, 3
global financial crisis, 114
Goodman, David S., 8
Guan Xinping, 72, 90, 91
guidance on the further regulation of the urban and rural resident MLG standard system and adjustment work (MCA, 2011), 34–5, 116–17
Guo Sujian, 11, 12
Guo Yu, 103

Han Deyun, 110
Harding, Harry, 8
harmonious socialist society discourse, 98, 99
household registration system (*hukou*)
agricultural (*nongye*) status, 23
non-agricultural/urban (*fei-nongye*) status, 23
rural–urban divide and, 43

Hu Jintao
harmonious socialist society discourse, 98, 99
values of the Hu regime, 90, 98–9
Huang Ju, 26, 47–50
Huang Xian, 138
Hubei province, 96

implementation
and adaptability to local conditions, 137
challenges to the implementation of urban *dibao*, 59–64, 68–9
China Society News' campaign on urban *dibao* implementation, 62–4
Duoji Cairang's personal intervention in *dibao* implementation, 54–6
within Fragmented Authoritarianism model, 10, 15–16
impacts of political structure on, 9–10, 14, 60
implementation process of urban *dibao* applied to the rural *dibao*, 100–2
institutional decision-making and, 10, 15–16
local government intransigence over, 86, 136–7
MCA strategies for (1997–9), 61–2, 65
MCA's lack of resources for, 72–3
newspaper coverage of the rural *dibao* implementation, 91–2, 94
and the 1997 Circular, 29, 52, 58, 59
problems at a local level, 136–7
resources for the urban *dibao* implementation, 61, 71–2
role of work units, 50
of the rural *dibao*, 33, 89–90, 94, 98, 101
slow implementation and uneven administration of the urban *dibao*, 68–70, 72
transitional implementation phase of urban *dibao* (1994–7), 27–8, 46, 51–9
of urban *dibao* (1997-99), 28–30, 46, 59–65

institutionalisation
  within the Chinese political system, 108
  defined, 108, 129–30
  of *dibao*, 107–8, 121
  of *dibao* through the Social Relief Law,
    110, 113
  dibao's lack of, 109
  impact of the fragmented state on,
    121–6, 130–1, 137
  of policy innovations, 108–9
  and the responsiveness of *dibao*, 115–17
  of the social relief system (Social Relief
    Temporary Measures), 117–19, 121,
    122–3
institutions
  decision making and implementation,
    10, 15–16
  defined, 9, 108
  in the Fragmented Authoritarianism
    model (FA), 9
  political structure of the state and, 9–10
  values and, 9
interventions in *dibao*
  by central government, 112
  by Duoji Cairang, 56
  first central intervention by central
    government, 74–6
  by Li Peng, 57–8, 60, 65, 135
  by Zhu Rongji, 76–82, 112
Iron Rice Bowl, 76, 77, 78

laid-off workers (*xiagang zhigong*)
  basic livelihood guarantee, 29, 77
  failure of national policies to cater for,
    77–8
  and the intervention of Zhu Rongji,
    78–9, 80, 83, 135
  local-level for discouragement of
    applications from, 69, 72
  problem of, 26
  provision for by the MLG, 6, 19, 30,
    76, 80–3, 86, 135
  re-employment service centres (RSCs),
    77–8

  as threat to social stability, 48, 78, 80–1,
    87
Lampton, D. M., 9, 10, 12
Leung, J. C. B., 4, 107–8
Li Peng
  intervention in MLG policy, 53–4,
    57–8, 60, 65, 135
  political authority of, 54, 135, 136
  speeches endorsing *dibao*, 7, 27, 29, 51
Lieberthal, Kenneth, 9, 10–11, 14, 73, 80,
  122, 133
local government
  compliance with the MLG, 86
  compromised implementation due
    to adaptation of the MLG to local
    circumstances, 86
  guidance for adjustments to the MLG
    line, 116
  guidance on application investigation,
    118–19
  impact of weak local finances on *dibao*
    funding, 60–1, 72–3
  intransigence over *dibao*
    implementation, 136–7
  local flexibility of *dibao*, 94, 114–17,
    124–5, 137
  malpractice by *dibao* administrators,
    119
  responsiveness to price increases via the
    MLG line, 115, 116
  rural development policies, 100
long-term sickness and MLG provision,
  77

MCA Circular Regarding Accelerating
    the Establishing and Completion of
    the Urban Resident MLG System
    (MCA Circular), 69
medical care
  before 1992, 22, 24
  basic medical cost relief through the
    MLG, 31, 33
  in the Constitution, 25
  in the draft Social Relief Law, 113

medical care (*cont.*)
  and the 'Five Guarantees', 24
  in rural areas, 99, 101
  and rural *dibao*, 103
  and urban *dibao*, 102
Mertha, Andrew, 12
Minimum Livelihood Guarantee (MLG)
  applicability of indexing solution to,
    128–9
  categorisation and conditionality
    criteria for, 127
  cost of living concerns and (2007–8),
    33–4
  emergence of (1992–3), 26
  first expansionary phase (2000–2),
    30–3
  as flexible policy, 94, 114–17, 124–5,
    126
  future research areas, 141–2
  groping type outcomes and, 16–17
  iterations of, 5–6, 6
  lack of institutionalisation of, 109
  means tested basis of, 2, 127
  motivations for the policy of, 6–7
  policies towards (2009–14), 34–40
  policy entrepreneurs influences on,
    16–17
  as poverty alleviation measure, 43–4,
    119–21, 125, 133
  provision for laid-off workers, 6, 19, 30,
    76, 80–3, 86, 135
  in relation to the priorities of the
    political elite, 137
  research on, 2–4, 7–8
  responses to changes in local
    circumstances, 114–17
  scope and reach of, 2, 30–3
  second expansionary phase (2003–7),
    33
  system of, 1–2
  total number of cities implementing
    MLG, 28
  see also MLG line (*dibao xian*); rural
    dibao; urban *dibao*

Minimum Livelihood Guarantee (MLG)
    line (*dibao xian*)
  30 per cent increase in (1999), 74
  in the 2007 Circular, 113
  consistency in and benefits of
    institutionalisation, 124
  in the draft Social Relief Law, 112
  guidance for adjustments to, 116–17
  impact on the numbers of recipients
    of, 70–1
  local government adjustments to, 115,
    116–17
  and problems with correct
    identification of recipients, 69
  regional variations in the calculation
    of, 70–1
  in relation to poverty alleviation, 97
  responsiveness to price increases,
    115–16
  for the rural *dibao*, 92, 93, 95, 100–1
  Shanghai MLG model, 26
  shopping basket method for the
    calculation of, 116
minimum wages, 26, 27, 79
Ministry of Civil Affairs (MCA)
  administration of the 'Ought to protect,
    fully protect' campaign, 82, 83–6
  bureaucratic rank issues, 15
  calls for local changes to the MLG line
    in response to price increases, 115
  China Society News information
    campaign, 65, 71
  computer systems, 85, 86
  data collection on the MLG, 85, 86
  development and implementation of
    classification guarantee measures,
    84–5, 86
  documentation on the adoption of rural
    dibao, 90–1
  expansion of the *dibao* programme, 31–3
  Guidance on the further regulation of
    the urban and rural resident MLG
    standard system and adjustment
    work, 34–5, 116–17

impact of price increases on those
    receiving payments, 34
lessons from the urban *dibao* applied to
    the rural *dibao*, 93, 100–2
official involvement in the draft Social
    Relief Law, 34, 110, 111
problems with allocation procedures,
    30, 69
promotion of the MLG, 27–30
promotion of the rural *dibao*, 33, 91
promotion of the urban *dibao*, 82–7
as resource-poor institution, 17, 60, 70,
    71, 72–3
responses to inconsistencies in
    implementation, 69
strategies to achieve implementation
    (1997–9), 61–2, 65
support for the classification guarantee
    measures, 83
Ministry of Finance (MoF)
    increases to MLG funding, 29, 34, 74,
        75, 80, 85
    increases to the MLG line, 115
    social assistance funding, 24

neo-institutionalism, 108
Ninth Five Year Plan (1996–2000), 28, 52,
    53, 57, 58
non-state actors, 11, 12

Oksenberg, Michel, 9, 10–11, 80, 133
'Ought to protect, fully protect' (*yingbao
    jinbao*) campaign
    administration of by the Department of
        Disaster Relief and Social Assistance,
        80, 82, 83
    funding for, 82
    MCA running of, 82, 83–6
    MLG expansion to help address, 30,
        76
    Zhu Rongji's involvement with, 78,
        79, 80
'Ought to protect, not protecting'
    problem (*yingbao weibao*), 69

pensions
    indexing solutions to, United
        Kingdom, 128
    non-payments of by SOEs, 77
policy actors
    behaviour of within the FA model,
        10–11, 82, 133
    constraints on, 16
    decision making and implementation,
        15–16
    generalist/specialist distinction, 80
    influence of values on the goals of, 14
    resources of, 15
    significance of the institutional
        positions of, 10, 15, 58–9, 133–5
    for the Social Relief Law, 111
    speech spaces, 9, 14
    structures of decision making and
        resource allocation, 14
    see also Duoji Cairang; Li Peng; Zhu
        Rongji
policy development
    by elite leaders in pre-reform China, 8
    Fragmented Authoritarianism model
        (FA) and, 8–9, 133, 138
    move to a more inclusive form of
        development across China, 98–9
    process of in the PRC, 4, 5
    in reform era China, 8–9
    sustainability of new policy
        experiments, 108–9
policy entrepreneurs (PE)
    concept of, 11, 16
    Duoji Cairang as, 54
    Huang Ju as, 48–9
    need for political authority and, 136
    Zhu Rongji as, 82
political structure
    and challenges to urban *dibao*
        implementation, 60
    impact of decision making and
        implementation, 9–10, 14
    impact of previous implementation
        announcements, 60

political structure (*cont.*)
    ranks of administrative agencies, 60
    ranks of policy actors, 15
poverty
    absolute poverty in rural areas, 41, 44,
        97, 100
    as a 'big wind' (*da feng*) policy area,
        119–20
    China-specific factors and, 42–3
    defined, 41
    dibao as poverty alleviation measure,
        43–4, 119–21, 125, 133
    ideological significance of in China, 40
    incidence of in China, 41–2
    Millennium Development Goal for, 40
    new poverty (*xin pinkun*), 25, 42, 44
    as a policy problem, 1
    political aspects to definition of, 40–1,
        44
    poverty alleviation for the disabled,
        120–1, 123
    quantification of, 42
    relative poverty, 41, 97
    rural *dibao* as poverty alleviation
        measure, 97, 100, 103, 119, 136
    rural–urban divide and, 43, 44
    social assistance provision for the
        alleviation of, 43–4
    as social illness, 22, 40, 42
    state attitudes towards in the early
        twentieth century, 22–3
    state intervention in rural areas, 42,
        119–20
    work as the means to alleviate poverty,
        23, 24, 42, 93

recipients of the MLG
    arbitrary allocation of rural *dibao*, 95
    classification guarantee measures (*fenlei
        baozhang cuoshi*), 84–5
    during different iterations of the MLG,
        5–6, 6
    eligibility criteria and benefits of
        institutionalisation, 124

    impact of the MLG line on, 70–1
    malpractices by, 119
    misallocation of rural *dibao*, 95, 102,
        104
    within the MLG discourse, 5
    numbers receiving rural *dibao*, 94
    problems with allocation procedures,
        30, 68, 69, 70, 72
    research on, 3–4
    self-reporting on changes in
        circumstances, 118
    total number of MLG recipients
        (1999–2003), 30, *31*
re-employment service centres (RSCs),
    77–8
rent subsidies, 33
Rogers, Sarah, 100
rural areas
    absolute poverty in, 41, 44, 97, 100
    attention to in developmental policy,
        early 21st century, 98–9
    'Five Guarantees' (*wubao*), 24
    introduction of household
        responsibility contracts, 25
    social assistance provision, 1
    state interventions for poverty
        alleviation, 42, 119–20
rural *dibao*
    annual income measurement, 95, 96,
        100–1
    average per capita spend and total
        cumulative expenditure for, 35, *37*
    challenges to day-to-day running of
        rural *dibao*, 94–5, 102–4
    confusion over the purpose of, 95–7,
        102–3
    developmental timeline, 90–1
    funding of, 93, 101
    impact of the fragmented state on,
        101
    lessons from the urban *dibao* applied to
        the rural *dibao* by the MCA, 100–2
    limited administrative capacity and,
        102

local flexibility of, 94
low level of compared to average wages, 120
misallocation of *dibao* payments, 95, 102, 104
national implementation, 33, 89–90, 94, 98, 101
newspaper coverage of implementation of, 91–2, 94
numbers receiving, 35, *36*
operation of alongside the Five Guarantees programme, 95–7
as poverty alleviation measure, 97, 100, 103, 119, 136
quotas for, 95, 102, 104, 120
as reflection of more inclusive development policies of the Hu-Wen era, 99
regulatory framework for, 92–3, 94
scope and reach of, 2, 94
in the State Council circular 2007, 92–3, 94–5, 97
see also Minimum Livelihood Guarantee (MLG)

Shanghai MLG
category based system problems, 49
emergence of (1992–3), 1, 5–6, *6*, 7, 26–7, 47–51
funding model, 50, 68, 70
impact of Shanghai's Municipality status, 50–1
locally set *dibao* line, 26
means tested basis of, 49–50
potential for social instability and, 48
role of the Bureau of Civil Affairs, 48
role of the work units, 50
state-facilitated innovation, 50–1, 133
Three Non-managed (*san bu guan*), 6, 27, 42, 48, 49
'Three No's/Withouts' (*sanwu*), 27, 49, 50
Shao Ting, 103

social assistance provision
adjustments to different social groups, 138
attitudes towards poverty, early twentieth century, 22–3
category based systems, 1–2, 120
and the changing nature of work, 129
in the Constitution, 25
during the dynastic era, 22
failed replacement of during SOE reforms, 76–8
'Five Guarantees' (*wubao*), 24
indexing solutions to, 128
institutionalisation of, 117–18
during the Mao era, 24–5
need for reform of, 25
before 1992, 22–6
for poverty alleviation, 43–4
prior to the Minimum Livelihood Guarantee, 1–2
reforms to in the 1990s, 25, 76–82
and regime stability, 138–9
rural–urban divide in, 23–4
for those able to work, 24
'Three No's/Withouts' (*sanwu*), 24, 26
workhouses, 22–3
Social Relief Law
applicability to *dibao*, 112–13
backbone law form of, 112
background to, 109–10
on central-level transfers for support for *dibao*, 112
coverage of in the *China Society News*, 110
definition of low-income households, 113
failure of as a result of the fragmented state, 122, 137
lack of adjustment and standardised mechanism and for the draft Social Relief Law, 113
process of drafting the law, 110–11
Social Relief Temporary Measures (State Council, 2014), 35, 117–19, 121, 122–3

social stability
  as one of the goals of the urban *dibao*,
    52–3, 54–5, 81
  rural areas as possible areas for social
    instability, 99
  threat to from laid-off SOE employees,
    48, 78, 80–1, 87
  urban areas as possible areas for social
    instability, 48
Solinger, Dorothy J., 3
speech spaces, 9, 14
State Council circular regarding the
    establishing of a national rural
    Minimum Livelihood Guarantee
    system (2007 Circular)
  on the MLG line, 113
  presentation of the rural *dibao*, 92–3,
    94–5, 97
  similarities with 1997 Circular and
    1999 Regulation, 92
State Council circular regarding the
    establishing of a national urban
    resident Minimum Livelihood
    Guarantee system (1997 Circular)
  finance details, 60–1
  Li Peng's involvement with, 57, 58
  on the MLG line, 113
  and the national implementation of
    MLG, 29, 52, 58, 59
  similarities with 2007 Circular, 92
  transition to Urban Resident MLG
    Regulations, 61–2
State Council 'Urban Resident Minimum
    Livelihood Guarantee Regulations'
    (1999 Regulations), 69
state structure, 10
state-owned enterprises (SOEs)
  the 'debt conflict' of, 78, 79, 132
  non-payment of pensions, 25, 77
  reforms to and potential for social
    instability, 48, 78
  transition of laid-off employees from,
    30, 52, 77–8
  see also laid-off workers (*xiagang zhigong*)

Thirteenth Five Year Plan, 119
'Three No's/Withouts' (*sanwu*)
  Bureau of Civil Affairs and, 49
  policy of, 24, 27, 50
  as pre-runner to the *dibao*, 1
  in relation to the urban *dibao*, 57, 96–7,
    127
2010 Development Goals, 57

unemployment insurance (UEI) benefits,
    74, 76, 77
urban areas
  recognition of relative poverty by
    policy makers, 97
  social assistance provision, 1
urban *dibao*
  bureaucratic mushiness of, 71
  challenges to implementation of, 59–64,
    68–9
  China Society News campaign for
    implementation of, 62–4
  compromised implementation due to
    variation through adaptation to local
    circumstances, 70
  as de facto unemployment provision, 77
  delegation of policy responsibility to
    local government, 72–3
  Duoji Cairang's personal intervention
    in, 56
  Duoji Cairang's promotion of, 53–4,
    56–7
  Duoji Cairang's tactics for tackling
    challenges to, 54–6
  emergence of (1992–3), 47–9
  as final security line, 79
  government subsidy of, 64
  human resources for implementation
    of, 61
  impact of Li Peng on development of,
    57–8
  impact of weak local finances, 61
  impact on from SOE reforms, 78
  implementation process applied to the
    rural *dibao*, 100–2

lack of resources for the
implementation of, 71–2
for laid off SOE employees, 83
links with social stability goals, 52–3,
54–5
MCA strategies for implementation of,
61–2, 65
national implementation (1994–7), 46,
51–9
national implementation (1997–9), 46,
59–65
numbers receiving, 35, *38*
potential for social instability and, 48
reasons cited for adoption of, 53
in relation to the Three No's
programme, 96–7
role of Civil Affairs bureaucracy, 52
scope and reach of, 2
slow implementation and uneven
administration of, 68–70, 72
sponsorship of by the MCA, 82–7
Three No's (*sanwu*), 57
total expenditure and per capita
expenditure on, 35, *39*
see also Minimum Livelihood
Guarantee (MLG)
Urban Resident Minimum Livelihood
Guarantee Regulations (1999
Regulations)
goals of MLG in, 29–30
implementation deadlines in, 59
similarities with 2007 Circular, 92
transition to from the 1997 Circular,
61–2

values
within the Chinese political system,
14
within the FA model, 9, 13–14
and the goals of policy actors, 14
of the Hu regime, 90, 98–9
and the ideological climate, 13–14
value judgements over policy
innovations, 108–9, 135

Wang Laizhu, 112
Weaver, R. Kent, 128
Wen Jiabao, 34, 90, 98
Wong, Linda, 68
Wong Yu-Cheung, 3, 7
work units
role in the nationwide implementation,
50
role in the Shanghai MLG, 50
workhouses, 22–3
Wuhan model, 68

Xi Ruixin, 28, 71
xiagang basic livelihood guarantee
(XGBLG)
failed reforms to, 76
increases in, 74
for laid off SOE employees, 77–8
Xiao Meng, 107–8
Xu Bing, 72, 90, 91

Yan Kun, 40, 41

Zeng Qun, 3, 7
Zhang Haomiao, 3
Zhao Liqiu, 103
Zhu Rongji
on the 'debt conflict'
concerning laid-off SOE employees,
78, 79
intervention in MLG policy, 76–82,
112
intervention in MLG policy to solve
the laid-off worker problem, 78–9,
80, 83, 135
'Ought to protect, fully protect'
campaign, 78, 79, 80
personal motivation for involvement
with the MLG, 81, 135
as a policy entrepreneur, 82
reforms to the SOE sector, 77, 81
as specialist policy actor, 79–80, 135,
136
support of the MLG, 78–80

EU representative:
Easy Access System Europe
Mustamäe tee 50, 10621 Tallinn, Estonia
Gpsr.requests@easproject.com

www.ingramcontent.com/pod-product-compliance
Lightning Source LLC
Chambersburg PA
CBHW071124280326
41935CB00010B/1110